Remembering Paradise

Harvard-Yenching Institute Monograph Series

31

'REMEMBERING PARADISE,

Nativism and Nostalgia in Eighteenth-Century Japan

PETER NOSCO

Published by COUNCIL ON EAST ASIAN STUDIES, HARVARD
UNIVERSITY and distributed by HARVARD UNIVERSITY PRESS,
Cambridge (Massachusetts) and London   1990

Library of Congress Cataloging-in-Publication Data

Nosco, Peter.
Remembering paradise : nativism and nostalgia in eighteenth-
century Japan / Peter Nosco.
p.   cm. — (Harvard-Yenching Institute monograph series : 31)
Includes bibliographical references.
ISBN 0-674-76007-7
1. Kokugaku.   2. Kada, Azumamaro, 1669–1736.   3. Kamo, Mabuchi,
1697–1769.   4. Motoori, Norinaga, 1730–1801.   5. Japan—Intellectual
life—1600–1868.   I. Title.   II. Series.
B5243.K6N67   1990
952'.025—dc20   89-29580
                                                                                 CIP

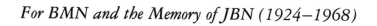

For BMN and the Memory of JBN (1924–1968)

Contents

Foreword and Acknowledgments

For several decades following the end of World War II, patriotism and nationalism were not fashionable sentiments among the vanquished countries, but, during the 1980s, numerous events attested to the presence in Japan as elsewhere of what the popular media termed a "new" nationalism. Among the more conspicuous indications of this in Japan are the founding in 1981 of the National Council to Defend Japan, which has as its first goal the reestablishment of the emperor as head of state; the Ministry of Education's authorization of textbooks which cast Japan's pre-war colonial and expansionist activities in a benign light; the official visit in 1985 by Prime Minister Nakasone with members of his cabinet to the Yasukuni Shrine where the spirits of the war dead are believed by some to be in repose; the remarks of the Prime Minister in 1986 (after the landslide election victory of his conservative party) concerning the effects of a heterogeneous society on U.S. statistics on education, remarks widely perceived outside Japan to be derogatory of America's racial minorities; and statements by Foreign Ministry and Cabinet Legislation Bureau officials in 1988, defending comments by Japan's ambassador to Britain, to the effect that Japan's ailing emperor was the nation's actual sovereign. There was also supporting evidence for this "new" nationalism within the social thought of Japan, and two such indications with particular relevance to this study were the *furusato buumu* (a renewed interest in visits to one's home place) and the *Edo buumu* (a new interest in the history and culture of the seventeenth through mid-nineteenth centuries). One element shared by these otherwise distinct "booms" or fads is that they are both nostalgic in character. The 1980s, however, are not the first time that patriotic and nostalgic constructions have existed side by side in Japan; their juxtaposition has a clear antecedent in the eighteenth century.

The most immediate, albeit simplistic, point of reference for understanding the patriotic and nostalgic sentiments of Japan in the 1980s is Japan during the decades preceding World War II, when the country as a whole was under the sway of an ultra-nationalist ideology with mythic qualities that helped propel Japan toward its international excesses. It is likewise understood that this ideology represented, at least in part, an updating of certain themes such as "revere the emperor" *(sonnō)* or "expel the barbarian" *(jōi)*, both of which propounded ahistorical ideals with pseudo-historical arguments; that these slogans represent part of the loyalist xenophobic ideology which contributed to the Meiji Restoration of 1868; and that these themes in turn have roots within the intellectual history of the Tokugawa period, particularly in the writings of the major nativist thinkers. It was, after all, figures like Motoori Norinaga—the most important nativist of the eighteenth century and one of Japan's most brilliant scholars—who asserted a privileged place for Japan and the Japanese within the world order as it was understood at the time and who argued for a nostalgic return to the "purer" ways of high antiquity.

For a variety of reasons, however, issues such as these and figures like Norinaga remain difficult for scholars of and within Japan to discuss, and this difficulty is reflected in the historiography of eighteenth-century nativism. During the decades prior to the war, the major nativists enjoyed sage-like respect from most Japanese historians, and their thought was regarded as "true," since, in substantial measure, it conformed to and buttressed the principal assumptions of the statist ideology. This, of course, made objective scholarly discussion of their writings all but impossible in Japan. Then, for roughly the first two decades of the post-war period, nativism became virtually a "taboo" topic within Japanese scholarly circles because of its perceived links to the discredited pre-war ideology. Thereafter, Japanese scholarship on the major nativists focused primarily upon their literary criticism, philological method, and affirmation of affective spheres of human experience (so-called "emotionalism" or *shujōshugi*); but a significant historiographical silence in Japan has substantially enveloped the patriotic and nostalgic themes of eighteenth-century nativism. Western scholarship on the subject has reflected this; there remains only one serious book-length study of the subject in English, Shigeru Matsumoto's psycho-biography of Motoori Norinaga.[1]

Besides breaking this silence, this book has four principal aims. First, it seeks to demonstrate that the major eighteenth-century nativists, frequently regarded as the formulators of a rabid xenophobic nationalism, were intellectuals engaged in a quest for meaning, wholeness, and solace in what they perceived to be disordered times. Second, it hopes to make historical sense of the emergence and development of their at times radical philosophies, on the one hand, by showing their slow and reasonable emergence over some one hundred years, and, on the other, by contextualizing this dynamic problematik both socially and ideologically. Third, this book attempts to identify elements of continuity into the eighteenth century from the singular Confucian-nativist discourse of the seventeenth century, and to indicate the appropriation of a new ideological space as a result of the rupture between nativism and Confucianism at the start of the eighteenth century. Finally, this study emphasizes the central role of the emotion of nostalgia throughout this quasi process.

The first part of this work (Chapters 1–3) discusses nostalgia in Japanese culture and contextualizes the development of eighteenth-century nativism by situating it socially and institutionally within the emergence of the popular culture of which the private nativist academy formed one part, and intellectually and ideologically in

---

[1] *Motoori Norinaga, 1730–1801.* H.D. Harootunian's *Things Seen and Unseen: Discourse and Ideology in Tokugawa Nativism,* which appeared as this volume was going to press, is concerned more with nineteenth-century nativism than its eighteenth-century forms.

terms of the disassociation of nativist concerns from those of Confucianism with which nativism had coexisted to mutual benefit during the preceding century. Specialists in seventeenth-century Japan will be familiar with much of the information in Chapters 2 and 3, but it is hoped that they will come to see familiar data in a somewhat novel context. The second part of this book (Chapters 4–7) traces the nostalgic and patriotic themes of eighteenth-century nativism through the careers and writings of its three major proponents: Kada no Azumamaro, Kamo no Mabuchi, and Motoori Norinaga. From their study of Japan's most ancient extant mythohistorical, poetic, and literary works, each sought to glean an understanding of what was "purely" Japanese about Japan in pre-Buddhist and pre-Confucian times. They called their constructed interpretations of Japan's past the "ancient Way" (*kodō*) and believed that the legacy of these idealized times was embodied within their contemporaries in the form of "true hearts" (*magokoro*). The intention of their studies was, first, to reenter the past and to reconstruct the "ancient Way," and second to reanimate the dormant "true heart" and thereby to reclaim within the fallen present those beatific qualities they believed to have characterized life in the primordially distant past.

Though less than one-fifth as long as the century it attempts to depict, the history of this book is longer than that of most monographic studies. My attention was first drawn to the subject of Tokugawa (1600–1868) nativist (*kokugaku*) thought by Carmen Blacker while I was a student in the early 1970s in the Faculty of Oriental Studies of the University of Cambridge.[2] I expected to work on other topics when I returned to the United States for doctoral studies, but, like an even then old friend, Tokugawa nativism came back to become the subject of my PhD dissertation, researched and written under the supervision of Wm. Theodore de Bary, Matsu-

---

[2] This early study resulted in a Tripos Essay (1973) titled "Nostalgia for Paradise in the Shinto Revival." I am grateful to Columbia College for providing me with the Kellett Fellowship that made possible my two years of study in England.

moto Sannosuke (then at the Faculty of Law, University of Tokyo), and the late Herschel Webb.[3] I intended at the time to revise this dissertation for possible publication, but I was distracted from the task of revision, first by the unanticipated rigors of starting full-time teaching, and then by a pair of projects from which I was finally liberated in the late summer of 1984.[4] In retrospect, I feel fortunate that these years intervened, because I came to understand some of the shortcomings of my earlier research on nativism, shortcomings my mentors had tried to call to my attention but which I resisted for reasons that now baffle me. Of these, by far the most serious was my disregard for the social, economic, and political background of the history of thought. I cannot pretend to have overcome this deficiency altogether, which, in any event, is a matter for the reader and not me to determine, but I am confident that the current version of my research on eighteenth-century nativism reflects a more mature understanding than my earlier ventures of the subtle and at times elusive relationship between thought and society.

Two grants made it possible for me to enhance my understanding of the background of eighteenth-century nativism, and I wish here to acknowledge my gratitude to the National Endowment for the Humanities for a summer stipend (1985) and the Fulbright Commission for a senior research award (1986), which enabled me to spend seven months at the Historiographical Institute (Shiryō Hensanjo) of the University of Tokyo and to visit sites relevant to this study. I also wish to acknowledge the ongoing support and invaluable criticisms I have received from Professors Blacker, de Bary, and

[3] The dissertation (1978) was titled "Remembering Paradise: Nostalgic Themes in Japanese Nativism, 1690–1823." I am grateful for the Fulbright-Hays and Japanese Ministry of Education grants that made possible my two years of research at Tokyo University, and to the U.S. Council of Higher Education for a grant that enabled me to write the dissertation while a research associate at Clare Hall, University of Cambridge.

[4] One was the translation of Ihara Saikaku's *Saikaku oritome,* a project originally suggested to me by Donald Keene, which resulted in the book *Some Final Words of Advice;* the other was the organization of a research conference on a topic suggested to me by Professor de Bary, and the subsequent editing of the papers from that symposium into the volume *Confucianism and Tokugawa Culture.*

Matsumoto, who have been model mentors to me long after I lost the privilege of sitting in their classrooms. I appreciate the supportive environment my research and I have found at the University of Southern California; my colleagues there, Gordon Berger, Mieko Han, George Hayden, Stephen Teiser (now at Princeton), and John E. Wills, Jr., have been kind enough to read parts or the whole of this work and to offer numerous helpful suggestions, as have "old friends" like R. Miriam Brokaw, Richard Rubinger, and Samuel Hideo Yamashita. It goes without saying but has become customary nonetheless to declaim that they in no way share my responsibility for those shortcomings which remain in my work.

Portions of this study represent revision of material which originally appeared elsewhere, and I wish to thank the editors of *Asian Thought & Society: An International Review*, *The Occasional Papers of the Virginia Consortium of Asian Studies*, and *Harvard Journal of Asiatic Studies* for their permission to use these materials.

Explanatory Notes

Japanese, Chinese, and Korean personal names are written in the native order with the surname first. The names Kada no Azumamaro and Kamo no Mabuchi often appear in Western-language scholarship without the (no) which is retained in this volume. Following the conventions of Japanese scholarship, these and other figures are most often referred in the following pages by their given names, i.e., Azumamaro, Mabuchi, and so on.

Commonly known placenames like Tokyo, Kyoto, Osaka, Honshu, and Kyushu are written without macrons, as are certain well-known terms like shogun and Shinto when they stand alone.

The place of publication for all Japanese language works is Tokyo, unless otherwise specified.

Dates prior to 1873 are given in the traditional manner according to the lunar calendar, e.g., the 4th month of 1736. Personal age is likewise reckoned in the traditional manner with a person's age counted as 1 on the day of birth, 2 on the first day of the lunar new year, 3 on the next lunar new year's day, and so on.

The following abbreviations are used in the notes and bibliography:

KKMZ:SH   *Kōhon Kamo Mabuchi zenshū: shisō hen*. Ed. Yamamoto Yutaka. 2 vols. Kōbundō, 1942.

KSRZK   *Kinsei Shintōron, zenki kokugaku*. Eds. Taira Shigemichi and Abe Akio. *Nihon Shisō Taikei, no. 39. Iwanami Shoten, 1972*.

KZ   *Kada zenshū*. 7 vols. Yoshikawa Kōbunkan, 1928–1938.

MNZ   *Motoori Norinaga zenshū*. Comp. Ōno Susumu and Ōkubo Tadashi. 20 vols., Chikuma Shobō, 1968–1975.

NST   Nihon Shisō Taikei. Comp. Ienaga Saburō, Inoue Mitsusada, Sagara Tōru, Nakamura Yoshihiko, Bitō Masahide, Maruyama Masao, and Yoshikawa Kōjirō. 67 vols. Iwanami Shoten, 1970–.

The "newness" in the individual psyche is an endlessly varied re-combination of age-old components. Body and soul therefore have an intensely historical character and find no proper place in what is new, in things which have just come into being. That is to say, our ancestral components are only partly at home in such things. . . . Once the past has been breached, it is usually annihilated, and there is no stopping the foreward motion. . . . Inner peace and contentment depend in large measure upon whether or not the historical family which is inherent in the individual can be harmonized with the ephemeral concerns of the present.
—C.G. Jung, *Memories, Dreams, Reflections*

Jam tomorrow and jam yesterday—but never jam *today*.
—Lewis Caroll, *Through the Looking Glass*

Remembering Paradise

Part One

ONE

Introduction: Ancient Way (Kodō) Themes and the Nostalgic Quest

The word *nostalgia* carries with it a complex set of identifications and associations, and, as it appears frequently in the pages that follow, it is perhaps best to begin by examining the history of the term's meanings and what is meant by it here. *Nostalgia* is a relative neologism which first appeared in the late-seventeenth century when it was used to refer to what one might today call "homesickness," that is, the pain associated with prolonged physical separation from what one identifies as one's primary abode. Writing in 1688, the physician Johannes Hofer coined the term from the Greek words *nostos* (return to native land) and *algos* (suffering or grief) and described nostalgia as a "continuous vibration of animal spirits through those fibers of the middle brain in which the impressed traces of ideas of Fatherland still cling."[1] In the nineteenth century, when technological advances made travel more rapid and common, and the study of the psyche aspired to greater precision, the word *nostalgia* acquired clinical connotations and was used for diagnosis with roughly the same meaning. Then, in the twentieth century, when life arguably became (or at least came to appear) more complex and the pace of change seemingly accelerated, *nostalgia* came to be identified with a temporal as well as spatial sense of dislocation; one

---

[1] Quoted in David Lowenthal, *The Past Is a Foreign Country*, p. 10.

might be nostalgic for a condition from which one is removed by
the passage of time as well as by space.

What is perhaps less well understood about nostalgia is that it is
an emotion like anger or joy, and that, like these other emotions,
it can be an altogether natural response to circumstances. When one
is dissatisfied with one's immediate situation, it can be a comforting
exercise to imagine and construct a more pleasing idealized environment. Depending upon the circumstances and the individual, this
may be nothing more than a personal exercise in imaginative fantasy, or it can take the form of entering into a preconstructed realm
through the medium of a book, poem, song, work of art, and so
on. Whatever one's approach or medium, however, one is transported by the nostalgic construct into an idealized realm whose
conditions provide a measure of solace in the here-and-now.

This idealized condition can be variously located. One can postulate its existence in the future, in the physically remote present,
or in the past. Though exceptions can be found, it is possible to
generalize a distinction between socalled "Western" and "Eastern"
approaches. It has been characteristic of European and recent North
American thought to situate the idealized condition in the future,
a tendency that might best be referred to as *utopian*. Conversely,
Asian thought has traditionally located the idealized condition in
the past, and it is specifically this "looking back" to those conditions believed to have existed *in illo tempore* that is meant in the
pages that follow by the term *nostalgia*.[2]

Such an exercise—the postulation of an idealized or paradisiac
state in the near or remote past—is inherently "escapist," though
it is important to dissociate this term from the negative connotations that have become attached to it. The fantasy, by its very nature, represents a disenchantment with and disengagement from the
here-and-now, and, since this disengagement is voluntary, it constitutes an egress from what is *(Sein)* into what one might wish to
be *(Sollen)*. This disengagement from the immediate and engage-

---

[2] It is an apparently universal phenomenon, however, to find, particularly in folk tales and
oral traditions, musings over a physically remote perfect society.

ment with the remote is not necessarily destructive in either a personal or social sense, though it has often been characterized as such. Psychologists and other social scientists might even argue that, through their capacity to vent otherwise potentially antisocial energies, and in their capacity to represent an idealized abstraction toward which an individual or a society can aspire, nostalgic or utopian fantasies may even serve a constructive role. To the extent, however, that one attempts either to reenter or to reconstruct the erected nostalgic fantasy, one is through this quasi action evidencing a degree of estrangement and attendant dissociation from one's environment, and is thereby articulating, however unconsciously or consciously, an implicitly critical posture toward that environment.

This inclination toward disenchantment is all the more evident when one considers the remarkable degree of similarity between depictions of an idealized past as they have been postulated over hundreds if not thousands of years in otherwise radically different societies. All of these constructions share most of the following characteristics. Harmony prevails without apparent effort, not only between persons in society but also between humans and other creatures in nature. There is an utter absence of guile or duplicity, as if such behavior were an impossibility, and social life conforms unconsciously to norms of universal benefit. All physical needs are met, that is, there is no hunger or thirst, and no discomfort from the elements. Nature itself is seemingly allied with human enterprise, creating an environment in which, without effort, one's most elementary physical requirements are satisfied. Though death still overtakes everyone, life spans are generally longer, and pain is nowhere evident. Time is suspended, and there is no yesterday or tomorrow but only a perpetual and changeless today, since, by the very nature of the idealized condition, change can only imply a falling away from that condition. In short, myths such as these generally depict the time of beginnings in idealized terms suggestive of an earthly paradise—humankind, nature, and the gods cooperate in a seamless hierophany, and this cooperation ensures that all human needs are met. It is, however, the nature of such idealized depictions of a primordial terrestrial order that they encounter a

Fall, most often as a result of some human offense—the umbilicus which once united humankind with the numinous cosmos is severed, the divine becomes remote, the timeless quality of the age of beginnings is disrupted, and historical time begins.[3]

As numerous scholars of ancient myths have observed, such accounts have enduring value extending well beyond archaic time, since they both explain and justify the existence of the world, humankind, and society. Furthermore, the "memory" of this idealized condition is sustained by the paradisiac myths into the fallen present in which it at times assumes the guise of a persistent nostalgia; and, if this nostalgia is sufficiently compelling, it may inspire one to embark upon a quest either to transcend one's environment by transporting oneself through time back to the idealized realm of the myths, or to transform the immediate world of yesterdays, todays, and tomorrows by resurrecting in the present the timeless paradisiac condition enjoyed by one's ancient forebears at the moment of their creation.

It is curious that there is no native Japanese word equivalent to the modern sense of the word *nostalgia,* and so, to refer to this in Japanese, one must use the coined (loan-word) term *nosutarujia,* which is all the more curious when one considers that, within Japanese culture, there is a long and distinguished literary tradition of nostalgic writings. To cite just a few examples selected from masterpieces prior to the early-modern Tokugawa period (1600–1868), many of the finest verses in the *Man'yōshū,* Japan's oldest extant poetry anthology, dating from the second half of the eighth century, and, in particular, the verses of its premier poet, Kakinomoto Hitomaro, express a nostalgic attitude toward times even then long past; Murasaki Shikibu's *The Tale of Genji (Genji monogatari),* the world's first psychological novel, dating from the first decade of the eleventh century, repeatedly expresses concern over the loss of courtly elegance identified with earlier times; and both Kamo no Chōmei's

---

[3] Among many studies of utopian or paradisiac constructions in the European tradition, two of particular value are Frank E. and Fritzie P. Manuel's *Utopian Thought in the Western World* and Harry Levin's *The Myth of the Golden Age in the Renaissance.* The "classic" comparative study of this subject is Mircea Eliade's *The Myth of the Eternal Return.*

An Account of My Hut (Hōjōki) of 1212 and Yoshida Kenkō's *Essays in Idleness (Tsurezuregusa)* of the 1330s lament the demise of manners and customs associated with the Heian period (794–1185). This tradition of longing for the past and attributing to it desirable qualities perceived to be lost in one's own times was so prevalent during the medieval (1185–1600) period of Japanese history that it became, during those centuries, a virtual literary conceit.

In Japan, as in many other countries, there is also a "primordial history" recorded in the most ancient sources. This begins with the cosmogonic myth, that is, the myth that describes the first, seminal state of the world and how that world came into being, and it continues with both narrative and episodic accounts of the gods' activities at this earliest stage of creation. The primordial or "true" history of early Japan is recorded in the *Kojiki* (712) and the *Nihon shoki* (720), whose so-called divine age chapters describe how Japan was created and the activities of the gods during this time of beginnings. In common with many other mythologies, those of Japan suggest the existence of a naive simplicity in this remotest antiquity—a beatitude born of all creation's spontaneous conformity to the dictates of a natural order infused with the divine. The myths depict the heavenly abode of the native gods as on or near earth, or more accurately Japan, and so the idealized ancient past in the Japanese tradition is a condition removed from the here-and-now temporally but not spatially. There are, however, three features of early Japanese myths that distinguish them from those of others according to the prevailing pattern described above: First, the idealized or "paradisiac" condition is implicit rather than explicit; second, the exodus from primordial time into historical time is gradual rather than abrupt; and, third, no earthly act is identified or singled out as bearing principal responsibility for the separation of heaven from earth.

In the eighteenth century, certain Japanese scholars engaged in the study of Japan's earliest literary and mytho-historical sources with new vigor. They depicted Japan's earliest ages in idealized and near-paradisiac terms, and they concluded that the beatific qualities of those times were terminated as a result of the contaminating effects of the introduction of foreign modes of thought into Japan. In particular, they blamed Confucianism, which they regarded as a pernicious invention of the human intellect and as a Way inferior to the native Way of Japan. Furthermore, since Confucianism originated in China, these same scholars also vilified Japan's formidable continental neighbor. They castigated China as a repository of wickedness; they maintained that the Chinese people had resorted to the invented teachings of sages because of their allegedly natural inclination toward disobedience and wrongdoing; and they concluded that Confucianism had not only repeatedly thrown China into upheaval—the antidote not transformed into the toxin—but that it also had the same effect in Japan where it offered the false hope of rescuing society from those very ills it had provoked.

These same eighteenth-century thinkers came to regard the possession of the attributes of the idealized past as a birthright or prerogative of being Japanese and the loss of these attributes as an event repeated afresh in each generation of Japanese. They asserted that the beatific qualities of life they believed their forebears to have enjoyed stemmed from their possession of a genetic element of perfection which they called the "true heart," that a Japanese at birth still possessed this true heart and its attendant attributes, and that the true heart was obscured or negated as a result of exposure to the vile contagion of Chinese modes of thought. They believed, however, that these effects were reversible—that the ancient glories of Japan and the Japanese were accessible through one's recovery or reanimation of the true heart a Japanese enjoyed as his birthright and by reuniting oneself thereby with the native Way. Though they differed as to how this reversal might be accomplished, they shared the belief that heaven need not be remote from earth, that is, that the glories and blessings of ancient Japan might be experienced anew in the present. Nonetheless, their racialist assumptions that these glories and blessings were purely and exclusively Japanese prerogatives distorted their patriotic themes into a distasteful xenophobia and narcissism characteristic of a significant corpus of later nineteenth- and twentieth-century thought in Japan.[4]

---

[4]On the nineteenth- and twentieth-century manifestations of these assumptions, see Bob

It has been the convention of both Japanese and Western scholarship to refer to the thinkers who formulated these propositions as members of the National Learning *(kokugaku)* movement, which, properly speaking, was, in the eighteenth century, not so much a movement as a lineage of schools. In its broadest sense, "National Learning" refers to all nativist studies in Japan, that is, studies focused on Japan as opposed to studies of China known as *Kangaku* (Chinese Learning); in this volume, the term is used in the narrower sense of referring to the philological enquiry into texts from the Japanese tradition in order to glean from those texts a native ancient Way, referred to variously as the natural Way of heaven and earth, the Way of the gods, the true Way, or simply the Way. During the eighteenth century, the major scholars engaged in this pursuit were Kada no Azumamaro (1669–1736), Kamo no Mabuchi (1697–1769), and Motoori Norinaga (1730–1801). Their preferred texts for the study of the Way were (respectively) the *Nihon shoki*, *Man'yōshū* poetry anthology, and *Kojiki*. The latter two texts in particular required philological elucidation, since they were written in a highly archaic and irregular form of Sino-Japanese, which was then and remains now unintelligible to a contemporary Japanese without the aid of extensive commentary and analysis.

Though the study of Japan by the Japanese represented a long and distinguished tradition——Hieda no Are and Ō no Yasumamaro, respectively the reputed narrator and compiler of the *Kojiki*, being the earliest major nativists in the broad sense of the term—the National Learning of Azumamaro, Mabuchi, and Norinaga had more immediate antecedents in the intellectual history of the late-seventeenth century. For example, National Learning shared much with the Confucianism it so reviled. Confucians also had a tradition of situating an idealized realm (the court of the Duke of Chou) in the remote past. Orthodox Neo-Confucians of the Chu Hsi school likewise believed that certain seeds of goodness, inherent but dormant within each individual, might be cultivated and animated with

Tadashi Wakabayashi, *Anti-Foreignism and Western Learning in Early-Modern Japan: The New Theses of 1825*, pp. 17–99; J. Victor Koschmann, *The Mito Ideology: Discourse, Reform, and Insurrection in Late Tokugawa Japan, 1790–1864*, pp. 56–80; and Carol Gluck, *Japan's Modern Myths: Ideology in the Late Meiji Period*, pp. 73–156.

beneficial consequences. The Ancient Learning *(kogaku)* schools of Confucianism had pioneered the development of linguistic and philological techniques in order to decipher faithfully the "true messages" encoded in ancient texts. The National Learning schools were institutionally patterned after the private Confucian academies, and both represented important forms of popular cultural activity during the Tokugawa period. Even the critical assumption of the Sorai school of Confucianism in the early-eighteenth century that the ancient Chinese sages were mere men was adopted by the major National Learning scholars *(kokugakusha)*, though with different intentions.

No less profound was National Learning's indebtedness to seventeenth-century nativist pursuits. Though it is possible to interpret National Learning as the irruption in the eighteenth century of a new discourse within an ideological field dominated by Confucianism, National Learning also represents the gradual narrowing and focusing of nativist activities with clear antecedents and prototypes in the seventeenth century. In this regard, the rediscovery by literary critics of both the Waka genre of poetry and the *Man'yōshū* poetry anthology, the remarkable expansion of Japanese historiographical enterprise, and the attempts by Shinto theologians first to reconcile their creed with Neo-Confucian "truths" and subsequently to divest Shinto from non-native assumptions and trappings (conspicuous features of the intellectual history of the seventeenth and early-eighteenth centuries) all figure prominently in the early emergence of National Learning, especially as nativist scholars began to attach normative value to these intellectual endeavors.

Chapters 2 and 3 in this volume explicate these various contexts for the emergence of eighteenth-century National Learning. Chapter 2 examines the multiplicity of forms of popular cultural activity in the seventeenth century, in particular the growth of the private Confucian academy of the Ancient Learning scholar Itō Jinsai (1627–1705), and describes a number of factors that arose in the first Tokugawa century and appear to have contributed to the new popular culture. Jinsai's career demonstrated the viability of the private urban academy, which may have provided the model for Kada no

Azumamaro's own less successful efforts to found a nativist counterpart. Chapter 3 concentrates on the harmonious relationship between Confucianism and nativism as constituent elements of a singular scholarly discourse during most of the seventeenth century and the first indications of the eventual rupture between the two as represented by the *Man'yō* studies of the Buddhist priest Keichū (1640–1701). By depicting Japan's ancient past as an unlettered age permeated by a Way later known as Shinto, Keichū articulated an image of the past that proved consistent with the idealization of the primordial past by later figures like Mabuchi and Norinaga. That Keichū arrived at this image through his study of the *Man'yōshū* and that he expressed it through the medium of a commentary on the anthology encouraged Mabuchi and Norinaga to identify Keichū as a pioneer of their own studies and conclusions.

Kada no Azumamaro, the subject of Chapter 4, was the first major eighteenth-century National Learning figure. As the intellectually gifted scion of one of Japan's oldest families of Shinto priests, he was in a distinguished position to formulate a nativist ideology with roots in Shinto theology. He emphasized the close reading of ancient Japanese works, articulated National Learning as a concept, endeavored throughout his adult life to establish an academy that might serve as a national center for such study, and sought with limited success, to enlist external support and patronage for his efforts. He was among the first to postulate an adversarial relationship between nativist and Confucian scholarship—a necessary step for the independent growth of National Learning—and his vilification of Confucian and Buddhist doctrines established the xenophobic tone of his principal successors. Furthermore, the aims of Azumamaro's National Learning, as he described them in a 1728 Petition to the shogun, Tokugawa Yoshimune, heralded the goals of roughly the next hundred years of nativist scholarship and activity.

Though it had been Azumamaro's intention to have his adopted son and designated intellectual heir, Kada Arimaro, carry on his efforts, Azumamaro's most famous student was Kamo no Mabuchi, the subject of Chapter 5. Keichū's goal of creating an accurate rendition of the cryptic verses of the *Man'yōshū* was no more than the

starting point for Mabuchi's efforts. Through his philological researches into the anthology, Mabuchi believed it possible to glean
from the archaic verses an ancient spirit which he regarded as deriv-
ative from the ancient Way or, as he styled it, the natural Way of
heaven and earth. He viewed this spirit as an evocation of all that
is purely Japanese about Japan, and he described life in ancient
Japan as being in perfect and spontaneous conformity with the natural cosmic order—humans lived in harmonious accord with each
other and with all other creations of nature, since, by virtue of their
"true hearts," human behavior and character were inherently guileless and direct. He argued that, as a consequence of their naiveté
and innocence, ancient Japanese turned to foreign Ways and thereby
lost both their true hearts and the attendant blessings of the primordial natural order, a process he believed to recur in each generation, even into his own age. Mabuchi insisted, however, that the
ancient Way was recoverable and that the true heart that lay dormant within all Japanese might be reanimated by a return to the
values that had inspired their ancient forebears, something he believed possible through immersion in the reading, study, and recitation of ancient verse. Mabuchi also reviled the Chinese for what
he described as their inherent propensity for immorality and unruliness, which had forced them to resort to the human invention of
a Way. Japan's superiority, he reasoned, lay in its possession of the
true ancient Way which had once enabled the country to enjoy the
blessing of untutored moral rectitude and which obviated the need
either to import or to fashion an alternative. That Mabuchi juxtaposed this ideality of Japanese superiority with a nostalgic orientation toward the past makes him the single most important figure
for an understanding of the emergence and development of eighteenth-century National Learning thought.

Kamo no Mabuchi only once met his own principal successor in
National Learning, Motoori Norinaga, regarded by many as the
greatest of all nativists in the Tokugawa period and the subject of
Chapters 6 and 7. Norinaga sought his ideals in the more distant
past and grounded his conclusions on the ancient Way in his study
of the *Kojiki,* a work to which he attributed scriptural status and to

which he maintained a fundamentalist's allegiance. Norinaga's ancient Way thought shared much with that of Kamo no Mabuchi, except that, where Mabuchi's thought emphasized the natural and spontaneous, Norinaga's focused more on the religious and deterministic. Norinaga styled the ancient Way as the Way of the gods, a Way neither created by human invention nor intrinsic to the natural order, but rather a Way fashioned by the native deities of Japan and bequeathed by them to their terrestrial delegates and successors. According to Norinaga, Japan's "golden age" was the divine age, a time before time when all was infused with the numinous and humans followed divinely imparted instincts. Furthermore, by grounding his arguments for Japanese superiority in the mythic cosmology of the *Kojiki*, Norinaga transformed Mabuchi's ideality of Japanese superiority into a more virulent set of articulations. He claimed that Japan's priority rested in the fact that it was created first among all countries by the native Japanese deities, and that all the world owed gratitude to the Japanese sun/sun goddess for her radiating warmth and sunshine. Like his predecessors in National Learning, Norinaga argued Japan's superiority primarily relative to the "whipping boy" of China, but Norinaga was the first Tokugawa nativist to assert Japanese superiority vis-à-vis all countries of the world, not just those of Asia. Though he was at best dimly (if at all) aware of it at the time, Japan was already embarked on a course that was to draw it ineluctably into a larger orbit of international relationships.

The writings of the major eighteenth-century *kokugakushu* covered a vast range of topics from poetry and literature, through ancient court ceremony and law, to theology and mytho-history. It appears that most of the students of Azumamaro, Mabuchi, and Norinaga were drawn more to their views on literature and verse than to those various subtopics subsumed under the rubric of the ancient Way. Nonetheless, following each eighteenth-century generational transition as the mantle of leadership in National Learning passed first from Azumamaro to Mabuchi and then from Mabuchi to Norinaga, it was the ancient Way that emerged as the thematic motive of National Learning thought. Though it is not always pos-

Kyoto in 1692 and Edo in 1698; the devaluation of metallic currency proved an effective short-term solution to economic problems; and some 150,000 perished in the Kantō earthquake of 1703—but, in most textbooks, all this is overshadowed by the emergence and development of the new popular culture. As George Sansom observed in his *History of Japan,* the Genroku was the age when Japan savored "la douceur de vivre."[1]

The term *popular culture* has a variety of meanings and implications. For example, the author of one recent study of eighteenth-century Japan uses it to refer to the political culture or "commoner consciousness" of the rural masses.[2] Most other writers have preferred not to define the term and to leave it to the reader to infer that the author intends popular culture to be understood vaguely as either non-aristocratic culture or the culture of merchant townsmen *(chōnin)*. None of these conveys the use of the term in this volume, where popular culture refers to those forms of secular urban culture that are self-supporting and sustaining, that is those forms that require neither the financial patronage nor independent wealth of the producer of the culture. More simply, popular culture is culture that pays for itself. It is financed by its consumers, thereby enabling its producers to create a livelihood through the marketing of the culture. Examples of such popular cultural activity—what might be called the "arts and letters business"[3]—include the author who gleans an income through the publication of his books, the playwright who profits through the production of his plays, the artist who earns a living through the sale of his art, or the intellectual who supports himself through the tuition of his students.

For the purposes of this volume, the most significant of these developments is that of the private academy, largely independent of external patronage or financial support and not requiring the independent wealth of the academy's head. The growth of this kind of nativist academy was slow by comparison with its Confucian or

---

[1]George B. Sansom, *A History of Japan,* III, 153.
[2]Anne Walthall, *Social Protest and Popular Culture in Eighteenth-Century Japan.*
[3]I am indebted to Philip Brown for this term.

Sinological counterpart, and, as shown in the chapters that follow, it represents a development that spanned most of the eighteenth century as nativism opened a new space on the impressive map of Tokugawa intellectual history. The nativist academy, thus, is not properly speaking a Genroku phenomenon; and yet it is evident that the same factors that contributed to the formation of the private Confucian academy in Genroku Japan fostered a cultural environment that allowed for the emergence of private nativist academies in eighteenth-century Japan.

The development of the popular academy in the Genroku—and the popular culture of which it formed but one part—is a remarkable phenomenon in the social history of Japan. It represents an important indication of cultural sophistication during an era that most historians regard either as pre-modern or, at best, early modern. Even more impressive, however, is the fact that, when viewed in the broader global context, Genroku popular culture is at least the contemporary of and is perhaps slightly prior to the comparable popular culture of England which emerged during the reigns of Queen Anne (1702–1714) and George I (1714–1727) as represented by the career of Daniel Defoe (1659–1731).[4] Thus, Tokugawa Japan may well have a legitimate claim to the world's oldest truly popular culture.

This chapter attempts to identify some of the social, economic, intellectual and political factors that appear to have contributed to the emergence of Genroku popular culture. The intention is twofold: on the one hand, to promote an understanding of the broader environment of urban Japan at the very start of the eighteenth century, the initial years with which this volume is principally concerned; and, on the other hand, to prepare for the examination of nativism in the chapters that follow by observing the relationship between popular culture and scholarship in the broadest sense. It is perhaps obvious but nonetheless necessary to state that these issues

---

[4] Defoe's key works in this context are *Robinson Crusoe* (1719), a work of "immediate and permanent popularity"; *Moll Flanders* (1722), "supreme as a realistic picture of low life"; and *The Complete English Tradesman* (1727), "that bourgeois classic." Quotations from George Sampson, *The Concise Cambridge History of English Literature*, p. 380.

represent an exceedingly complex problematik, and that a comprehensive examination of the matters considered in this chapter alone would require hundreds of pages and, ideally, multiple authorship.[5] Nonetheless, it is hoped that even a relatively cursory exploration will illuminate certain themes developed later in this volume and perhaps contribute to their further refinement and elaboration by others.

There are at least five features that characterized Genroku society and contributed to the emergence and development of its popular culture. (1) It included areas of high population density brought about through urbanization. (2) Its populace enjoyed a measure of surplus wealth distributed broadly if not equitably. (3) The society seems to have achieved high rates of literacy, at least in its population centers. (4) It had a developed transportation and communications infrastructure. (5) In addition to a high level of political stability, Genroku society demonstrated an attitude of conspicuous cultural liberality. The first four of these features are all more or less quantifiable, though not in each case with the accuracy one might desire; the fourth, though demonstrable, requires at least a measure of subjective evaluation; the fifth is the most subjective but perhaps the most important. The remainder of this chapter examines these features of Genroku Japan in greater detail, describes their relationship to the nascent popular culture, and concludes with a brief examination of the Confucian Ancient Learning academy of Itō Jinsai (1627–1705), one of the earliest and most successful examples of a self-sustaining private academy in Genroku Japan. It is hoped that this vignette of Jinsai and his academy will demonstrate his role—at once pioneering and paradigmatic—in the development of the private academy as well as his status as an exemplar of popular cultural activity not unlike his better-known contemporaries—the author Ihara Saikaku (1642–1693), the artist Hishikawa Moronobu (d. 1695?), and the playwright Chikamatsu Monzaemon (1653–1724).[6]

---

[5] One recent example of such a study is David Johnson, Andrew J. Nathan, and Evelyn S. Rawski, eds., *Popular Culture in Late Imperial China.*
[6] For an examination of Saikaku, Moronobu, and Chikamatsu within the context of popular culture, see my "The Requisites for Popular Culture in Genroku Japan"

Urbanization in Genroku Japan is the most easily quantifiable of the various features to be explored, and its relevance to popular culture perhaps the most obvious. Population centers encourage communication and concentrate the potential consumers of popular culture within a given and relatively accessible area, thereby facilitating the marketing of popular culture by its producers. Not surprisingly, therefore, popular culture always develops nationally first in those areas of highest population density from which it may later spread to less densely populated areas.

It is thus for our purposes significant that Tokugawa Japan was, if not the most, then certainly one of the most highly urbanized societies in the world by the start of the eighteenth century.[7] It may be assumed that 10 percent or more of Japan's population lived in communities with populations of 10,000 or greater by the year 1700; the populations of Nagoya and Kanazawa at over 100,000 each ranked with such cities as Rome and Amsterdam; the populations of Kyoto and Osaka, approximately 400,000 and 350,000 respectively, rivaled the population of Europe's two largest cities at that time, London and Paris; and, with a population of over 1 million, the political center of Edo was the world's largest city.

Furthermore, this urbanization of Japan was a phenomenon that occurred relatively quickly during the century and a quarter preceding the year 1700. The percentage of residents in settlements of over 10,000 increased 10-fold during those years, and as the historian John Hall has observed, since most of Japan's major cities and castle towns were founded during the years 1580 to 1610, it would be "hard to find a parallel period of urban construction in world history."[8] Edo itself grew from the proverbial "mere village" to Japan's major metropolis during those years by virtue of its status as the shogun's designated castle town and thus the political center of Tokugawa Japan.

---

[7] The major study of this phenomenon is Gilbert Rozman's *Urban Networks in Ch'ing China and Tokugawa Japan.* A useful introductory essay is John W. Hall's "The Castle Town and Japan's Modern Urbanization." A valuable case study of one castle town is James L. McClain, *Kanazawa: A Seventeenth-Century Japanese Castle Town.* Unless otherwise noted, the statistics concerning population come from McClain, *Kanazawa,* pp. 1–2.

[8] Hall, "Castle Town," p. 176.

Further comparisons with Europe are fruitful for comprehending the enormous significance of Japan's urban development at the close of the seventeenth century. Whereas between 5 and 7 percent of Japan's total population of some 30,000,000 by that time resided in cities of 100,000 or more population, only 2 to 3 percent of Europeans lived in such centers. In all Europe, only the Netherlands and England-Wales matched Japan's level of urbanization, and even such second-tier Japanese cities as the castle towns of Nagoya and Kanazawa ranked among the 20 largest cities of Europe and Japan.

Tokugawa popular culture emerged in the last two decades of the seventeenth century in Kyoto and Osaka and soon thereafter irrupted in Edo, whose population eventually outstripped its older rivals. Kyoto, of course, had been the traditional seat of the medieval culture that formed the crucial foundation for the nascent popular culture of the Genroku, and the displacement of much of this cultural activity to Edo was part of one of the more dramatic cultural movements in world history. But, for our purposes, the key element is the correlation between population density and the locus of popular cultural activity.[9] Concentrated population settlements are the breeding ground for popular culture. By their very nature, they attract the wealthiest, most literate, and cosmopolitan elements of a society, and they demand a more sophisticated infrastructure than rural environments. Therefore, the fact that Genroku Japan represented an extraordinarily urbanized society is of critical significance to this discussion.

A second element necessary for the development of a self-sustaining popular culture is a measure of surplus wealth dispersed in a relatively broad manner throughout the society. Popular culture requires consumers no less than producers, and, the broader the pool of potential consumers, the more successful the marketing of such culture. In fact, the content of Genroku popular culture suggests targeting by its producers at those sectors of society with the highest disposable income.

---

[9]On the cultural shift from the Kansai to the Kantō, see my *"Man'yōshū* Studies in Tokugawa Japan," pp. 124–140, 144.

Prior to the Tokugawa period, of course, there was surplus wealth in Japan, but it was concentrated in the hands of three main sectors of the society: first, the conglomeration of military elites, whose wealth derived from their control of land and the foodstuffs worked from that land by peasant agriculturalists; second, the hereditary aristocracy, socially centered on the Imperial Court in Kyoto, whose wealth, like that of the military elites, derived from the control of land, though the scale of aristocratic landholdings was smaller, as was their power; third, a group formed by those large Buddhist institutions that enjoyed sizable landholdings exempt from taxation, profitable involvement in a variety of economic activities, and the control and manipulation of religious symbols. It is no coincidence that these three groups, otherwise in various forms of competition with each other, were the custodians of medieval Japanese culture.

During the Tokugawa period, however, wealth was more broadly distributed across a wider range of social strata. In the seventeenth century, a variety of improvements in agronomy increased the annual national agricultural yield by an estimated 40 percent,[10] and, with the exception of occasional periods of famine attributable to either natural disasters or climatic irregularity, one can observe a small but steady improvement in the lot of the peasant agriculturalist throughout the seventeenth century.[11] Even more significant, however, was the growth in the manufacturing and service sectors of the seventeenth-century economy. With the emergence of Edo as the political center and the alternate attendance requirement for daimyo known as *sankin kōtai*, there was an extraordinary increase in the demand for the services of artisans such as carpenters, porcelain and paper manufacturers, metalworkers, weavers, and so on.[12] Under the *sankin kōtai*, daimyo were obliged to reside for part of each year in Edo where their families remained as semi-permanent

---

[10] Walthall, p. 5.

[11] See Susan B. Hanley and Kozo Yamamura, eds., *Economic and Demographic Change in Preindustrial Japan, 1600–1868*, p. 320.

[12] For an exceptionally insightful article on this phenomenon in Edo and several other Japanese cities in the seventeenth century, see Yoshida Nobuyuki, "Chōnin to machi."

hostages under a formula intended to preserve domestic peace. In order to create a residential environment appropriate to their social status, elaborate dwellings and estates were required for daimyo families within the precincts of the political center, and this required the extensive services of artisans and workers with an attendant transfer of untaxed wealth into their hands.[13]

However, no group in seventeenth-century Tokugawa society experienced a more dramatic economic advance than merchants. In theory, merchants were consigned by the dictates of Neo-Confucian social principles to the lowest rank of society, by virtue of that philosophy's perception that they were not engaged in either primary or secondary modes of production. Merchants grew, however, in wealth, power, and prestige throughout the Tokugawa period as their banking, warehousing, wholesaling, and brokerage services proved essential to the vitality and well-being of the expanding Tokugawa economy.[14]

Members of the samurai class, of course, enjoyed the greatest social prestige as well as the broadest measure of wealth, but two factors inhibited their economic growth. Large numbers of the class were disenfranchised by their lords during the seventeenth century since it was supposed that their martial services were no longer required in such large numbers during an age of prevailing peace. This resulted in the well-known *rōnin* or masterless samurai phenomenon, with occasionally tragic social consequences.[15] And samurai lived on fixed incomes or stipends which, while generous by contemporary standards, did not generally increase, giving rise to a tendency for samurai indebtedness. This indebtedness was almost always to the merchant class, creating the awkward situation of

---

[13] For a detailed discussion of the impact of this upon artisan organization, see Yokota Fuyuhiko, "Shokunin to shokunin shūdan."

[14] See Charles D. Sheldon, *The Rise of the Merchant Class in Tokugawa Japan, 1600–1868: An Introductory Survey.*

[15] The most dramatic instance of this in the seventeenth century was the Shimabara Rebellion of 1638. See Ivan Morris, *The Nobility of Failure: Tragic Heroes in the History of Japan,* pp. 143–179.

having those at the highest ranks of Tokugawa society in economic dependence upon those whom they regarded as their social inferiors.

The samurai, merchants, and artisans lived for the most part in the major cities and castle towns, and they were the market for the emerging popular culture. The stories and plays that reached large audiences in the Genroku recounted not only the exploits and misadventures of samurai but also those of greengrocers and other shopkeepers, clerks and apprentices, carpenters and potters, women of pleasure and their customers, and so on. The prints that circulated depicted scenes from their lives, or adorned their homes with colorful portrayals of a stylized world of nature. And the private academies were taught and staffed and attended at this time either by merchants who relished the opportunity to purchase the previously inaccessible culture or by disenfranchised samurai who found educational activities an appropriate vocation as well as a source of needed income.

It is remarkable how often economic themes enter into the plots of Ihara Saikaku's tales or Chikamatsu Monzaemon's plays. This is evidence not only of the impact of the cash economy upon daily life in Genroku Japan but also of the degree to which such popular writers—themselves products of urban environments— crafted themes that mirrored the concerns of their audience. It is a commonplace to assert that only the "middle classes" suffer from worries about money, and, though it would be anachronistic to depict the *chōnin* as a new middle class, the prevalence of economic anxieties in the popular literature of the time attests in a most convincing manner to the distribution of wealth in Genroku Japan and the expectations and concerns that attend such wealth.

The expanded distribution of surplus wealth throughout various sectors of Genroku society broadened the potential audience for popular culture. Generally, during the second half of the seventeenth century, members of the samurai class were the producers of most of the various forms of popular culture discussed here, while members of the merchant and artisan classes were among the primary consumers of that culture. But, by the end of the first half of the eighteenth century, members of the merchant class formed the largest sector for both the production and the consumption of this new culture. The Genroku years anchored this transitional stage and therefore mark a time of unprecedented social and cultural interaction among the various classes in Tokugawa Japan.

The expansion of literacy and the development of printing technology were likewise significant for facilitating the emergency of the new popular culture. Though it is obvious that one need not be literate to enjoy the performance of a play or piece of music, or to appreciate a painting or print, the central position popular literature occupies within popular culture justifies the inclusion of literacy among the most prominent features of Genroku society that appear to have contributed to the emergence and growth of a self-sustaining popular culture.[16] In addition, the distribution of texts at a more readily affordable per-unit price requires the use of printing technology. Genroku Japan had the technology, and all evidence points to its also having the literacy.

The best estimates for literacy rates at the end of the Tokugawa period suggest male literacy of 40 to 50 percent, and female literacy perhaps half that of males. These rates, which may appear low by contemporary standards, are most impressive when one considers that they were probably higher than those of any other place in the world at that time, with the possible exceptions of England and Holland.[17] Unfortunately, estimates of comparable quality and reliability for literacy rates in the late-seventeenth and early-eighteenth centuries are not available. Since there is no hard evidence for an explosion of literacy during the eighteenth century, one must turn to other sources for information about literacy in Genroku Japan.

The evidence contained within the popular literature itself may be the most illustrative; there one finds frequent references to the reading and writing of letters by altogether ordinary characters. To cite just one example from a short story by Ihara Saikaku, in a

---

[16] See Ian Watt, *The Rise of the Novel* pp. 37–40.
[17] See Ronald P. Dore, *Education in Tokugawa Japan*.

chapter devoted to anecdotes about pawnshops, Saikaku describes the ingenious scheme of one pawnbroker who catered to the women of the licensed pleasure quarters. In exchange for a personally addressed love letter, the pawnbroker would advance a fixed sum of cash. His loans were invariably repaid, according to the story, since the threat of exposing the "love letter"—and the catastrophic impact such exposure would have upon the woman's livelihood—was always sufficient to inspire timely settlement of the debt.[18] The story, of course, was intended to amuse rather than edify, but nowhere in the story is it suggested that it might be odd or exceptional for a courtesan to be able to write a love letter, and, if the courtesan could write, then of course she could read as well.

Such references are so common in the literature of the Genroku that it encourages one to consider the possibility that an actual majority of those who resided or made their living within Japan's major metropolises had the ability at least to read, if not also to write. Further, since the stories and plays themselves often provide the best clues as to their intended audiences—under the assumption that people then, as now, enjoyed reading about or viewing the exploits of persons not unlike themselves—there is further reason to suspect that literacy was not at all unusual for precisely those urban clerks and shopkeepers, samurai and attendants, brokers and wholesalers, and even those courtesans and habitués of the demimonde of the licensed quarters who figure so prominently in the literature.

The question of how so large a percentage of Genroku urban population may have acquired literacy is difficult to answer, but it is possible to construct a composite of the typical circumstances. The offspring of the wealthiest—the daimyo, high-ranking samurai, aristocrats, and prosperous merchants—were usually taught to read by private tutors, such training beginning at about age 6. Those from slightly more humble circumstances generally were taught to read within the home and received instruction from women, most often their mothers or close female relatives. Others from still hum-

---

[18] See Ihara Saikakiu, *Some Final Words of Advice*, tr. Peter Nosco, pp. 202–204.

bler backgrounds were taught either in the *terakoya* (originally Zen temple schools) or by village tutors who were themselves often disenfranchised samurai earning a living in a manner appropriate to their social station.[19]

A further indication of the increased literacy of Tokugawa Japan is the rise of private academies during the second half of the seventeenth century and their maturation in the eighteenth century. The contribution of these academies to adult continuing education has often been noted, but the evidence they provide of a literate public that derived either personal or professional benefit from training in Confucianism, Shinto theology, nativism, versification, and so on is no less impressive.[20]

Of course, neither a literate public nor a popular literature can be created without readily available texts of relatively low per-unit price, and such texts can be produced only through printing technology. In virtually all societies, the printing or publication of texts with religious or ideological significance precedes secular popular literature, and, throughout East Asia, this pattern has been upheld.[21] The printing of doctrinal works can be regarded as paving the way for other works and thereby contributes indirectly to such publication; but a developed popular culture requires the publication of secular literature.

The first non-religious work published in Japan, the *Setsuyōshū* dictionary, was printed in 1591. It was nearly two decades, however, before the first commercial publication began in Japan, in 1609. With the success of this initial venture, commercial printing rapidly spread throughout the major metropolises of Kyoto, Osaka, and Edo. One irony in this development was that commercial print-

---

[19] Virtually all literate persons in Tokugawa Japan were taught to read using a Neo-Confucian curriculum, beginning with the *Primary Learning (Hsiao-hsueh)* and *Thousand-Character Classic (Ch'ien-tzu wen)* and advancing through the Four Books.
[20] See Richard Rubinger, *Private Academies of Tokugawa Japan*. The prototype for these academies was the Tung-lin Academy founded in China in 1604 by Ku Hsien-ch'eng (1550–1612).
[21] In China, the earliest printed texts were the Confucian classics, while, in Japan, the oldest printed work was the Buddhist Lotus Sutra.

ing in Japan did not rely upon the newly introduced movable type technology Japan had acquired as a result of its ill-advised invasion of Korea in the 1590s,[22] but instead reverted to the traditional carved block printing, for reasons probably more aesthetic than practical.

The next breakthrough came in 1682 with the publication in Osaka of Ihara Saikaku's *Life of an Amorous Man (Kōshoku ichidai otoko)*, which captured the interest of a receptive reading public while opening up an entirely new concept in Japanese fiction. Cast in 54 chapters like the classic *The Tale of Genji* nearly seven centuries earlier, the work recounted the romantic misadventures of a Japanese cross between Don Juan and Robinson Crusoe, as he proceeds through a sexual career beginning at age 7 to make love to thousands of women and hundreds of men. In a curious parallel to Crusoe in one of the earliest commercial successes in the history of European popular literature, the work's hero, Yonosuke, finally sets sail aboard the vessel SS *Lust (Kōshoku maru)* bound for a mythical Isle of Women. The first printing of some 1,000 copies sold out almost immediately and ushered in the first of two major bursts of publishing activity in Tokugawa Japan.[23]

The commercial success of *Life of an Amorous Man* marked the first time in Japanese literary history that it became possible for an author of non-religious fiction to support himself through the publication of his work. The themes of these earliest "bestsellers" most often centered on adventure, travel, sexual escapades and their consequences, and guides to personal wealth and betterment. They were tailored and calculated to satisfy the desires of a broad literate public, thus representing a new relationship between author and audi-

---

[22] Though the invasion was a failure, printing was only one of its benefits for Japan. Another was the discovery of the vitality of the Neo-Confucian tradition on the mainland as a result of Japan's plundering numerous Korean libraries—a discovery that transformed the intellectual history of the next three centuries in Japan.

[23] The first such burst lasted from roughly 1680 to 1730; the second came about a century later. For additional information on Tokugawa publishing, see G. Raymond Nunn, "On the Number of Books Published in Japan from 1600 to 1868."

ence in Japanese literary history; this new relationship rested in substantial measure upon the capacity of commercial publishers to produce texts in sufficient numbers and at relatively moderate cost.

The development of commercial publication was, of course, just one part of a broader communications and transportation infrastructure in Genroku Japan, which had developed considerably during the sixteenth century in order to meet the logistical requirements of armies on the march; it did not reach full form until the early decades of the seventeenth century under the Tokugawa peace.[24] As a military man, the first Tokugawa shogun, Tokugawa Ieyasu, understood the strategic value of overland transportation routes, and he moved quickly to control and regulate their use. He established a national network of five major highways (the Gokaidō) and consolidated numerous regional networks, widening the roads and erecting post stations *(shukueki)* and distance markers. The post stations served a variety of functions—providing porters and post horses to official travelers and their goods, offering the facilities of a rest stop and recreation area, and fulfilling the function of an information-communications center.[25]

The quality of this highway system, at least relative to that of Europe at the time, is attested to by the German physician Engelbert Kaempfer, who was in the employ of the Dutch in Japan during the early 1690s. Kaempfer found "scarce credible" the number of daily travelers on the Tōkaidō, the principal highway linking Kyoto to Edo, and proclaimed the route to be "on some days more crowded than the public streets in any of the most populous towns of Europe."[26] Though it is not possible to estimate the number of daily travelers on routes like the Tōkaidō with precision, it is clear that the travelers were numerous and included not only officials like

---

[24] John Saris's (1579–1643) description of travel on the Tōkaidō in 1613 is included in Michael Cooper, ed., *They Came to Japan: An Anthology of European Reports on Japan. 1543–1640,* pp. 283–284.

[25] The information above on transportation comes from Constantine N. Vaporis, "Post Station and Assisting Villages: Corvee Labor and Peasant Contention," especially pp. 378–381.

[26] Quoted in Sansom, III, 136. Kaempfer's 3-volume *The History of Japan* (Glasgow, 1906) is an invaluable source on daily life.

daimyo and their retinues en route to and from Edo but also great numbers of ordinary citizens. The volume of goods transported along the route was extraordinary; no less remarkable was the presence of sojourners and religious pilgrims, who on occasion numbered in the thousands.

These aforementioned features of Genroku society which contributed to the emergence of a self-sustaining popular culture have all been (at least to some extent) quantifiable, though often not with the precision one might desire. The last feature to be examined, however—a climate of cultural liberality—does not lend itself to quantification but may be the most critical component of the social and intellectual environment which conduced toward the emergence of a successful popular culture during the Genroku. The term *cultural liberality* is, of course, a difficult one. Charles Frankel spoke of cultural liberalism as "an affirmative interest in the promotion of the diversity and qualities of mind which encourage empathetic understanding and critical appreciation of the diverse possibilities of human life."[27] This kind of cultural liberalism was certainly present in the Genroku when, as a possible response to the influence of Neo-Confucian philosophy's belief in the world's comprehensibility, an impressive variety of social, ethical, and cosmological discourses circulated among informed circles.[28]

More significant, however, for the emergence of the private academy within the popular culture was the fact that culture during the Genroku was not perceived to be the monopolized prerogative of any particular class or group within the society; it is this sense that is intended here by the term *cultural liberality*. During the centuries of classical and medieval civilization prior to the Tokugawa period, "high" or aristocratic culture had been the exclusive possession of the ruling classes and the major Buddhist institutions. Initially centered upon the imperial court, this high culture spread during the medieval period to the courts of various shoguns and the other military elites who were the country's masters. In fact, at all times prior

---

[27] See the transcript of Charles Frankel's talk "The Foundations of Liberalism."

[28] See Wm. Theodore de Bary, "Some Common Tendencies in Neo-Confucianism."

to the Tokugawa, the possession of this aristocratic culture was part and parcel of the aura of legitimacy whereby successive elites used the trappings of culture to justify the authority they had seized through cunning and force.

Though it is now clear that the process of breaking down the walls of this cultural hegemony had begun in and accelerated during the sixteenth century,[29] it is clear that the process reached maturity during the Tokugawa. The new combination of relatively broadly distributed surplus wealth, population density, and the other factors we have examined resulted during the Genroku era in an unprecedented degree of access to the traditional high culture. For example, in a list of the attributes and skills the otherwise wayward son of a merchant had acquired, Ihara Saikaku listed the following: training in the traditional musical instruments for Nō drama accompaniment, linked verse and *haikai* composition, flower arrangement, *kemari* football, tea ceremony, Neo-Confucianism, *go*, archery, distinguishing and combining incenses, court etiquette, *biwa* and *koto* performance, singing, improvisation, and mimicry.[30] Saikaku's intent was satirical, since he sought to convey a father's disappointment over his son's inability to earn a living despite the attention lavished upon his upbringing and his otherwise impressive accomplishments. Nonetheless, the list indicates an unprecedented degree of access by Japan's newly wealthy to a broad range of culture which, prior to the Tokugawa, had been inaccessible to all but a privileged few.

One key development in this new spirit of cultural liberality was the weakening of the system of esoteric transmission that had been characteristic of the medieval attitude toward virtually all forms of knowledge. In earlier centuries, if one wished to acquire knowledge of, say, the arts of poetry or tea, and was of a class for whom such knowledge was regarded as appropriate, one then sought out a master; if accepted and gifted, one might eventually be privileged to

---

[29] Several helpful articles may be found in George Elison and B. L. Smith, eds., *Warlords, Artists and Commoners: Japan in the Sixteenth Century* and John W. Hall, et al., eds., *Japan Before Tokugawa: Political Control and Economic Growth, 1500–1650*.
[30] *Some Final Words of Advice*, pp. 41–42.

learn the secrets (quite literally) of the art. Without such esoteric knowledge, one's level of accomplishment could never advance beyond the elementary.[31] These esoteric transmissions began to lose their exclusivity at the very start of the Tokugawa. For example, in 1603, just three years after the decisive Battle of Sekigahara and the same year in which Ieyasu was accorded the title of shogun, Hayashi Razan (1583–1657), a pioneering scholar of Neo-Confucianism, began a series of unprecedented public lectures on the key texts of that tradition. Just one year later, Matsunaga Teitoku (1571–1643) lent further respectability to Razan's experiment by himself giving equally unprecedented public lectures on two literary classics, the *Tsurezuregusa (Essays in Idleness)* and *Hyakunin isshu (One Hundred Poems by One Hundred Poets)*. As Donald Keene has observed, "The new approach to learning represented by the public lectures did not put an end to the secret traditions, but the characteristic literary arts of the Tokugawa period were remarkably free of the old secrecy."[32]

What changed was the degree of access to the various components of Tokugawa secular culture. Those who would once have been denied access for reasons of class or background could, by the Genroku period, purchase access from altogether willing purveyors. Ihara Saikaku, our by now oft-quoted observer of the follies of his age, remarked on the ease with which the untrained might gain reputations as *haikai* masters and the untutored qualify as their students: "Recently . . . *haikai* have grown so popular in our society that every last apprentice and scullery maid tries his or her hand at them . . . But look at the persons who pass themselves as markers [tu-

---

[31] One illustration of the seriousness these esoteric transmissions were accorded concerns the scholar Hosokawa Yūsai (1534–1610), who, in 1600, was the sole possessor of the esoteric *Kokin denju* tradition on the *Kokinshū* poetry anthology. In that year, the siege of the castle at Tanabe where Yūsai was staying was lifted at the request of Emperor Goyōzei (r. 1586–1611) who was prevailed upon by Yūsai's students, fearing permanent loss of the *Kokin denju* if harm befell their master. See Donald Keene, *World Within Walls: Japanese Literature of the Pre-Modern Era, 1600–1867*, pp. 24–26.

[32] Teitoku was responding in this to pressure from not only Hayashi Razan but also Razan's father and uncle. See Donald Keene, "Characteristic Responses to Confucianism in Tokugawa Literature," p. 121.

tors] today! If you think about it carefully, *haikai* masters now seem
so foolish because they are crooks."[33] Of course Saikaku's loss, so
to speak, was popular culture's gain, since the traditional culture of
the few had become the popular culture of the many. Daniel Defoe
recognized that the gentility previously attainable only through birth
had become acquirable, for, if being a gentleman in Defoe's England meant that one possessed both wealth and breeding, then trade
could bring his "true-bred merchant" the wealth and a liberal education could produce his cultivation. While for Defoe this was reason to rejoice, Saikaku and others of his age found cause to lament
a perceived loss of that dignity they identified with culture.[34] But,
access to culture in Japan would never again be as restricted as it
had been.

The popular culture of Genroku Japan thus represented an entirely new class of producers, a new class of consumers, and a new
relationship between the two. Fostered and nurtured by the various
features described above, culture was now something that could be
marketed to a broad and enthusiastic audience. If there was an attendant loss of "dignity," there was also a wealth of colorful richness
and pluralism as the new popular culture addressed themes and
concerns nowhere evident in the high culture of classical and medieval Japan. To regard this as a bloodless cultural "revolution" is
in no way inappropriate, and, like all revolutions, it had its "heroes." Figures like Ihara Saikaku, Chikamatsu Monzaemon, and
Hishikawa Moronobu were pioneers in the popularization of a broad
range of cultural arts and activities. In various ways, they took existing genres and modes and refashioned them to suit the interests,
tastes, and preferences of newly diversified audiences.

Though they have generally not been regarded in this context,
the activities of the Confucian scholar Itō Jinsai were also an important indication and part of the expansion of popular culture during
the Genroku. Jinsai's academy, the Kogidō, was not the first self-

---

[33] *Some Final Words of Advice,* pp. 128–131.
[34] Saikaku's lament echoes that of Yoshida Kenkō in his fourteenth-century *Tsurezuregusa,*
where he confesses that in all things he yearns for the past. See Donald Keene, tr., *Essays
in Idleness* (New York, Columbia University Press, 1967), p. 23.

supporting private academy in Tokugawa Japan, but it was the most successful prior to the eighteenth century. What is more, just as the respective successes of Saikaku, Chikamatsu, and Moronobu inspired scores of others to emulate their activities, the success of the Kogidō appears to have been inspirational for not just other Confucian scholars but also for nativists like his fellow Kyoto resident Kada no Azumamaro. In this sense, Jinsai is no less an exemplar or paradigm of Genroku popular culture than his better-known contemporaries in literature and the arts.

The rise of the private academy was closely related to the "civilianization" of the samurai class during the middle decades of the seventeenth century, that is, the vocational rehabilitation of significant numbers of this class as their martial skills were discovered to be of less practical value in an age of enduring peace. This transformation of the samurai class was so radical that one scholar has remarked how, by "the end of the seventeenth century, a high degree of literacy was expected of the samurai and advanced study in Confucian classics had become part of their training for leadership." [35] The formal codification by Yamaga Sokō (1622–1685) just prior to the Genroku of the centuries-old martial code of *bushidō* was itself an ironic indication of the fossilization of the samurai class and its values in an age that had less need for its services.

The Confucian studies of various sorts which members of the samurai class taught and studied were, of course, nothing new in Tokugawa Japan, but their direction and influence were. Confucianism had been studied and taught in Japan for over a thousand years prior to the seventeenth century, but it was not until the arrival of new Confucian texts in the 1590s—another ironic byproduct of the invasion of Korea—that Confucianism, or rather its updated Neo-Confucian form, acquired an independent stature and began an extraordinary transformation of the terms of intellectual discourse. [36] During the seventeenth century, government authori-

---

[35] Rubinger, p. 50.
[36] See Nosco, "Introduction: Neo-Confucianism and Tokugawa Discourse," in *Confucianism and Tokugawa Culture*, pp. 3–26.

ties took an increasingly active role in sponsoring such activities. The 5th Tokugawa shogun, Tsunayoshi, whose reign covered the last two decades of the seventeenth and the first decade of the eighteenth century, was particularly remarkable in this regard. Not only did he directly patronize a number of Confucian scholars; he even lectured himself on Neo-Confucian texts and issues and raised the status of the Hayashi family's school on those doctrines to that of a quasi-official government academy. Numerous daimyo followed suit by establishing domainal schools for instruction in the orthodox tradition of Ch'eng-Chu Neo-Confucianism.[37] For our purposes, however, such officially and semi-officially sponsored or patronized scholarship does not quality as true popular culture; for that we must turn to the growth of private academies founded by townsmen like Itō Jinsai.

Jinsai was born in Kyoto, the eldest son of an unsuccessful merchant.[38] His formal education began at age 10 under the supervision of his uncle, a celebrated physician, and followed what soon became the standard Neo-Confucian curriculum. Jinsai continued his studies of these works during his teens, using his family's unusually good collection of books. He also briefly attended lectures on the subject by Matsunaga Sekigo (1592–1657). In all these pursuits, Jinsai apparently went against the advice of his relatives and friends who "all warned that Confucianism would not make me any money and that medicine would be more profitable."[39]

It was during the 1660s and 1670s that Jinsai broke with the orthodox Ch'eng-Chu traditions of Neo-Confucianism, turned briefly to the heterodox teachings of Wang Yang-ming (1472–1528), and finally began to recommend the direct study of such seminal works as the *Analects* of Confucius and the *Mencius*. Jinsai started a discus-

---

[37] Named for the commentaries by the brothers Ch'eng Hao (1032–1085) and Ch'eng I (1033–1107), and those of the master Chu Hsi (1130–1200).

[38] Biographical information on Jinsai in this book comes from Samuel Hideo Yamashita, "The Early Life and Thought of Itō Jinsai." The only Western-language book-length monograph on Jinsai is still Joseph John Spae's study first published in 1948, *Itō Jinsai: A Philosopher, Educator and Sinologist of the Tokugawa Period*.

[39] Quoted in Yamashita, p. 457.

sion group in 1661 called the Dōshikai (Society of the Like-Minded), and, one year later, he founded a private academy in Kyoto known as the Kogidō (Hall of Ancient Meaning).[40] Here he taught the new methodology of *kogaku* (Ancient Learning), which emphasized the study of ancient classical Chinese in order to dispense with commentaries on the core texts of Confucianism and to allow those texts to communicate their truths in their most direct form.

As mentioned above, Jinsai's academy was not the first private Confucian academy in seventeenth-century Japan but it was the most successful, and its development followed what later became a pattern among such ventures. As early as the 1630s and 1640s, Nakae Tōju (1608–1648) had established a small academy, the Tōju Shoin, in Ōmi. At the school, which probably had fewer than 60 students, Tōju taught an eclectic range of subjects including Confucianism, history, poetry, and calligraphy, while also arranging for individual instruction in other subjects for students with special interests.[41] It appears, however, that Tōju, who was of samurai ancestry, never gleaned more than a meager income from his students' tuition and was supported in large measure by their gifts of food and clothing. By contrast, Jinsai's school began as a study and reading group and was only later formalized as a successful private academy, establishing a pattern followed by such other academies as the Kaitokudō in Osaka and the Suzunoya in Matsusaka.[42] Jinsai's school had as many as 215 students by 1687 and continued to grow even after Jinsai's death, when the mantle of leadership passed to his son, Itō Tōgai.[43] Like the Kaitokudō, Jinsai's Kogidō also continued with its traditional curriculum until well into the nineteenth century.[44]

---

[40] Jinsai's school is also known as the Horikawaha (Horikawa Group) after the section of Kyoto in which it was located.

[41] Rubinger, p. 46.

[42] On the Kaitokudō and this institutional pattern, see Tetsuo Najita, *Visions of Virtue in Tokugawa Japan: The Kaitokudō Merchant Academy of Osaka,* esp. p. 62.

[43] Rubinger, p. 55. Itō Tōgai estimated that as many as one thousand students had come into contact with his father. See Spae, p. 90n.

[44] Spae, p. 93. Unlike the Kaitokudō, which repeatedly changed heads and turned to bakufu support in the eighteenth century, the Kogidō remained under the headship of the Itō and independent of government support throughout these centuries.

One of Jinsai's primary teachings was his insistence that one's emotions, which orthodox Neo-Confucianism taught one to distrust, were part and parcel of the natural and innate moral disposition. He interpreted the cardinal Confucian virtue of humanity (C. *jen,* J. *jin*) as virtually synonymous with love *(ai)* and insisted, in the best Confucian tradition, that knowledge of morality was of no consequence if not translated into actual moral behavior. This affirmation of the emotional and emphasis on the practical manifestation of virtue were much attuned to the intellectual tastes and dispositional preferences of the Genroku townsman, and an examination of the Kogidō's student registry during the 1680s confirms this. As one might expect in terms of the transformation or "civilianization" taking place among the samurai class, 39 percent of his students during those years were of either samurai or *rōnin* backgrounds, but even more impressive is the fact that fully 50 percent were of either the merchant, artisan, or medical professions.[45]

The success of Jinsai's private academy inspired scores of others to try comparable ventures. In a diatribe reminiscent of that of Ihara Saikaku against the profusion of self-proclaimed authorities on versification, a work called *Gion monogatari (Tale of Gion)* complains of the ease with which young monks, no longer interested in their Buddhist vocation, return to lay life and establish themselves as authorities on Confucian texts.[46] Furthermore, the Kogidō was the first private academy in Japan in which the mantle of leadership successfully passed from one generation to the next upon the death of the founder. Jinsai's son, Itō Tōgai (1670–1736), continued the direction his father had set for the school, and the school continued to prosper. This success, in turn, may have proved instrumental in the attempt by Kada no Azumamaro (1669–1736) to found a nativist counterpart to the Kogidō in Fushimi, a southern ward of the city of Kyoto.[47]

Jinsai's career exemplifies the successful, albeit unconscious, ex-

---

[45] Rubinger, p. 55.
[46] See Royall Tyler, "The Tokugawa Peace and Popular Religion: Suzuki Shōsan, Kakugyō Tōbutsu, and Jikigyō Miroku," pp. 93–94.
[47] See Nosco, "*Man'yōshū* Studies in Tokugawa Japan."

ploitation of those criteria we have identified as supportive of the emergence and development of popular culture. His academy was urban and situated in the ancient seat of learning of Kyoto, though, within a decade of his death, similar ventures began to appear in Edo and elsewhere. His students were drawn overwhelmingly from the samurai, merchant, and artisan classes, those classes which enjoyed the greatest measure of the newly dispersed surplus wealth. The expansion of literacy as well as the new expectation of literacy, particularly among the samurai, defined and refined Jinsai's potential audience, since it is apparent that many of his students derived professional advantage from their training. The communications and transportation infrastructure made possible the circulation and eventual publication of his major works throughout Japan and enabled him to draw his students from literally all over the country.[48] And, the climate of encouragement of learning and cultural liberality provided a new degree of access to teachings such as those of Jinsai, while it also permitted him to express non-orthodox views of a sort that would have been disallowed prior to the Genroku.[49]

Itō Jinsai's career contains some interesting parallels with and divergences from the careers of Ihara Saikaku, Chikamatsu Monzaemon, and Hishikawa Moronobu. All were active in Japan's largest cities, and, with the exception of Moronobu, all were active in the Kansai metropolises of Kyoto and Osaka.[50] Their class backgrounds were different—Chikamatsu was the son of a *rōnin,* Moronobu the son of an artisan, and controversy still surrounds the question of whether Saikaku's father was a merchant or a samurai—but their class origins replicate those of their audiences. They were, of course, contemporaries; three of the four achieved their first prominence with works completed in either 1682 or 1683,[51] and three of the

---

[48] See the map of the geographical distribution of Kogidō students by province in Rubinger, p. 54. Note that Ezo (present Hokkaido), from which no Kogidō students came, was not in any meaningful sense Japanese during Jinsai's lifetime.

[49] Yamaga Sokō (1622–1685) was exiled to Ako in 1666 for publishing an attack on orthodox Neo-Confucian teachings in the previous year. He remained there until 1675.

[50] Saikaku was born in Osaka; Chikamatsu moved to Kyoto around 1663; and Moronobu was born and raised in Edo.

[51] Saikaku wrote his first commercial success, *The Life of an Amorous Man (Kōshoku ichidai*

four also achieved their first fame in ventures somewhat removed from those that later earned them their greatest acclaim.[52] To different degrees each may be credited with the invigoration of a traditional genre through stylistic and thematic innovation, and, of course, each contributed to a further obfuscation of the traditional distinction between "high" and 'low" culture.[53]

Perhaps most significant in terms of their popularization of culture, however, all four of these figures represent a new realism in their respective areas of activity, and this realism contributed to the relevance of their cultural production. Saikaku's fiction treated such themes as sexuality, violence, and social disobedience, on which the earlier literature had been, for the most part, silent. Chikamatsu's plays addressed and even glorified the love suicides (*shinjū*) which became something of a vogue in his age. Moronobu's paintings and prints often contained an erotic dimension whose appeal to the Genroku townsman requires no explanation. And Jinsai's affirmation of the affective and emotional spheres of human experience seemed to many to be attuned to the new realities of urban life in an age of both prosperity and peace.

Like the contributions of Saikaku, Chikamatsu, and Moronobu, Jinsai's contribution to Genroku popular culture has both qualitative and institutional aspects. The excellence and originality of his teachings are self-evident and represent an important chapter in Japanese intellectual history, but the unprecedented success of Jinsai's private academy opened a new set of educational opportunities by meeting the intellectual and vocational needs of a segment of late-seventeenth-century townsmen and thereby added one more facet to the already brilliant gem of Genroku popular culture.

---

otoko), in 1682; Chikamatsu wrote his first major play, *The Soga Heir (Yotsugi Soga),* in 1683; and, in the same year, in response to a bakufu request, Jinsai wrote his *Gomō jigi,* a summary of the doctrines of his school, which circulated widely in MS form.

[52] Both Saikaku and Chikamatsu won their first acclaim as composers of *haikai* verses, while Moronobu's first signed and dated works are a set of book illustrations and a painted scroll.

[53] Saikaku's *Life of an Amorous Man* revitalized the novel; Chikamatsu, who wrote for both the *kabuki* and *jōruri* theaters, gave respectability to the former and rescued the latter; Moronobu significantly expanded the thematic range of the monochrome painting and print; and Jinsai legitimized the study of the Chinese classics on their own terms.

Various features—urbanization, surplus wealth, literacy, communications infrastructure, and cultural liberality—proved relevant to the development of Genroku popular culture in general and, in particular, to the career of Itō Jinsai and his academy as an exemplar of that culture. One feature of Genroku popular culture already noted was the manner in which traditional genres and styles were invigorated by infusing them with thematically new materials attuned to the tastes and preferences of the townsman. Saikaku was not the first novelist in Japanese history, nor was Chikamatsu the first dramatist, Moronobu the first painter, or Jinsai the first scholar; each used existing media in a refreshingly new manner and with unprecedented popular success. Thus, while their originality may not appear so extreme when they are correctly situated within their historical context, their achievements were nonetheless revolutionary, and their contributions both enduring and profound.

There is a certain "truth" of intellectual history demonstrated in this, namely, that, no matter how original one's message may be, one cannot be successful with it in a popular sense unless that message is communicable in the existing idiom. Thus, all popular pioneers share much with their forebears, irrespective of the apparent originality of their achievement. In this sense, pioneers also share much with forerunners in that they are at once harbingers of the new while contextually products of the past. It is, of course, probable that, had popular culture been regarded by the Tokugawa bakufu as a destabilizing force, the government's response would have been to censor its production and thereby obstruct its consumption. With few exceptions, however, the government did not regard the popular culture as much more than a costly amusement for those with wealth to squander.[54] It is somewhat ironic, then, that, though this culture did not actively destabilize the feudal structure, it did transform with enduring effects the society that was its habitat.

The "space" Jinsai opened—that of the private Confucian academy with a classical curriculum and emphasis on philological method—was appropriated during the next century by the private

---

[54] An example of one bakufu attempt to proscribe popular culture is discussed by Donald H. Shively in his *"Bakufu* versus *Kabuki."*

nativist academy with a curriculum of classics from the Japanese tradition and a comparable focus on philology. Before this became possible, however, nativism had, first, to disentangle itself from Confucianism, with which it had coexisted harmoniously as scholarship *(gakumon)* during most of the seventeenth century, and, second, to articulate an adversarial relationship toward it. If the rise of the private academy as an aspect of a new popular culture represents one interpretive context for the formation of the ideological nativism known as National Learning, then the disassociation of nativism from Confucianism represents a second such context.

THREE

Creating a Context (II): Confucianism, Nativism, and Keichū (1640–1701)

One of the most conspicuous features of nativist thought in eighteenth-century Japan was its vilification of Buddhism and Confucianism as "foreign" creeds alleged to have had a deleterious impact upon the national character and polity. Of the two doctrines, Confucianism was singled out for special criticism, as the major nativists denounced what they regarded as its misplaced but nonetheless seductive confidence in the capacity of the human intellect to arrive rationally at ultimate truths.

Setting aside the question of whether it was either appropriate or accurate in the eighteenth century to castigate as "foreign" doctrines that had existed in Japan for over a thousand years, the nativists did have a point concerning Confucian rationalism and humanism. Virtually all modern students of the subject agree that these were among the enduring influences Confucian discourse exercised during the Tokugawa period. There remained within a variety of Tokugawa scholarly circles an abiding faith in positivistic and quasi-scientific approaches to learning, and a confidence that the world was comprehensible in rational terms, though of course the nature of such understandings often differed from one scholar to another. Furthermore, Tokugawa political discourse was colored by the Confucian assumption that the responsibility for maintaining the delicate balance at the heart of both state and cosmos rested squarely on the shoulders of human beings who were expected to maintain correct loyalties and duties in their relationships with others.[1]

As a result of the adversarial relationship between Confucianism and nativism in eighteenth-century Japan, there has been an understandable tendency among scholars to overlook the fact that Confucianism and nativism coexisted harmoniously and to mutual benefit as constituent elements of scholarly discourse in the seventeenth century. Leading Confucian thinkers sought verification for Confucian premises in Japanese history, attempted to reconcile Confucian "truths" with the native "truths" of Shinto, tried to apply Confucian political principles to the realities of Tokugawa government, and even argued that the Japanese experience might reflect such Confucian themes as loyalty and obedience in a manner superior to that of China.

Conversely, the assimilation of Confucian terms and assumptions into much of the popular literature and thought of the Genroku and later eras reflects the extent to which Confucianism had become an integral part of the culture—popular and otherwise—of Tokugawa Japan. While it had long been assumed that Confucianism was the dominant, if not the sole, component in the construction of a Tokugawa ideology during the seventeenth century, the researches of Ishida Ichirō and Herman Ooms in particular have demonstrated that Confucianism was just one element among many in this process, and that Shinto and Buddhist elements figure no less prominently.[2] Nonetheless, by virtue of its own intellectually compelling qualities as well as the measure of official interest accorded to its teachings during the seventeenth century, Confucianism exerted considerable influence in various arenas of intellectual endeavor.

This chapter examines some examples of the seventeenth-century

---

[1] See de Bary, "Some Common Tendencies in Neo-Confucianism"; Ryusaku Tsunoda, et al., comps., *Sources of Japanese Tradition,* I, 342–344; and Nosco, *Confucianism and Tokugawa Culture,* pp. 23–26.

[2] See Ishida Ichirō, "Zenki bakuhan taisei no ideorogii to Shushigakuha no shisō," in Ishida Ichirō and Kanaya Osamu, eds., *Fujiwara Seika, Hayashi Razan,* pp. 411–448. See also Herman Ooms, *Tokugawa Ideology: Early Constructs, 1570–1680;* my review of this work in *Harvard Journal of Asiatic Studies* 47.1: 341–349 (1987); and Ooms's "Neo-Confucianism and the Formation of Early Tokugawa Ideology: Contours of a Problem."

coexistence of Confucian and nativist scholarship, suggests a number of possible factors in the Japanese disenchantment with China both as a reality and as a metaphor, and looks closely at the life and intellectual career of Keichū (1640–1701), a Buddhist priest of the Shingon denomination. Keichū has been recognized since the eighteenth century as a forerunner of the ideological nativism known as National Learning, and his career and thought represent both the convergence and the initial rupture between the goals of Confucian and nativist scholarship.

Though one can find examples of extreme Sinophiles among Tokugawa intellectuals—scholars like Dazai Shundai (1680–1747) whose attraction to Confucian wisdom and the Chinese sages who communicated it was so great that they found little to admire within their own tradition—it is remarkable that virtually all the major seventeenth-century proponents of Confucianism devoted a significant measure of attention to nativist concerns. One is justified in regarding this, as Kate Nakai has done, as part of a deliberate attempt by Japanese Confucians to "domesticate" Confucianism in its Tokugawa setting by diluting its Sinocentric qualities and demonstrating its relevance to contemporary Japanese concerns.[3]

One area in which this interaction between Confucian and native elements is apparent is in the field of Shinto theology. Such seeming paragons of seventeenth-century Neo-Confucian orthodoxy as Hayashi Razan (1583–1657) and Yamazaki Ansai (1618–1682) formulated their own Shinto theologies in which they sought to reconcile the Neo-Confucian ontology with the Shinto creed. Even Kumazawa Banzan (d. 1691), identified with the heterodox Neo-Confucian teachings of Wang Yang-ming (*Yōmeigaku*), engaged in a comparable endeavor. By doing so, these scholars were able both to challenge the insinuation that their doctrines were alien and to demonstrate Confucianism's compatibility with long-held native truths.

---

[3] Kate Wildman Nakai, "The Naturalization of Confucianism in Tokugawa Japan: The Problem of Sinocentrism."

For their part, leading Shinto theologians like Watarai Nobu-yoshi (1615–1690) and Yoshikawa Koretaru (1616–1694) embraced these efforts by constructing their own syncretic Confucian-Shinto formulations. Though their endeavors often resulted in creeds that were virtually indistinguishable from those of their Neo-Confucian counterparts, the benefit to these Shinto theologians rested, on the one hand, in an apparent updating of their ancient creeds and, on the other, in enabling them to distance Shinto doctrines from those of Buddhism, which had for centuries exerted a profound influence upon Shinto teachings.[4]

Confucian and Neo-Confucian teachings also exerted a less obvious but not less important influence upon the world of the arts in seventeenth-century Japan. The exoteric traditions of Confucianism appear to have contributed significantly to breaking down the old barriers of secrecy that characterized the esoteric transmission of all the arts in pre-Tokugawa Japan; such Confucian concepts as the inherent tension between one's social and moral duties (*giri*) and the dictates of one's emotions (*ninjō*) became major themes in the popular stories of Ihara Saikaku and the plays of Chikamatsu Monzaemon.[5]

Literary criticism and the objects of literary investigation were likewise affected. In its most traditional and orthodox forms, Confucianism tended to reinforce the same didactic norms within literary criticism—known as *kanzen chōaku,* or "praising the good and chastising the evil"—that had arisen during the medieval period in response to Buddhist influence. However, part of Confucianism's domestication in Tokugawa Japan involved its acceptance and advocacy of critical norms that esteemed literature and verse more for their artistic merits than their supposed capacity to improve human character.[6] Furthermore, it appears that the status Confucianism accorded the oldest extant Chinese poetry anthology, the *Book of*

---

[4] For further information on the above two paragraphs, see my "Masuho Zankō (1655–1742): A Shinto Popularizer Between Nativism and National Learning," in *Confucianism and Tokugawa Culture,* especially pp. 169–178.
[5] See Keene, "Characteristic Responses to Confucianism in Tokugawa Literature."
[6] These issues are discussed both below in Chapter 5 and in my "Nature, Invention, and National Learning: The *Kokka hachiron* Controversy, 1742–46."

Songs (Shih ching), may have inspired a comparable reawakening of interest in seventeenth-century Japan in its own oldest extant anthology of verse, the *Man'yōshū*.[7]

No field of scholarly endeavor, however, blossomed under Confucian influence during the seventeenth century more than historical writing. One of the principal tendencies of Confucian thought in China had been an inclination toward historical mindedness, as Confucian scholars sought verification of their assumptions concerning the polity within the copious records of the past and scoured those records for insights on contemporary policy.[8] When transplanted into its Tokugawa setting, the Confucian and Neo-Confucian teachings of the East Asian mainland initially inspired a renewed interest in the study of Chinese history. For example, as early as 1592, Tokugawa Ieyasu was attracted to the example of the founder of the T'ang dynasty in China, Emperor T'ai-tsung (r. 627–649), whose policies toward his ministers and subjects had been recorded by Wu Ching in the *Administrative Essentials of Chen-kuan (Chen-kuan cheng yao)*, and he invited Fujiwara Seika (1561–1619), a Zen priest who was expert in Neo-Confucian teachings, to lecture on the work.[9]

As part of Confucianism's domestication during the Tokugawa period, however, Japanese Confucians turned toward the study of their own country's past; and Confucianism proved to be the catalyst for a veritable explosion of historical writing during the seventeenth and early-eighteenth centuries.[10] Long before the Tokugawa period, the Japanese had demonstrated a passion for record keeping, but there was a dearth of analytical or interpretive histories in Japan from the late-fifteenth to the early-seventeenth centuries.[11] In 1657,

---

[7] See my *"Man'yoshū* Studies in Tokugawa Japan."

[8] See de Bary, "Some Common Tendencies in Neo-Confucianism."

[9] As Herman Ooms points out *(Tokugawa Ideology,* p. 112n), emperors and shogun had heard lectures on the work in the past, but not really "many times" as he claims. There are only two recorded instances of such lectures in the two centuries preceding Fujiwawa Seika's lecture.

[10] See Kate Wildman Nakai, "Tokugawa Confucian Historiography: The Hayashi, Early Mito School, and Arai Hakuseki."

[11] The only Japanese work of any historiographical significance between 1482 and 1610 was the *Tenshōki* (Chronicle of the Tenshō era [1573–1591]), commissioned by Toyotomi

a watershed year in Japanese historiographical enterprise, Tokugawa Mitsukuni (1628–1701), grandson of Ieyasu and daimyo of Mito, ordered the commencement of work on the mammoth *History of Great Japan (Dai Nihonshi)*. It is believed that Mitsukuni's inspiration for this project was Ssu-ma Ch'ien's *Records of the Historian (Shih-chi)*, an early model of Chinese historiography written during the Former Han dynasty. Mitsukuni was assisted during the early stages of compilation by the Chinese scholar and refugee, Chu Shun-shui (1600–1682), who had fled to Japan following the collapse of the Ming dynasty. It was also said that fully one-third of the Mito budget was devoted to this project.[12]

Mitsukuni's *History of Great Japan* epitomized both the Confucian notion of regarding history as a source book of vice and virtue and the patriotic Japanese conviction that moral lessons of equal validity could be gleaned from the study of Japan's own past. Reflecting the newly domesticated ethnocentricity of Confucian historiography, Mitsukuni asserted: "It is perfectly natural for people from Moro-koshi [China] to refer to their country as the 'central flower' *(chūka)*, but it should not be called this in Japan. We should speak of our own capital of Japan as this central flower. Why should we call a foreign country by that name?"[13]

Other examples of Confucian-inspired historiography in the second half of the seventeenth century and early-eighteenth century include Yamaga Sokō's (1622–1685) *Truth About the Central Kingdom (Chūchō jijitsu, 1669)*, a comparable attempt to validate Japanese claims to a central position within the East Asian orbit, and his *Records of the Affairs of the Military Houses (Buke jiki, 1673)*; the Hayashi family's *General History of Our Kingdom (Honchō tsugan)*, begun by Hayashi Razan in 1644, completed by his son Gahō (1618–1680) in 1670, and modeled on Chu Hsi's *T'ung-chien kang-mu*;[14]

Hideyoshi to celebrate his own exploits during those years. See Maruyama Masao, ed., *Rekishi shisō shū*, pp. 486–491.

[12] Nakai, "Tokugawa Confucian Historiography," pp. 72–73.

[13] Quoted in Matsumoto Sannosuke, "Kinsei ni okeru rekishi jojutsu to sono shisō," in Matsumoto Sannosuke and Ogura Yoshihiko, eds., *Kinsei shiron shū*, p. 588.

[14] Chu Hsi's work was itself a redaction of Ssu-ma Kuang's *Tzu-chih t'ung-chien*, in which

Hayashi Gahō's *Perusing Sovereign Reigns* (*Ōdai ichiran*, 1652); and
Arai Hakuseki's (1657–1725) *Lessons from History* (*Tokushi yoron*,
1712) and *Understanding Ancient History* (*Koshitsū*, 1715), a remarkable analysis of ancient myth as historical allegory.[15]

Though generalizations on such a diverse range of historiographical efforts are difficult, these works shared at least two assumptions. The first was the conviction that the way things were was the
way things were likely to remain for a very long time. The power
of the bakufu and its centralized feudal administration as well as
the Tokugawa peace, intended to endure for ten thousand generations, were perceived, with gratitude, to be irreversible. The second
assumption was that an objective Way or set of principles underlay
all historical transition, providing continuity and coherence to the
national historical experience. Though this notion had antecedents
in Japan as far back as the thirteenth-century writings of Jien in his
Gukanshō,[16] to Tokugawa historians it represented evidence that the
past was by no means estranged from the present.[17]

The renewed enthusiasm scholarly circles in Japan were exhibit-
ing for the study of their own nation's past was but one aspect of a
broader shift in the Japanese perception of China. China had traditionally been the center of the East Asian orbit of countries and, for
over a millennium, had served as the primary point of reference for
Japanese comparisons of themselves with others. Japanese percep-
tions of China, however, had begun to shift during the sixteenth
century for a variety of reasons. First, as a result of problems in the
treatment of their embassies to China—problems that arose at least
in part as a result of unruly behavior by the two Japanese embassies
in 1523—Japan stopped sending embassies altogether after 1547;
thus, official contacts between the two countries all but ceased.

Chu Hsi attempted to edit Ssu-ma Kuang's voluminous materials so as to strengthen their
didactic impact.
[15] Joyce Ackroyd has translated the *Lessons from History: Arai Hakuseki's Tokushi Yoron*. On
the political implications of Hakuseki's historiography, see Kate Wildman Nakai, *Shogunal Politics: Arai Hakuseki and the Premises of Tokugawa Rule*, pp. 242–297.
[16] Translated by Delmer Brown and Ishida Ichirō as *The Future and the Past: A Translation
and Study of the Gukanshō, an Interpretive History of Japan Written in 1219*.
[17] Based on Uete Michiari, "Edo jidai no rekishi ishiki," pp. 64–66.

Second, though unofficial and technically illegal trade contacts continued for several more decades, the problem of piracy was so severe that, after 1572, few Japanese ventured to China for any reason; thus, after the early 1570s, Sino-Japanese relations were mediated principally by Chinese who traveled to Japan. Third, the debacle of the Japanese invasion of Korea in the early 1590s and the fall of the Ming dynasty in China to the alien Manchu on the one hand reinforced the isolationist sentiments of the early Tokugawa shoguns and, on the other, diminished the lustre of Chinese prestige in Japan. There were, in short, no more Japanese pilgrims to China like those who in earlier centuries had returned home with tales of the magnificent empire of Japan's continental neighbor; and those Chinese who did come to Japan were mostly merchants in pursuit of a quick profit from what was often a clandestine trade.[18]

China the reality was replaced in the popular culture of late seventeenth-century Japan by China the metaphor. Part of this metaphor construed China in terms of its immenseness by comparison with Japan; as an example, when, in a depiction of the almost unbelievable honesty of a particular salt vendor, Ihara Saikaku wrote, "Why, you wouldn't even find someone like that in all of China."[19] Japan's image of itself as a small country, an image that persists into the present, was in this sense shaped by its historical preference for comparing itself with China.

The metaphor of China, of course, also included a regard for China as the home of the sage and his wisdom, though this was not always a flattering identification. As Donald Keene has observed, "The Japanese of the Tokugawa period tended to think of the Chinese as learned and eminently dignified but lacking in Japanese spontaneity," and Chinese wisdom was often juxtaposed in the popular literature against Japanese bravery.[20] Typical of this characteriza-

---

[18] I am indebted for much of the information in this paragraph to an unpublished paper by John E. Wills, Jr., "The Waters Red With Blood: Maritime China in Japanese Perspective, 1550–1700" (used with permission).

[19] From the story, "Mr. Happiness, the Salt Vendor," in *Some Final Words of Advice*, p. 110.

[20] Donald Keene, "Characteristic Responses to Confucianism in Tokugawa Literature," pp. 122, 131.

tion is that found in Chikamatsu's play *The Battles of Coxinga* (1715), in which the half-Japanese and half-Chinese protagonist, Watō-nai—whose name means betwixt China and Japan—prevails miraculously against the Tartar usurpers; throughout the play that which is Japanese is depicted as young and clever, while that which is Chinese is portrayed as old and devious.

The metaphor of China in seventeenth- and early-eighteenth-century Japan was thus an image of a land that merited admiration but not envy. During the preceding hundred or so years, Confucianism had been transformed from an originally and prevailingly Chinese philosophy into something more attuned to its Japanese setting, and in the process had begun to offer essentially Japanese solutions to Japanese concerns. By successfully displacing Buddhism as the dominant mode of thought in Tokugawa scholarly discourse, Confucianism expanded its influence among intellectual circles and subsumed within itself such fields of inquiry as Japan's historical study of itself and even Shinto theology. There thus was no fundamental tension between nativism and Confucianism during most of the seventeenth century, since the scholarship of the former was essentially incorporated within the broadened horizons of the latter as components of a singular scholarly discourse.

However, in the same way in which Confucianism was unable to achieve independent status in Tokugawa Japan until it disassociated itself from the Zen Buddhist monasteries in which it had been institutionally housed during the medieval period, nativism in Tokugawa Japan was obliged—in order to distinguish itself from Confucianism—to articulate itself in terms of an adversarial relationship with those doctrines with which it had for decades coexisted so comfortably. The rupture between the two became evident during the 1680s and 1690s, and its initial traces are evident in the thought of Keichū, one of the most interesting yet little-known figures in Tokugawa intellectual history.

Keichū (1640–1701) was an amateur classicist and the premier nativist philologist of his age, even though he had no particular instructor in his ancient studies; he was also a Shingon Buddhist priest who contributed unwittingly to the founding of an anti-Buddhist movement.[21] The circumstances of his life demonstrate the convergence of Confucian and nativist goals during the seventeenth century, though his writings betray the initial traces of the eventual rupture between these two modes of thought and herald the advent of the more ideological nativism of the eighteenth century known as National Learning.

Keichū was born in Amagasaki in what today is known as Hyōgo prefecture.[22] His grandfather, Shimokawa Motoyoshi, had served the celebrated warrior Katō Kiyomasa (d. 1611), who had distinguished himself during Toyotomi Hideyoshi's invasion of Korea. At the time, Keichū's grandfather received the generous annual stipend of 5,000 *koku* (1 *koku* = roughly 5 bushels of rice). As a former ally of Hideyoshi, however, the Katō family declined sharply under the new Tokugawa government, and Keichū's grandfather was obliged to transfer his allegiance to the Kiyoyama family in Amagasaki from whom he received the much reduced though still handsome stipend of 250 *koku*. Keichū's mother came from the Azama family, retainers to the Hosokawa, with an annual stipend of 800 *koku*.

Keichū's pedigree was thus solidly samurai, and in all likelihood he would have perpetuated his family's martial traditions had it not been for certain extraordinary circumstances in his youth. In 1646, while still a boy, Keichū became critically ill. His parents' recourse to physicians proved fruitless, and, as their son's condition worsened, they began a 37-day series of prayers to Tenman Tenjin, the deity worshiped as the spirit of the celebrated calligrapher and statesman, Sugawara no Michizane (843–903).[23] The deity is said to have appeared to Keichū's parents in a dream, offering to have the child spared in exchange for his parents' promise to have their son given over the next day to a Buddhist temple in order to be

---

[21] Abe Akio, "Keichū, Azumamaro, Mabuchi," *NST* p. 559.

[22] All biographical information on Keichū comes from two works by Hisamatsu Sen'ichi: his *Keichū;* and his *Keichū den,* esp. pp. 17–101. For his own biographical information on Keichū, Hisamatsu, in turn, relied in both these works principally on Andō Tameakira's *Gyōjitsu*.

[23] On the Sugawara legend, see Robert Borgen's *Sugawara no Michizane and the Early Heian Court*.

trained as a priest. His parents agreed, and Keichū was cured, though he did not learn of his parents' vow until years later. It is said that the still young Keichū pleaded with his parents to allow him to fulfill their pledge, but they initially denied him permission and relented only after becoming convinced of their son's sincerity by his refusal to take nourishment. In 1650, accordingly, Keichū entered the temple Myōhōji in Osaka.

Keichū's early education was rigorous and demonstrates the concern for literacy prevalent among the samurai class and the Buddhist community. He had received instruction in reading from his mother as early as 1644, using the *Hyakunin isshu* poetry anthology as one of his primers. Then, after Keichū left home, the abbot (*jushoku*) of Myōhōji, Kaijō, instructed the still young lad for two years in the Buddhist classics. In 1652, Keichū took the tonsure and moved to Mt. Kōya, headquarters of the Shingon denomination of Buddhism, where he studied for ten years and was eventually ordained. His instruction there included the reading of Buddhist scriptures in both classical Chinese and Sanskrit. Now in his early twenties, Keichū was assigned to priestly duties at the Mandarain in Osaka where, in 1663, he attained the rank of *ajari,* or high priest.

Keichū's conversion to the religious vocation places him squarely within one of the sub-traditions of the Tokugawa civilianization of the samurai class known as the *inshi,* or "sequestered samurai." In contrast to the better known *rōnin,* masterless warriors who retained their samurai right to wear the two swords, the *inshi* voluntarily relinquished this privilege and dedicated themselves to literary, artistic, or religious pursuits. The *inshi* were often dilettantes of sorts—dabblers rather than professionals—though contributions by *inshi* figure with particular prominence in the history of seventeenth-century poetics.

During his early years at the Mandarain, Keichū developed a more serious interest in Waka verse and began his long association with Shimokōbe Chōryū (1624–1686), another samurai with literary interests resident in Osaka. Chōryū admired the poetics of Kinoshita Chōshōshi (1569–1649), a pioneering figure in seventeenth-century studies of the *Man'yōshū,* and is said to have been instructed in linked verse by the founder of Danrin school *haikai*, Nishiyama Sōin (1605–1682), both likewise *inshi*. As a result of his studies of the *Man'yōshū*—a pair of works on *Man'yō* placenames and difficult words, and a commentary on 73 selected verses—Chōryū gained a reputation as the leading authority on the anthology during the 1660s and 1670s.[24] Though he also had a reputation as something of a misanthrope, Chōryū's friendship with Keichū appears to have been a close one, and the two exchanged numerous verses and letters.

Keichū's father passed away in 1664; it appears that, at about this time, Keichū began to question his fitness for the religious vocation. In 1666, he left the Mandarain, spent a brief period in aimless wandering, and attempted suicide by smashing his head against a rock near Mt. Muro. Disillusioned with both his life and ministry, he returned briefly to Mt. Kōya to recuperate. He spent the next decade staying first at the home in Hisai (near Osaka) of Tsujimori Yoshiyuki, a former acquaintance from Mt. Kōya, and then at the home of Fuseya Chōzaemon in nearby Manchō. During these years, Keichū continued to work on his Sanskrit studies while also taking advantage of both households' excellent libraries of Chinese and Japanese classics. It is believed that Keichū met the elderly Nishiyama Sōin when Sōin spent the night at the Fuseya household.

In 1678, Kaijō, Keichū's first teacher in Buddhism, retired from his position as abbot of the Myōhōji, a post he had held for over half a century, and recommended Keichū as his successor. Though Keichū was reluctant despite the web of disciple-teacher obligations involved, Kaijō's death the next year made the offer impossible to decline. Hence, Keichū returned to the Myōhōji, a move that brought him closer to his aged mother, and assumed the abbotship which he held until his own retirement in 1690. Keichū's eleven years at the Myōhōji constitute the greatest period of his intellectual and

---

[24] Shimokōbe Chōryū's major studies of the *Man'yōshū* were his *Man'yōshū kanken, Man'yōshū shō*, and *Man'yō koji narabi ni kotoba*. See my "*Man'yōshū* Studies in Tokugawa Japan," pp. 114–115.

scholarly productivity, since he converted the previous decade of intensive study into a decade of serious writing.

At this juncture in his life, Keichū's scholarly career intertwined with the careers of Tokugawa Mitsukuni and Shimokōbe Chōryū. It will be recalled that Tokugawa Mitsukuni had initiated work on the *History of Great Japan* project in 1657. For reasons that remain obscure but may be related to a perception of the *Man'yōshū* as the Japanese counterpart to the Chinese *Book of Songs*, Tokugawa Mitsukuni turned his attention in the early 1670s to the possibility of a full commentary on Japan's earliest extant anthology of verse. The problems inherent in this project were formidable—there were numerous variant manuscripts of the anthology; linguistically, its archaic language and method of transcription had made it virtually unintelligible within roughly a century of its compilation;[25] and there was a dearth of credible expertise on the anthology.

Nonetheless, after arranging for copies to be made of various manuscripts of the anthology, Mitsukuni ordered two scholars already in his employ, Shimizu Sosen and Yamamoto Shunshō, to produce an authoritative edition of the *Man'yōshū* and to begin work on a commentary.[26] It soon became apparent, however, that the two were unlikely to complete the project assigned to them, and so, in 1673, Mitsukuni invited Shimokōbe Chōryū as an "outside" expert to take over work on the commentary. Chōryū worked on a commentary for nine years while a palsy-like disease slowly took its toll and brought his work to a halt, whereupon Chōryū recommended to Tokugawa Mitsukuni that another scholar, his friend

---

[25] Here the evidence is formidable: There are no fewer than 12 *Man'yō* verses included in the *Kokinshū* anthology (c. 907), despite instructions to its compilers to select verses not previously included in other anthologies; and, in 951, Minamoto Shitagō (911–983) was assigned to the newly established Wakadokoro (Office of Japanese Verse) in order to compile glosses for selected *Man'yō* verses. See my *"Man'yōshū* Studies in Tokugawa Japan," pp. 110–111.

[26] The 4 editions that figured most prominently in the final version were the Ano, Nakanoin, Asukai, and Kishu manuscripts, referred to collectively as the *Shiten Man'yōshū*. Shimizu Sosen also produced his own edition of the anthology known as the *Kaitei Man'yōshū*.

Keichū, take over the project. Mitsukuni accepted the suggestion and dispatched Andō Tameakira to the Myōhōji to present the offer to Keichū.

It appears that Keichū had mixed feelings about accepting the position. On the one hand, it is evident that he sensed a deep personal obligation to complete the work begun by his closest friend, Chōryū, and it is likely that Keichū found the intellectual challenge compelling; on the other hand, it appears that Keichū had reservations about serving a scion of the Tokugawa house, since the reversal of his family's fortunes in earlier generations was attributed to their loyalties to a rival of the Tokugawa. In the end, Keichū compromised—he accepted the task but declined the status of a Mito-household scholar and insisted that he be allowed to perform the work at the Myōhōji. Tokugawa Mitsukuni accepted these terms, and, in early 1683, Keichū began work for Mitsukuni on the *Man'-yōshū*.

Four years later, in 1687, Keichū presented Mitsukuni with a first draft of his efforts. This draft was, for the most part, an unrevised extention and completion of the scholarship of Shimokōbe Chōryū, who had passed away the previous year. It was also handicapped by the fact that Shimizu Sosen and Yamamoto Shunshō had not yet completed their preparation of a more definitive edition of the anthology based on the comparative study of variant manuscripts. Their work, however, was also completed in 1687, and, using their text called the "Four Man'yōshū" *(Shiten Man'yōshū)*—a reference to the four major manuscripts utilized by them—Keichū returned to his labors and in 1690 presented Mitsukuni with his revised final commentary. Like the first draft, it was titled *A Stand-in's Chronicle of the Man'yōshū (Man'yō daishōki)* in acknowledgment of Keichū's completion of the work begun by his late friend. Though Keichū in later years also produced important studies of the *Tales of Ise, The Tale of Genji, Hyakunin isshu,* and other works, it is on his commentary on the *Man'yōshū* that Keichū's reputation as a nativist primarily rests.[27]

---

[27] Hisamatsu Sen'ichi (1894–1976), the primary twentieth-century authority on Keichū,

Keichū's scholarship in general and his work on the *Man'yōshū* in particular are significant in terms of later eighteenth-century nativism for three main reasons. First, Keichū's attitude toward verse combined a near-mystical reverence for the genre of the Waka with rigorous objectivity in his poetics and literary criticism. Second, the quality of his philology was without precedent in Tokugawa-period analyses of literature from the native tradition and for the first time placed nativist philology on a par with comparable endeavors within the Ancient Learning schools of Confucianism. Third, Keichū's depiction of Japan's ancient past as a naive and unlettered yet self-sufficient age was largely consistent with those of his eighteenth-century successors in nativist pursuits.

Keichū's poetics represented a combination of both progressive and traditional elements. For example, his interest in the Waka placed him squarely within the broader rediscovery of the genre during the first half of the Tokugawa period, and, like many others in his age, Keichū argued that the 31 syllables of the Waka were uniquely suited to the expression of poetic sentiments.[28] His rejection of the medieval notion that literature's primary value was its didactic capacity to instruct in matters of good and evil was likewise representative of late-seventeenth-century literary criticism at its best.[29]

---

wrote that "The *Man'yō daishōki* is so representative of Keichū's scholarship that his other writings may be regarded as secondary to it" (*Keichū*, p. 116).

The Stand-in's Chronicle has a complex textual history. The version that circulated during the Tokugawa period was copied by Keichū's disciple Imai Jikan (1657–1723) from the first draft. It appears that Imai Jikan and Keichū's other major disciples never saw the revised version, which remained within the Mito Shōkōkan library until its discovery by Kimura Masakoto (1827–1913) in the Meiji period, when it was also first published. The major nativists of the eighteenth century—Kada no Azumamaro, Kamo no Mabuchi, and Motoori Norinaga—all formulated their positions vis-à-vis Keichū's scholarship on the basis of their familiarity with the first draft of the *Stand-in's Chronicle*. See Hisamatsu, *Keichū den*, pp. 130–134.

One irony of this textual history is that, since the first draft was more indebted than its revision to Shimokōbe Chōryū's efforts, Chōryū exerted a far greater influence on later Tokugawa nativist scholarship than has generally been either understood or acknowledged.

[28] On the rediscovery of the Waka, see Donald Keene, *World Within Walls: Japanese Literature of the Pre-Modern Era, 1600–1867*, pp. 300–333.

[29] Keichū's rejection of literary didacticism is evident in the following quotation from his

By comparison with these positions, however, Keichū's near-mystical reverence for the Waka appears positively archaic. According to Keichū, the Waka partook of the divine: He followed the mythological interpretation of the Waka's invention by attributing it to the deity Susanoo, the unruly brother of the sun goddess Amaterasu, and he claimed that this divine attribution of the genre was responsible for a numinosity latent within the Waka itself. He further claimed that this element of the divine within the Waka was more responsible for the genre's survival than the poetic accomplishments of such Waka masters as Ki no Tsurayuki (868?–945?) or Fujiwara Teika (1162–1241), and that the achievements of such masters were due only in part to their skills at versification but more in that, by composing Waka, they were participating in what was originally a divinely instituted activity.[30] Keichū even insisted, in a discussion of why a Waka has 31 syllables, that such matters were ultimately mysteries beyond human ken, since "the ordinary human mind is not equipped to judge the lofty actions of the gods."[31] This posture made rational and objective poetics impossible, and it contrasts sharply with Keichū's relatively progressive stance rejecting didacticism as a criterion in literary criticism.

Nonetheless, most of the major eighteenth-century National Learning scholars found much in Keichū's poetics to their liking. Kada no Azumamaro shared Keichū's devaluation of the exalted status of Fujiwara Teika in the hagiography of Japanese verse. However, Azumamaro's more progressive adopted son and heir, Arimaro, bristled at theories that asserted a mythological genesis for the Waka, which he believed evolved from primitive songs.[32] Kamo

---

1696 study of *The Tale of Genji* titled *Genchū shūi:* "The didacticism *(hōen)* of the *Spring and Autumn Annals* [attributed to Confucius] rests in the fact that it records incident after incident in which good men do good and evil men do evil, and it is precisely this insistence that this is good and that that is bad that constitutes 'praising good and blaming evil' *(kanzen chōaku)*. *The Tale of Genji* shows that both evil and good can be combined in a single person. Why would anyone compare it with the *Spring and Autumn Annals?*" In Hisamatsu Senichi, et al., comp., *Keichū zenshū,* VI, 394.

[30] See Keichū's *Man'yō daishōki: zassetsu* in *KSRZK,* pp. 310, 313.
[31] Ibid., p. 310.
[32] For Azumamaro's views on Teika, see his *Ise monogatari dōjimon,* in *Kada zenshū,* I, 315

no Mabuchi agreed with Keichū's regard for verse's seemingly un-canny capacity to communicate heartfelt emotion as well as the at-tribution of the genre to divine invention.[33] Motoori Norinaga like-wise made a critical point of the wondrous mysteries of life and the human inability fully to fathom the operations and machinations of the divine.[34]

Keichū's scholarship on the *Man'yōshū* was also significant in terms of its philological analysis. Keichū was the first Tokugawa-period scholar to practice nativist philology that compared favorably with the Chinese philology of the Confucian schools of Ancient Learning. The quality of his philology was so high, in fact, that accounting for it has become something of a problem for contemporary schol-ars. Keichū's principal biographer, Hisamatsu Sen'ichi, has sug-gested a number of possible factors in this regard: Keichū had ap-parently immersed himself in the study of classics from the native tradition during his years at the Tsujimori and Fuseya households, mastering the intricacies of the historical variations in the use of Japanese syllabaries *(rekishiteki kanazukai)*; he was familiar with the *Man'yō* scholarship of the medieval Tendai Buddhist priest Senkaku (1203–1272), whose studies included comparisons of the available *Man'yōshū* manuscripts, a critical commentary on the work, and the correction of certain older transcriptions as well as the addition of new transcriptions for previously unintelligible verses; and his study of Sanskrit, another ancient language, had familiarized him with the application of grammatical principles to linguistic study.[35] It is also apparent that Keichū possessed a measure of genius and applied a remarkably scientific approach to his task.

The study of the *Man'yōshū* posed certain distinctive linguistic challenges. Since the anthology was compiled in the late-eighth

---

and below, Ch. 4, p. 88; for Kada Arimaro's views on the origins of verse, see his *Kokka hachiron*, in Nakamura Yukihiko, ed., *Kinsei bungakuron shū*, pp. 47–52, and below, Ch. 5, p. 115.

[33] On Mabuchi's views, see his *Kokka ron okusetsu*, in *KKMZ:SH*, I, 23, and below, Ch. 5, pp. 114–116.

[34] For Norinaga's views, see his *Kuzubana* in Tsunoda, II, 21–22, and below Ch. 7, pp. 179–181.

[35] Hisamatsu, *Keichū*, pp. 116–117.

century, before the Japanese written language had reached its standard classical form, Chinese characters were used in an irregular fashion without the rules of consistency that made later written Japanese comprehensible. At times, Chinese characters were used for their semantic value so that a reader substituted in rebus-fashion the correct reading of the equivalent word from the native vocabulary—the character for tree, for example, being pronounced in its native equivalent of "ki." At other time, however, Chinese characters were used to designate approximations of their phonetic value in a manner resembling that used a century later in the standard *kana* syllabaries. In addition, these two uses of Chinese characters might appear within a single verse or even a single word, typically in verbs, though again without the fixed rules that made later written Japanese intelligible. Thus, the linguistic deciphering of the anthology posed a formidable challenge.

Keichū's methodology in his analysis of the *Man'yōshū* rested upon his comparative study of vocabulary in other relatively ancient texts. He recognized that, ideally, he should include the study of vocabulary from texts older than the *Man'yōshū*, like the *Nihon shoki* (720) and *Kojiki* (712); but, aside from a handful of verses and phrases from the former, Keichū relied more upon texts such as the *Kaifūsō* (751) anthology of Chinese verse composed by Japanese poets, the *Shoku Nihongi* (797) history, the *Kogo shūi* (807) chronicle of the Inbe family's ancient exploits, the *Kanke Man'yōshū* (893) collection of Waka with Chinese translations, and the *Wamyōshō* (c. 938) dictionary of names, words, and (often pseudo-) etymologies.[36] Keichū compared the usages and transcriptions of words and names in these texts in order to glean a sense of their comparative usages within the *Man'yōshū*, and thus he attempted, bit by bit, to reconstruct the meaning and phonetic value of entire verses. This highly scientific and objective linguistic methodology had no precedent in Tokugawa-period examinations of texts from the native tradition.

Further, Keichū attempted to enhance the quality of his philol-

---

[36] *Man'yō daishōki: zassetsu*, in *KSRZK*, p. 313. Note that the *Kojiki* was still an inaccessible text and remained so for another century until the work of Motoori Norinaga.

ogy through a kind of sympathy for the task and personal identification with the text. In a statement that reveals not only the complexity of the philologist's mission but also his emotional involvement with a text, Keichū wrote that, "in order to obtain an understanding of the verses in this anthology, one should approach them in much the same fashion as a mother who accustoms herself to the garbled speech of an infant and soon understands what the child means."[37] He also recognized the necessity of objectifying one's perspective in the analysis of a text and advised readers of the *Man'-yōshū* "to try to forget the spirit *(kokoro)* of your own age and become part of the spirit of ancient man."[38] It should be noted that Keichū's purpose in this counsel was clearly neither escapist nor normative, since he nowhere implies—as Kamo no Mabuchi did some six decades later—that the spirit of ancient man as represented by the *Man'yōshū* was either superior to the spirit of his own age or worthy of acquisition through emulation. Rather, it appears that Keichū regarded the establishment of this kind of intimate sympathy with one's text as an essential aspect of the philologist's understanding of a work within its social and historical context, an understanding intended, on the one hand, to enhance the quality of his linguistic study of the text and, on the other, to deepen the reader's appreciation of the work.

Numerous twentieth-century scholars have commented upon Keichū's apparent ability to distance himself from both the mistaken *Man'yōshū* transcriptions of earlier generations of *Man'yō* scholarship and the assumptions of his own Shingon Buddhist background. One example is Keichū's transcription of a verse by the celebrated poet Yamanoue Okura (660–733):

Should a man's existence	Onoko ya
Have proved so meaningless	munashikarubeki
That he will not have made a name	yorozu yo ni
That will endure	kataritsugubeki
For a myriad of ages?	na wa tatazu shite

---

[37] Ibid., p. 315.
[38] Ibid.

The traditional gloss of the first two lines had been *hito nareba munashikarubeshi,* or "because I am human, I must die," a statement of the classic Buddhist perspective on the transience of life and the emptiness of existence. Keichū was the first *Man'yō* commentator to correct the error by revising the transcription of the first line and adjusting the grammar of the second. Though, in its revised form, the verse's message is not significantly less Buddhist—a Buddhist's name being no less ephemeral than his life—Keichū's corrections of numerous traditional *Man'yō* glosses indicate his impressive ability to avoid repetition of the errors of the past, irrespective of the Buddhist theological implications of such revision.[39]

Keichū's eighteenth-century nativist successors were likewise impressed by the quality of his *Man'yō* philology. Kada no Azumamaro's commentary, the *Man'yō hekian shō,* borrowed liberally from the *Stand-in's Chronicle* without acknowledging Keichū's work;[40] Kamo no Mabuchi wrote that "Keichū's *Stand-in's Chronicle* should be regarded as the first commentary on the *Man'yōshū;*"[41] and Motoori Norinaga felt that, even though Keichū's nativist scholarship was limited by what Norinaga regarded as an excessive concentration on poetry, Keichū nonetheless founded the nativist methodology of using the philological analysis of ancient texts to examine the basic features of high antiquity.[42] Norinaga also seized upon the near-contemporaneity of Keichū's *Man'yō* scholarship with that of Itō Jinsai and the other early leaders of Confucian Ancient Learning to claim that nativist classicism was not methodologically indebted to Confucian classicism. Norinaga wrote: "While Itō Jinsai and the other founders of Confucian Ancient Learning were near contemporaries of Keichū, Keichū has a slight priority and Jinsai was later.

[39] This example is cited in Muraoka Tsunetsugu, *Studies in Shinto Thought,* pp. 80–81. Note that, in Brown and Araki's transcription of the verse, *tatazu* is misprinted as *tatezu.*
[40] See Hisamatsu, *Keichū den,* pp. 388–391, and below, Ch. 4, p 83. Azumamaro's *Ise monogatari dōjimon* bears the same unacknowledged relationship to Keichū's *Seigo okudan.*
[41] *Tatsu no kimie Kamo no Mabuchi toikotae,* in *KKMZ:SH,* II, 1105.
[42] *Uiyamabumi,* in *MNZ,* I, 15.

Ogyū Sorai was later still. Why would anyone state that our Ancient Learning is patterned after the Confucian one?"[43]

Of course, Norinaga had something of a vested interest in denying Confucianism a role in the founding of nativist ancient studies, and so his claim requires scrutiny, even though it does call attention to a nascent classicist discourse in late-seventeenth-century Japan in which both Confucian and nativist concerns were addressed. While it is indisputable that Keichū's classical scholarship preceded that of Ogyū Sorai, most of Itō Jinsai's major writings were completed prior to 1685, though his thought was not well known outside the circle of his students at the Kogidō until after 1683 when he wrote the *Gomō jigi* summary of his school's teachings in response to a bakufu request. Tokugawa Mitsukuni's interest in the *Man'yōshū* dates from the early 1670s, but Keichū did not join the project until 1683. It is, however, likely that Mitsukuni, as the greatest patron of scholarship in seventeenth-century Japan, was aware of Confucian ancient studies early on and may have perceived the applicability of Ancient Learning's methodology to texts from the native tradition at a time when sharp lines had not yet been drawn between nativist and Confucian scholarship.

Even though Keichū nowhere suggests an antipathy toward Confucianism or Buddhism as foreign modes of thought, the opening sentences of a section titled "Various Theories" (*zassetsu*) in his *Stand-in's Chronical* depict ancient Japan in a manner suggestive of the eighteenth-century divergence of nativist ideals:

> Japan is the land of the gods. Therefore, in both our histories and our administration, we have given priority to the gods and always placed man second. In high antiquity, our rulers governed this land exclusively by means of Shinto. Since it was not only a naive and simple age but an unlettered age as well, there was only the oral tradition which was called "Shinto," and there was no philosophizing of the sort one finds in Confucian classics and Buddhist writings.[44]

---

[43] *Tamakatsuma*, in *MNZ*, I, 257.
[44] *Man'yō daishōki: zassetsu*, in *KSRZK*, p. 310.

By 1690, when Keichū completed work on the *Stand-in's Chronicle,* the notion of Japan as the "land of the gods" or "divine country" *(shinkoku)* was virtually a conceit. The phrase has its *locus classicus* in the *Nihon shoki,* where the Korean King of Silla is quoted as saying, "I have heard that there is a divine country to the east and that it is called Japan (Nippon),"[45] and the phrase also appears variously in such diverse writings as the *Tale of the Heike (Heike monogatari)*, Kitabatake Chikafusa's *Chronicle of Gods and Sovereigns (Jinnō shōtōki)*, and Hayashi Razan's *On Japanese Shrines (Honchō jinja kō)*. Thus, the phrase's impact on a reader was largely to announce that what followed represented a Shinto perspective, as when Keichū declared the priority of the divine over the human in the governing apparatus and writing of history in Japan. It appears that by "histories" Keichū was referring to the Six National Histories *(rikkokushi)* which began with the *Nihon shoki* and covered early Japanese history through the year 887. Since these histories were imperially sponsored and centered on the imperial institution, and since the emperor represented the living manifestation of the divine at the center of the Japanese polity, Keichū accurately attributed a concern with the divine to the early histories, though, with the exception of the Divine Age chapters of the *Nihon shoki,* the Six National Histories were of negligible relevance to Shinto theology. Keichū's assertion of the priority of the divine in administration, in turn, is probably a reference not to imperial rule but to the fact that, in the early Japanese court bureaucracy, one difference from the Chinese T'ang-dynasty court practices on which it was patterned is that the Japanese court gave priority to the Bureau of Shrine Affairs (Jingikan) over the Council of State (Dajōkan); hence, officially at least, the human realm was administratively subordinate to the divine.[46]

Keichū continued his depiction of Japan's high antiquity by characterizing it as a naive, simple, and unlettered age in which men knew nothing but the oral tradition of Shinto, the Way of the

---

[45] Cf. W.G. Aston, *Nihongi: Chronicles of Japan from the Earliest Times to A.D. 697,* I, 230.
[46] This follows the analysis of Abe Akio in *KSRZK,* p. 310.

gods; yet this Way proved sufficient for all men's needs, including ordering their lives and governing the state. He described the age as devoid of the intellectuality identified with Confucian teachings or Buddhist doctrines. While Keichū stopped short of criticizing these doctrines or the "philosophizing" he identified with them, he implied that the naiveté and simplicity of high antiquity in Japan were either diminished or lost altogether in the wake of their introduction.

Keichū did not idealize high antiquity or yearn nostalgically for a return to ancient ways—his depiction of Japan's ancient past, in fact, is in most respects consistent with chacterizations found in survey histories today[47]—and yet later nativists whose purposes were normative and ideological were struck by points of agreement between their own and Keichū's perspectives on the past. They agreed with Keichū that Japan is the land of the gods or divine country; in Japan, the divine realm has traditionally merited priority over the secular or temporal realm; a Way existed in ancient Japan, and this Way was called Shinto, that is, the Way of the gods, this Way was solely responsible and altogether sufficient for the ordering of men's lives and the administration of government; and life changed in ancient times in response to the introduction of Confucianism and Buddhism from abroad. When these points are considered in conjunction with the previously noted endorsement of Keichū's methodology and poetics by the major eighteenth-century National Learning figures, it is understandable that they (like modern scholars) tended to regard Keichū's seventeenth-century nativist scholarship as a forerunner of their own more ideological nativism.[48]

In addition to the completion of his magnum opus, the *Stand-in's Chronicle,* Keichū's years at the Myōhōji also bore fruit in a

---

[47] In a virtual paraphrase of Keichū, Shuichi Kato has described the early Japanese worldview as "neither an abstract nor theoretical view, but [one which] tended towards the material and the practical; it did not involve a comprehensive philosophical system . . . [and] there was no question of any universal system of values. . . ." In Shuichi Kato, *A History of Japanese Literature,* I, 20–21.
[48] On Keichū as a forerunner, see my "Keichū (1640–1701): Forerunner of National Learning."

number of short essays on words, their definitions, etymologies, and pronunciation; the composition of numerous Waka; and preliminary studies of tale *(monogatari)* literature. But, 1690 proved to be a personal as well as scholarly watershed year for Keichū. In the first month of that year his mother died, and, a few months later, he submitted to Mitsukuni the revised draft of the *Stand-in's Chronicle.* With his obligations to his mother terminated, those to his teacher Kaijō satisfied, and those to the late Shimokōbe Chōryū fulfilled, Keichū resigned his position at the Myōhōji and withdrew to a life of relative seclusion in the precincts of the Enjuan in Osaka's Esahimachi district. It appears that he lived comfortably there, supporting himself with the assistance of a pension from Mitsukuni and the donations of the small group of students to whom he lectured on literature and verse from the native tradition.

Keichū continued his scholarly researches during these years of retirement. He produced a number of fine studies on the *Kokinshū* and other imperially sponsored anthologies of verse, treatises on ancient words, and essays on both literary and historical prose works. He also maintained contact with the scholars at Mito by whom he was commissioned to write a 1691 commentary titled *Kōganshō* on verses in the *Kojiki* and *Nihon shoki,* and with whom he corresponded regularly concerning their own ongoing efforts in the study of the *Man'yōshū.* In 1700, Tokugawa Mitsukuni again dispatched Andō Tameakira to Keichū, this time to inquire if Keichū would honor the Mito school's partially completed commentary on the *Man'yōshū* by writing its Preface. It was to be the last request of Keichū by Mitsukuni, who died in the 12th month of that year; just one month later, in the new year of 1701, Keichū likewise breathed his last.

Keichū's achievements are remarkable in their own right and distinguish him as one of the premier scholars active in the closing years of the seventeenth century; they acquire additional significance when regarded in the context of the relationship between Confucianism and nativism in the Tokugawa period. During most of the seventeenth century, these two modes of thought were intertwined in a nearly seamless web of scholarship that perceived no contradiction between the mastery of Confucian and Neo-Confucian principles and the application of those principles to such diverse fields as nativist historiography or Shinto theology. Confucian thought had indeed been "domesticated" within its new Tokugawa setting during the early decades of the seventeenth century.

Despite his vocation as a Buddhist priest, Keichū's scholarly career was in many ways emblematic of this convergence of nativist and Confucian goals. His magnum opus had been commissioned by the Tokugawa period's greatest patron of Confucian historiography; the methodology he applied to the study of the most ancient Japanese verse was one he shared with the pioneering figures of Confucian Ancient Learning, at the time and for several decades to follow the most compelling development in Japanese Confucian thought; and, though they do not reveal a specifically Confucian influence, his researches fell within the mainstream of the rediscovery of the Waka, a new fascination with Japan's oldest extant anthology of verse, and a renewed interest in the non-didactic analysis of classical prose literature, developments that all figure prominently in the literary history of the seventeenth century.

Many of the same originally Confucian assumptions about man, the sage, the Way, the past, and even the methodology for retrieving the Way were seemingly destined to reappear in a new guise during the century following Keichū's work on the *Man'yōshū*. The major eighteenth-century nativists—as described in succeeding chapters—shared the following premises with their Confucian colleagues: that there was a Way and that conformity to the Way brought blessings to both the individual and the polity; that human beings contained within them qualities that inclined naturally toward goodness, and that, by animating or cultivating those qualities, life might be lived in spontaneous conformity to the Way; that life in the past was not only preferable to life in the present, but also that, at certain identifiable periods in the past, life was virtually paradisal, and hence one's quest entailed the resurrection of the elements of this ancient perfection within the present; that the sages who invented the Way in China were mortal and not superhuman creatures; and that the Way was encoded within the most ancient classics, whose true message was decipherable through the philological study and recitation of and immersion in those classics as well as the temporally removed realm they represented.

When National Learning scholars of the mid- and late-eighteenth century depicted the same ancient era Keichū had described in the "Various Theories" section of his *Stand-in's Chronicle,* they did so in terms that idealized that ancient past; they blamed the disruption of the ancient perfection upon the introduction of foreign doctrines like Buddhism and Confucianism which, they alleged, had not only disrupted the spiritual harmony of the primordially distant past but continued to do so in generation after generation of the fallen present; and they asserted that verification of their claims lay within the study of ancient texts, using the philological commentary on texts like the *Man'yōshū* and *Kojiki* as the primary medium for communicating their theories. Keichū's depiction of the ancient past did not represent a nostalgic idealization of that period. Nor did he regard the "philosophizing" identified with Buddhism and Confucianism as responsible for a Fall from a primordial state of grace. But, he did write—in the context of a philological commentary on Japan's most ancient extant anthology of verse—of an ancient Way called Shinto, the sufficiency of this Way for all human concerns at that time, the historical priority of the divine over the secular in the Japanese tradition, and the disruption of an implied ancient harmony by the introduction of moral and ethical teachings from abroad.

In this sense, Keichū stands somewhere between the broadly defined and non-normative nativist scholarship of the seventeenth century and the ideological nativism of the eighteenth century known as National Learning. By writing as he did while in the service of Tokugawa Mitsukuni—that paragon of historical-mindedness and patron of historical scholarship, which represent part of Confucianism's legacy in the intellectual world of Tokugawa Japan—Keichū's thoughts on the past thus indicate the initial traces of a fissure in the melded nativist and Confucian scholarship of the first Tokugawa century; and they foreshadow the disjoining of these two modes of thought and the attendant creation of a new space in the intellectual world of the second Tokugawa century.

One area in which nativism still lagged behind Confucianism was in the successful development—the "marketing" as it were—of the private nativist academy; in this sense, it is evident that nativism was in certain institutional respects lagging behind the popularization of scholarship that characterized the cultural activity of the late-seventeenth and early-eighteenth centuries. Itō Jinsai and other Confucians were demonstrating the viability of the unofficial private Confucian academy during the Genroku years when Keichū was in the most productive period of his scholarship. Nonetheless, Keichū—like many other *inshi* and perhaps for comparable personal reasons—chose to lecture to only a small group of students who gathered around him during the last half-dozen years of his life, and seems to have disdained the more public life required of the leader of an academy. Nonetheless, the goal of founding a successful self-supporting nativist academy became a major priority for nativists like Kada no Azumamaro, who was largely unsuccessful in this venture; Kamo no Mabuchi, who enjoyed a measure of success in Edo; and Motoori Norinaga, whose achievements in this regard were all the more striking for their setting in a non-urban environment. Part of nativism's success in asserting its independence from Confucianism devolved from its articulation of an adversarial relationship with Confucianism. The pioneering figure in this regard was the Shinto priest Kada no Azumamaro.

Part Two

FOUR

Discovering the Past: Kada no Azumamaro

(1669–1736)

Nowadays, the precincts of the Inari Shrine in Fushimi, a southern ward of Kyoto, are lined with souvenir shops, small houses serving refreshments, and numerous inns to lodge those visiting the shrine on religious pilgrimages. Throughout the day, a steady stream of visitors passes through its impressive lacquered *torii* entranceway proceeding to, or more accurately under, the shrine's most distinguishing feature—its thousands of smaller votive *torii*.[1]

The history of the shrine includes some of the most famous figures and events in the history of Japan. It dates at least as far back as 901, when Fujiwara Tokihira, an able administrator known in legend as the ruthless rival of Sugawara no Michizane, was chancellor of the realm *(dajō daijin)*. In 1438, the original buildings were removed to their current site by Ashikaga Yoshinori, sixth son of the celebrated shogun Yoshimitsu and chief abbot *(daisōjō)* of the Tendai denomination of Buddhism, who had become shogun himself a decade earlier through the drawing of lots. Then, ravaged by fire during the outbreak of the Ōnin War (in 1467), the shrine buildings were rebuilt in 1499. Most of the present shrine complex

---

[1] The principal deities believed to be enshrined there are Ukanomitama no ōkami, Sadahiko no ōkami, and Ōmiyanome no ōkami.

dates from 1589, when it was further expanded by order of Japanese history's most popular dictator, Toyotomi Hideyoshi.

Like the Ise Shrines and Mt. Kōya, the precincts of the Fushimi Inari Shrine are often said to impress the visitor with a sense of the presence of the divine. Proceeding along the exhausting circuit of the grounds, one comes eventually to a small sub-shrine built in 1890 to house the spirit of Kada no Azumamaro, the most famous of all the Kada who have served for over a thousand years as the hereditary wardens of the shrine. The Kada family took pride in its ancestry, which it traced back as far as the fifth century, claiming descent from Emperor Yūryaku (r. 456–479); Azumamaro was born on the 3rd day of the 1st month of the new year 1669, the second son of his father Nobuaki (1625–1696).[2]

Azumamaro's contributions to the development of nativism as a distinctive field of scholarly enquiry are impressive, as is his status in its hagiography. Within a century of his death in 1736, Azumamaro was revered as the first of National Learning's "great men" (*taijin* or *ushi*). Hirata Atsutane (1776–1843), the nineteenth-century popularizer of nativism, was the first to accord this appellation to Azumamaro in 1824, though it was soon codified further by Ōkuni Takamasa (1792–1871) in his *Gakutō benron (Discourse on Scholarly Lineage)* of 1857 and represents a perspective shared as well by much Western scholarship.[3]

Azumamaro was indeed a pivotal figure in the history of Japanese nativist thought. He was the first major figure to dissociate nativism from the Confucian thought with which it had coexisted so comfortably during the previous century. He articulated nativism in terms of an adversarial relationship with such non-native doc-

---

[2] Unless otherwise noted, all biographical information on Kada no Azumamaro comes from Miyake Kiyoshi, *Kada no Azumamaro*.

[3] Hirata Atsutane's views are recorded in Chapter 3 of his revised *Tamadasuki*. Ōkuni Takamasa's codification of this hagiography can be found in Tahara Tsuguo, Seki Akira, Saeki Arikiyo, and Haga Noboru, eds., *Hirata Atsutane, Ban Nobutomo, Ōkuni Takamasa*, p. 460. Among English-language studies, Tsunoda, et al. uses this approach (II, 1–46). In his pioneering and still definitive works on Keichū, Hisamatsu Sen'ichi (1894–1976) has challenged this perspective by giving Keichū priority as the first of National Learning's "great men." See his *Keichū den* and *Keichū*.

trines as Buddhism and Confucianism and thereby set the tone for
the next century of nativist thought. He established, with modest
success, the first private academy for the study of nativist topics on
the familiar grounds of the Inari Shrine in Fushimi. And, his students dominated and expanded the field of nativism during the decades following his death. In short, Azumamaro was in many ways
the complete scholar-administrator, which makes the relative pau-
city of information on him all the more puzzling.[4]

There are few verifiable data on the first three decades of Azumamaro's life. The boundaries of his physical world at that time
were principally those of the Inari Shrine, while intellectually the
only slightly broader spheres of Shinto circles appear to have defined
his horizons. His father appears to have had a lively interest in
contemporary culture, and, since both his parents were literate, it
is believed they instilled in their second son that fondness for learning that distinguished his later career. It appears that his parents
frequently took him on visits to other shrines. The family's library
is known to have contained works on selected verses from the *Man'-
yōshū* and *Nihon shoki*, legends of the divine age, essays on the *Kokinshū*, and treatises on historical phonology.

It is also clear that, by 1694, when Azumamaro began to take a
full role in the affairs of the Inari Shrine, the financial condition of
both his family and their surrounding community were straitened.
Ihara Saikaku (1642–1693), that wry observer and chronicler of the
follies of his day, wrote movingly near the end of his life on Fushimi's plight:

> The town of Fushimi down alongside the Capital, with the single exception
> of its main boulevard, now has a lonely and desolate air. The sadness of
> things there is especially evident in the autumn, the time of year when tea
> masters once plucked blossoming morning glories from hedges and fence
> rows for use in the tea ceremony; these days no one pays much attention to
> the old ceremonies, and the bucket from the well lies in disarray, entangled

---

[4] To my knowledge, the most useful published scholarly discussion of Azumamaro in any
Western language remains pp. 2, 5–9 of Vol. II of *Sources of Japanese Tradition*. In his *The
Japanologists: A History*, pp. 313–356, Sajja A. Prasad offers a more extensive and subjec-
tive evaluation.

in its own rope. . . . Where banks once lined the broad avenues, there is
not a single home left that gives the appearance of having a hundred cop-
pers. The place is barren except for the odd shop selling oil . . . and the
only time of year when one can find even salted sardines is at New Year's.[5]

It is apparent that Fushimi did not partake of the economic growth
that otherwise characterized the early years of the Genroku and that,
even though much of the Inari Shrine's budget derived from the
contributions of visitors, it was nonetheless dependent upon the
financial well-being of its surrounding community.[6]

It was thus all the more fortunate for the Kada family that their
son Azumamaro proved to be as gifted as he was and that his gifts
were recognized by others. In 1697, Azumamaro won the extraordinary honor of appointment as poetry tutor to Prince Myōhōin,
son of the abdicated Emperor Reigen (r. 1663–1687). Nothing is
known of how this appointment came about or what might have
qualified Azumamaro for it, since he is believed not to have had any
formal training aside from what he received from his parents, and
he belonged to no single school of versification.[7] Azumamaro's lessons must have pleased the prince since he honored the Kada family
with a personal visit in the spring of 1698, but, just as mysteriously
as they had begun, the lessons ended in the summer of the next
year, apparently at Azumamaro's request.

Then, under circumstances shrouded with ambiguity, Azumamaro arrived in Edo in 1700 where he remained in residence until
1713.[8] Azumamaro nowhere recorded his purposes in making this
move; one can only surmise his intentions from his activities in Edo
and from what one may assume he had heard about recent developments there. By 1700, Edo had surpassed Kyoto in population

---

[5] Adapted from *Some Final Words of Advice*, pp. 200–201.

[6] Despite the general aura of prosperity at this time, the bakufu treasury was in poor shape,
owing at least in part to the extravagance of the shogun, Tsunayoshi. The debasement of
gold and silver currency in 1695 provided a short-term solution to the problem, but it
also generated the first of several inflationary cycles that caused widespread hardship.

[7] As attested to by Azumamaro's student, Kamo no Mabuchi, in his *Tatsu no kimie Kamo
no Mabuchi toikotae*, in *KKMZ:SH*, II, 1022.

[8] For a discussion of the various theories on the exact date of his departure from Kyoto and
arrival in Edo, see Miyake Kiyoshi, pp. 48–52.

and had become the world's largest city. Kyoto still retained its reputation as Japan's center of cultural activity, but the business of arts and letters was clearly expanding at a faster pace in Edo under the government of the 5th Tokugawa shogun, Tokugawa Tsunayoshi (r. 1680–1709). The poet-scholars Toda Mosui (1629–1706) and Kitamura Kigin (1624–1705) had moved there, the latter by invitation of the bakufu in 1689. Tsunayoshi built, in 1690, a new home, the Shōheikō (School of Prosperous Peace), in nearby Yushima to lodge the Hayashi school of Neo-Confucianism, and promoted its chief spokesman at that time, Hayashi Nobuatsu (1644–1732), to the new position of Head of the University *(daigaku no kami)* with court rank.[9] Tsunayoshi not only sponsored debates among the various proponents of Confucianism but even lectured himself on the classics before assembled audiences of feudal lords and scholars and read poetry at the home of his chamberlain, Yanagisawa Yoshiyasu (1658–1714). Of course, the shogun's sponsorship and patronage of various cultural activities encouraged numerous daimyo to follow suit. Looking back on the Tsunayoshi years a century later, one scholar observed that "literature and learning flourished widely. Every house read and every family recited [the classics]. Such a thing has not happened since."[10]

Azumamaro's activities in Edo lend support to the speculation that he may have already been seeking to establish a network of contacts among the samurai elite to support his study of nativist topics, but the majority of his students at this time came from the ranks of the Shinto clergy to whom he lectured on *norito* prayers and liturgy, Shinto theology, the ancient histories, and early verse including the *Man'yōshū*.[11] The numbers of his students, however, grew steadily at this time with some 27 registrants by the close of 1705 in the small school he operated within his home.

---

[9] Known posthumously as Hayashi Hōkō, Nobuatsu was Hayashi Razan's grandson. The court rank was junior 5th rank (of 9 ranks, each divided into senior and junior).

[10] From the *Sentetsu sōdan* of Hara Masaru (1760–1820), quoted in Maruyama, *Studies in the Intellectual History of Tokugawa Japan*, p. 115.

[11] Several of his works on the *Man'yōshū* date from this period, including *Man'yō mondō* (c. 1708), *Man'yōshū Wakana kun* (1709), and *Man'yō kunshaku* (1710).

Upon the death of the shogun, Tsunayoshi, in 1709, his nephew Tokugawa Ienobu became the 6th Tokugawa shogun (r. 1709–1713) and brought into the bakufu as his advisor the scholar who had been his tutor for many years, Arai Hakuseki (1657–1725). Hakuseki continued to serve the bakufu through the regime of Ienobu's successor as shogun, the boy Ietsugu (r. 1713–1716), and sought with varying degrees of success to apply Confucian theories of economics and statesmanship to the complex fiscal and administrative issues confronting the bakufu at that time.

In the 4th month of 1713, Azumamaro moved back to Fushimi only to return to Edo some six months later at the invitation of Makino Suruga no kami, lord of the castle at Nagaoka in Echigo, who supported Azumamaro's year-long stay in Edo with a stipend. Aside from a final year-long trip to Edo in 1722–1723, when he lectured to the bakufu vassal Shimoda Kōtayu and others on a broad variety of subjects, Azumamaro spent the rest of his life back in Fushimi endeavoring to expand and promote his school.[12]

These were also fateful years for the bakufu. In 1716, Yoshimune became the 8th Tokugawa shogun and continued in that position until his retirement in 1745, revoking many of the reform measures instituted by Arai Hakuseki and relying upon the more conservative Confucian guidance of Muro Kyūsō (1658–1734). Inflation had continued to plague the economy years after Tsunayoshi's debasement of the currency, and Yoshimune's policies—known as the Kyōhō reforms, after the era in which they were implemented (1716–1736)—represented a fiscal retrenchment and return to those practices believed to have characterized the early decades of the Tokugawa. Open to solutions from previously untapped sources, Yoshimune, in 1720, even relaxed the ban on imported books, so long as they contained no mention of the proscribed doctrines of Christianity.

Despite this openness to foreign learning and the boldness of his

---

[12] Azumamaro's discussions with Shimoda and the others included such topics as the administrative structure of the imperial court and the bakufu, Shinto, and domainal administration and are recorded in Azumamaro's *Reimondō* (1723).

reform efforts, however, the prevailing intellectual tone of the Yoshimune years was one of overt restorationism—a hearkening back to an idealized past, the parameters of which were defined by the rule of the 1st Tokugawa shogun, Ieyasu. Ogyū Sorai, who advocated the wholesale restoration of the institutions and practices of remote antiquity, enjoyed the attention of Yoshimune and even submitted two memorials on policy to him—the *Proposal for a Great Peace (Taiheisaku)* and *Discourse on Government (Seidan)*—yet even Sorai was eventually disappointed by the fact that Yoshimune's reforms did not go farther or hearken back to a sufficiently remote past. Sorai's lament, "Alas, the spirit needed to effect a restoration was absent," spoke movingly about the limits of conservative reform in the 1720s, a disappointment Kada no Azumamaro shared by the end of his own life.[13]

The available sources allow only a frustratingly unclear picture of Azumamaro's years and activities in Edo, but the image of him is clearer once he returned to his native Fushimi. He continued his efforts to cultivate contacts with bakufu officials by providing them with access to his library of rare books, answering their questions on the past, and offering his services as a consultant on ancient language. For example, following a request from bakufu officials in 1724 for a list of books in his library, Azumamaro loaned personal copies of the *Izumo fudoki* and *Ruijū kokushi* and answered queries on the *Shin kokushi*.[14] In the same vein, he wrote several times in 1724 to Shimoda Kōtayu on interpretations of the *Kojiki*, and numerous other works exchanged hands between Edo and Fushimi during the years 1724 to 1727.[15]

Azumamaro emerged during these years as a primary authority for bakufu officials on a broad range of antiquarian matters. He

---

[13] Sorai is quoted in Maruyama, *Studies in the Intellectual History of Tokugawa Japan*, p. 133.

[14] Dated 733, the *Izumo fudoki* is the only extant gazetteer from those compiled by order of Emperor Genmei (r. 707–715). The *Ruijū kokushi* (892) is attributed to Sugawara no Michizane and contains a topically arranged history of early Japan with chapters on Shinto, Buddhism, ancient ceremonial, and the imperial family. The *Shin kokushi* (950–954) by Fujiwawa Saneyori is non-extant and was regarded as the last of the official, i.e., imperially sponsored, histories.

[15] Miyake, pp. 95–110.

provided answers to their questions on the institutions, customs, regulations, and ceremonial of the ancient imperial court, including such specific matters as the *ritsuryō* laws and ordinances, the system of cap ranks instituted by Prince Shōtoku in 604 and patterned after the practices of Sui-dynasty China, the *Engi shiki* legal codes of 905, and a number of ancient prohibitions and taboos with roots in Shinto beliefs. In linguistic and textual matters, Azumamaro addressed such issues as the correct glossings for ancient words and the names of deities who appear in the *Nihon shoki,* glossings for the *Ryō no gige* legal commentary of 834, and commentaries on the ancient Shinto *norito* prayers and liturgies. In particular, Azumamaro established a reputation as an authority on the *Nihon shoki* which for him served as the primary source on ancient history, mythology, and tradition; and he wrote numerous essays and letters which expounded on such issues as the divine descent of the imperial line, the identities of various deities, and details of the ancient cosmogony.

From the late-1720s on, when his health began to deteriorate, Azumamaro began increasingly to entrust these relations with bakufu officials to his gifted adopted son and intellectual heir, Kada Arimaro (1706–1751), who, despite his youth, showed an aptitude for such matters. Arimaro began to function as an emissary of sorts for his step-father. The best known instance of this is believed to have occurred in 1728 when Arimaro is said to have delivered the "Petition to Found a School" ("Sō gakkō kei") to the shogun, Yoshimune. During the remaining eight years until his death in 1736, Kada no Azumamaro had few respites from the chest pain and palsy-like disease that tempered his enthusiasm for writing and finally took his life. He did, however, play a major role in the activities of his school in Fushimi, touching the intellectual lives of several of his students in a manner that in significant measure shaped the tone and direction of nativist pursuits in Japan for decades after his death. Azumamaro was buried near his home where, in 1890, the latter-day followers of Hirata Atsutane erected a memorial as their recognition of his role as the founder of National Learning.

Azumamaro's writings run the gamut of nativist subjects and range from criticism and commentaries on verse and tale (*monogatari*) literature to linguistic analysis of ancient legal codes, and from antiquarian researches in the customs, ceremonial, and material culture of the past to the diverse concerns of Shinto. He was in many ways the most "complete" of the major eighteenth-century nativists, but, since his "world" had for so long been that of Shinto circles, it is understandable that Shinto and Shinto-related topics form the nucleus of his thought. [16]

One misunderstanding of Azumamaro's achievements, however, which persists with surprising tenacity in modern Western scholarship, has been the tendency to regard him as the pioneering figure of a "Shinto revival." Scholars who have depicted him as such have tended to underestimate the vitality of early eighteenth-century Shinto circles and have overstated Azumamaro's achievement. [17] The Shinto Azumamaro taught represented an advance over the Inari Shinto he had learned as a youth; yet its theology was not sufficiently removed to merit being regarded as a new "school" of Shinto; it remained much attuned to and consistent with the major Shinto theologies in circulation in his own age. The novelty of Azumamaro's Shinto lay, rather, in its concern with scriptural authority and his stated intention of applying the methodology of philological analysis to ancient texts in order to elucidate the archaic roots of his faith and creed. In that sense, Azumamaro's Shinto represented not a Shinto revival but rather "Restoration Shinto" (*fukko Shintō*), as Japanese scholarship often refers to it, since its central concern was the restoration of Shinto in its pristine form, a form believed to be unaffected by interaction with such non-native forms of thought as Buddhism and

---

[16] Ibid., p. 235.

[17] To cite just one example from among many, *Sources of Japanese Tradition* discusses National Learning in a chapter titled "The Shinto Revival." The tendency in English-language scholarship to regard National Learning as a Shinto revival probably stems from a misunderstanding of an article by Ernest Satow titled "The Revival of Pure Shin-tau," in which Satow accurately described National Learning in terms of its concern with "reviving" Shinto in what its proponents believed to be its most archaic form.

Confucianism. That Azumamaro was ultimately unsuccessful in dissociating himself from the Shinto assumptions of his age—assumptions based on more than a century of experimentation in reconciling the "truths" of Shinto with those of Neo-Confucianism—in no way diminishes the valiance or significance of his efforts.[18]

At the start of the eighteenth century, it was widely accepted among intellectual circles that three texts—the *Kujiki (Sendai kuji hongi)*, *Kojiki* and *Nihon shoki*—spoke authoritatively on Japan's most ancient past and its Shinto traditions. For example, Azumamaro's contemporary, the Shinto popularizer Masuho Zankō (1655–1742), wrote in 1716 that, "if you know the message of the *Kujiki, Kojiki, and Nihon shoki*, then what you know is nothing other than the Way of Japan."[19] As late as 1688, Azumamaro accepted the authenticity of the *Kujiki*,[20] though he later came correctly to dismiss it as a forgery which postdated its purported seventh-century authorship and asserted that "to speak of the *Kujiki, Kojiki, and Nihon shoki* as the three fold writings is folly for persons in later ages."[21]

As the scion of a rival denomination, it is understandable that Azumamaro did not base his theology upon the Five Shinto Classics *(Gobusho)*—a thirteenth-century invention of the Watarai family, hereditary custodians of the Outer Shrine at Ise—and between the *Kojiki* and the *Nihon shoki*, Azumamaro by far preferred the latter, perhaps because of its compilation by imperial order and status as the first of the Six National Histories *(Rikkokushi)*,[22] but just as plausibly because of its relative accessibility by comparison with the slightly older and linguistically more complex *Kojiki*.[23] He wrote

---

[18] I discuss these experiments in *Confucianism and Tokugawa Culture*, pp. 166–187.

[19] From Zankō's *Uzō muzō hokora sagashi*, quoted in Takeoka Katsuya, "Kokugakusha to shite no Masuho Zankō no chii," p. 111.

[20] According to his *Jindai bunsho*, quoted in Miyake Kiyoshi, p. 144.

[21] See his *Nihon shoki jindai no maki shō* in KZ, VI, 151.

[22] In addition to the *Nihon shoki*, the Six National Histories include the *Shoku Nihongi, Nihon kōki, Shoku Nihon kōki, Nihon Montoku tennō jitsuroku,* and *Nihon sandai jitsuroku.* Written in classical Chinese, the 6 works represent a narrative account of Japanese history from earliest times to 887.

[23] Of all pre-Heian native texts, the *Nihon shoki* had the most commentaries written on it.

that "the divine age chapters [of the *Nihon shoki*] are all one needs
in order to know the Way,"[24] and he revered the history's compiler,
Prince Toneri, as a "religious sage for ten thousand generations" for
his preservation and elucidation of Shinto teachings.[25] Azumamaro's decision to give priority to the *Nihon shoki* for his discourse on
ancient Shinto exemplified what later became a characteristic of the
major eighteenth-century nativists—the selection of a primary text
on which to base or from which to extrapolate their speculations
concerning an ancient Way.

Azumamaro was keenly aware that nearly a thousand years of first
Buddhist-Shinto syncretism and then (closer to his own age) Confucian-Shinto syncretic formulations had significantly colored interpretations of the native creed. He observed that "the divine age
chapters are scriptural writings of great antiquity, and their message thus differs from that of later Confucian writings"; he cautioned accordingly that, "unless one inspects the writings of high
antiquity with the spirit of high antiquity, their purport will
be lost."[26] Accordingly, the fact that Azumamaro's Shinto teachings conform so closely in their Confucian coloration to those of
his immediate Shinto predecessors and contemporaries indicates
how powerful the grip of quondam Confucian-Shinto discourse was
even upon one who sought to leave such syncretic formulations
behind.

Azumamaro regarded Shinto as the most basic creed of Japan, a
distinctive teaching of great antiquity. He wrote:

Since the teachings of our land are ancient teachings dating from the Divine Age, they constitute a singular Way which includes elements that

---

Pre-Tokugawa commentaries on the work include: Kenshō (1130–1210), *Nihongi kachū;*
Jakue, *Nihongi kashō;* Urabe Kanekata (mid-Kamakura), *Shaku Nihongi;* Inbe Masamichi,
Jindai no maki kōketsu; Ken'a, *Nihongi shishō;* Dosa, *Nihon shoki shikenbun;* Ryōyo Shōkyō,
Nihon shoki shisho; Ichijō Kanera (1402–1481), *Nihon shoki sanso;* Yoshida Kanetomo (1435–
1511), *Nihon shoki jindai shō;* and Kiyohara Nobukata (1475–1550), *Nihon shoki kansui
shō.* Of these, Azumamaro preferred the commentary by Ichijō Kanera but warned that
even this one "should be used with caution, since it includes many theories based on
Buddhist writings." From his *Gogimon jōjō,* quoted in Miyake Kiyoshi, p. 252.
[24] *Ise monogatari dōjimon,* in *KZ,* I, 290.
[25] From his *Nihon shoki mondō sho,* quoted in Miyake Kiyoshi, p. 251.
[26] From his *Gogimon jōjō,* quoted in Miyake Kiyoshi, p. 253.

cannot be found in Confucian texts and cannot be learned from Buddhist
writings. We call our country the land of the gods; we call our Way the
Way of the gods; and we call our teachings the teachings of the gods.[27]

In other words, according to Azumamaro, the presence of Shinto
deities and the possession of the Shinto Way and teachings contribute to the definition of the "Japaneseness" of Japan. Azumamaro
also described what he perceived to be the ongoing impact of these
teachings upon Japanese history and national character:

> Our imperial institution *(teii)* is different from the system of rule in other
> lands where violence is used to seize power. From the time of Kunitoko-
> tachi no Mikoto to our present emperor, rule has not changed from one
> family to another. We have Shinto as a legacy from the imperial line, and,
> since there is this divine doctrine, it is inconceivable to use human effort
> to seize power. Ten thousand generations from now it will still be like
> this.[28]

Here Azumamaro reiterated what was for centuries held in Shinto
circles to be the normative value of the creed—its capacity to sta-
bilize imperial rule and to preserve a single imperial lineage believed to descend from the creator deity via the sun goddess Amaterasu—which in itself contributes further to the definition of national
polity and character. Shinto is thus, for Azumamaro, a primordial
Way native to Japan and bequeathed by divine authority; to be
Japanese, in this context, was to be an heir to these teachings and
the moral character they were believed to impart.

Azumamaro's avowed methodology in his reconstruction of the
native ancient Way was the philological analysis of the earliest extant texts, in particular the divine age chapters of the *Nihon shoki,*
and his insistence that one use the "spirit of high antiquity" to
analyze such texts was fully consistent with the nascent classicism
of much early eighteenth-century thought. As observed in the preceding chapter, in his analysis of the *Man'yōshū,* Keichū had likewise counseled in 1690 that one "try to forget the spirit of one's

---

[27] From his *Nihon shoki mondō shō,* quoted in Miyake Kiyoshi, pp. 241–242.
[28] *Man'yōshū hekian shō,* in *KZ,* I, 462–463.

own age and enter into the spirit of ancient man";[29] it is certain that Azumamaro was familiar with at least two of Keichū's works, including the one from which this quotation is drawn, probably through Keichū's disciple Imai Jikan (1657–1753), who lived in Kyoto and with whom Azumamaro is believed to have had contact.[30] Furthermore, the methodological similarities between Azumamaro's work and that of his counterparts in Confucian Ancient Learning are such that his principal biographer, Miyake Kiyoshi, has acknowledged that Azumamaro's methodology may be regarded as the conscious application of the Ancient Learning methodologies of Itō Jinsai and others to the field of Japanese studies.[31]

One problem Azumamaro encountered in his attempts to retrieve the ancient Way was that of the conflicting accounts that existed, not just between such texts as the *Kojiki* and the *Nihon shoki,* but even within the *Nihon shoki* itself. For example, the *Nihon shoki* offers nine alternative accounts of the creation of the first islands, a reflection of the composite nature of the earliest myths and the compiler's aspiration to a measure of comprehensiveness appropriate to a history written at imperial request.[32] Azumamaro sought to reconcile these conflicting narratives and contradictory accounts by using that legerdemain characteristic of the gifted theologian. He insisted that all texts relevant to the task of reconstructing the native Way contain at least two levels of meaning—a straightforward literal meaning and an inner meaning or "essence" underlying the words—and that "it is when both levels of meaning are amalgamated and used to illuminate each other that one achieves an understanding of those themes that span the Divine Age."[33] Thus, where variants conflicted at the literal level, Azumamaro sought to

---

[29] *Man'yō daishōki: zassetsu,* in *KSRZK,* p. 315.

[30] Azumamaro's *Man'yō hekian shō* and *Ise monogatari dōjimon* have been demonstrated to be closely based on Keichū's *Man'yō daishōki* and *Seigo okudan.* See Hisamatsu Sen'ichi, *Keichū den,* pp. 388–393. The speculation that Azumamaro, in 1701, made a bedside visit to the failing Keichū and received from him the "mantle" of Japanese nativism is spurious.

[31] *Kada no Azumamaro,* p. 579.

[32] See *Nihongi: Chronicles of Japan,* pp. 16–18.

[33] *Nihon shoki jindai no maki satsuki,* in *KZ,* VI, 87.

glean an essential transcendent level of meaning in order to reconcile such variants into a singular "truth."

Significantly, it is clear that, despite his attempts to penetrate
through to this "essential" level of meaning, Azumamaro relied
principally upon his own subjective preconceptions gleaned from a
variety of contemporary Shinto theologies, and that his analysis of
the Divine Age chapters of the *Nihon shoki* contributed little if anything to the formulation of the fundamentalist theology to which
he aspired.[34] This is evident in his conception of *kami,* of human
beings, and of the relationship between the two.

All the syncretic Confucian-Shinto formulations of the seventeenth century reflected, to varying degrees, the rationalistic and
humanistic tendencies inherent in Confucian thought; these are
likewise reflected in Azumamaro's views on *kami.* As a young man,
he found significance in the similarity between the words *kami* and
kagami (mirror)—one of Japan's imperial regalia and a traditional
Confucian metaphor—and wrote of *kami* as being like mirrors of
human activity and character,[35] a pseudo-etymologizing strategy
common to much seventeenth-century Shinto thought and particularly prominent in the Suika Shinto of Yamazaki Ansai.[36] In his
middle and later years, Azumamaro refined this view by interpreting deities and humans as, in effect, obverse sides of the same coin
in which *kami* represented the concealed aspects of humans while
humans represented the revealed aspects of *kami*—a view of deities
as superior but not altogether transcendent alter-egos to human
beings, and again a view common in contemporary Shinto circles
and particularly evident in the writings of Masuho Zankō.[37] He
wrote in this regard: "Since men make mistakes, the *kami* also make
mistakes. The difference between them is in the correction of these

---

[34] Miyake Kiyoshi, p. 291.
[35] From his *Jindai bunsho* of 1688.
[36] See Ooms, *Tokugawa Ideology,* pp. 240–250.
[37] See Miyake Kiyoshi, pp. 266–267; and Nosco, *Confucianism,* pp. 170–187. On the
distinction between the "concealed" and "revealed" in Tokugawa thought, see Muraoka
Tsunetsugu, *Studies in Shinto Thought,* pp. 171–202.

errors. The *kami* recognize their mistakes and correct them, which is one respect in which they are superior to men."[38]

Azumamaro recognized that, within the legends of the divine age, one finds *kami* who represent the entire spectrum of human behavior from extremes of benevolence to extremes of malevolence, and he also recognized depictions of the deities' fallibility as evidence of the *kami*'s lack of omniscience. "The ultimate truth," he wrote, "is that what they did not see they did not know, and what they did not hear, they just did not hear. . . . They never claim to know the future."[39] The beneficence and virtue of the deities could, he believed, be perceived in fellow humans,[40] so that, like other Tokugawa Shinto theologians, Azumamaro concluded that the native Way described in the divine age chapters was "none other than the Way of man."[41]

According to Azumamaro, what separates gods from humans is that the deities dwell in the spiritual realm of the soul or spirit *(tamashii)*, while humans reside in the material world of forms or shapes *(katachi)*; and what binds these dimensions together is that they partake of a common metaphysical principle through the indwelling of the divine spirit within the human. "Originally there was one spirit of heaven, earth, man, and all things,"[42] but, in the cosmogonic process, a bifurcation occurred resulting in two forms of spirit: a "heavenly spirit" *(amatsu tamashii)* which is perfectly pure, and a "material spirit" *(katachi no tamashii* or *katachi ni tsuki-taru tamashii)* which varies from person to person and contains impurities. The heavenly spirit is abstract and immaterial, though it partakes of the sun and is therefore universal.[43] This spirit, he wrote, "is lord over our bodies, and thus the Way of our land is to respect

---

[38] From *Azumamaro jindai tōki,* quoted in Miyake Kiyoshi, p. 271.

[39] *Nihon shoki jindai no maki satsuki,* in *KZ,* VI, 54.

[40] Ibid., p. 11.

[41] From his *Gogimon jōjō,* quoted in Miyake Kiyoshi, p. 268. Yoshida Shinto had written of Shinto as the Way of man as early as the fifteenth century; in the Tokugawa period, Hayashi Razan, Yamazaki Ansai, and Masuho Zankō shared this perspective.

[42] *Nihon shoki jindai no maki satsuki,* in *KZ,* VI, 37.

[43] Ibid, VI, 42, 114, 135.

the spirit like a master. To do otherwise is an offense."[44] Accordingly, Azumamaro described Shinto as a doctrine that can help persons not only to overcome those thoughts, emotions, and desires that bind them to the material but also to approximate the superior character of the divine.

Unlike virtually all other contemporary Shinto theologies and most Confucian perspectives on the matter, Azumamaro regarded human nature as a mixture of good and bad elements. He wrote that "good and evil are intermingled, and human nature will forever partake of both. They say that human nature is good, but within human nature evil elements are automatically included as part of its essence."[45] Goodness thus requires a deliberate effort, first, to overcome the wicked inclinations inherent in one's nature and, second, to act in accordance with the divinely imparted spirit. However, before one can conform to the dictates of the spirit or emulate the *kami,* one must first learn about the *kami*'s divine deeds, and the way to do so, Azumamaro counseled, was through study of the divine age chapters of the *Nihon shoki.*[46]

One element in Azumamaro's cosmology that figured prominently in a number of Confucian ontologies but appeared rarely in Shinto formulations was the element of material force or ether (J. *ki,* Ch. *ch'i*). Ether, according to Azumamaro, fills heaven where it is non-material and congeals on earth in order to form the material in which it subsists. Unlike spirit, which is quiescent, ether is active, moving, and changing constantly within the material realm.[47] "Without receiving the ether of heaven," he explained, "there is no birth or growth."[48] This ether is also, however, part of Azumamaro's explanation of human misbehavior, for, just as clouds are capable of obscuring the radiance of the sun, so too, "when one's specific ether becomes willful, one becomes incapable of distin-

---

[44]*Nihon shoki jindai no maki shō,* in *KZ,* VI, 155–156.
[45]*Nihon shoki jindai no maki satsuki,* in *KZ,* VI, 61.
[46]Miyake Kiyoshi, pp. 271–272.
[47]Ibid., pp. 277–279.
[48]*Nihon shoki jindai no maki satsuki,* in *KZ,* VI, 38.

guishing between good and evil or even of perceiving the difference
between right and wrong."[49]

It is at this juncture, however, that Azumamaro's cosmology becomes extraordinarily complex, rivaling Yamazaki Ansai's Suika
Shinto in its intricate interweaving of Shinto and Neo-Confucian
elements, though lacking Suika Shinto's internal consistency and
rarified intellectual appeal. Having proposed an ontology with three
constituent parts—spirit, ether, and forms—Azumamaro drew upon
the ancient Five Elements (J. *gogyō,* Ch. *wu hsing*) theory to provide
that dynamic catalyst to the transformation of the pure and immaterial to the impure and material. He postulated that it was through
the catalytic action of water that spirit responds to the transformative life-giving ether, resulting in a tangible world of forms and
shapes full of vitality and activity.[50]

There was, of course, ample precedent within the Shinto tradition for attempts to reconcile the cosmogonic myths of Shinto with
the originally Chinese ontologies of Yin and Yang and the Five
Elements,[51] but Azumamaro's is the only one to have attributed so
critical a role to water, and, while one might admire the novelty of
Azumamaro's formulations, it is evident that they go far beyond
what might be gleaned from a close reading of the divine age chapters of the *Nihon shoki.* Azumamaro's Shinto theology bears a far
more familiar resemblance to the syncretic Confucian-Shinto formulations of his immediate contemporaries and seventeenth-century forebears in the tradition than it does to the ancient Way constructions of his eighteenth-century successors in nativism like Kamo
no Mabuchi and Motoori Norinaga. It was, rather, in the tone that
he set and in his methodology of seeking, however unsuccessfully,
to ground his speculations on the ancient Way within a single text
that one finds intellectual affinities between Azumamaro and the
later major figures in National Learning.

---

[49] Ibid.

[50] Miyake Kiyoshi, p. 282.

[51] Ooms's *Tokugawa Ideology* contains an excellent discussion of the Five Elements theory
in Ansai's Suika Shinto, as well as several precedents for it.

Azumamaro's work in classical literature and verse likewise offered little that might be termed "new" in his times. The main literary works he studied and commented upon were the *Man'yōshū*, *Kokinshū*, and *Ise monogatari*. He described the *Man'yōshū* as "the branches of that tree whose trunk is the *Nihon shoki*" [52] and extolled the anthology as an unexcelled work which deserved regard as the fountainhead of Japanese poetics, going so far as to suggest that what he perceived to be a decline in Japanese versification was attributable to its deviation from the standards and precedents of the *Man'yōshū*. [53] Just as Keichū had done, though with greater vehemence, Azumamaro even vilified the premier medieval poet in Japan, the virtual saint Fujiwara Teika (1162–1241), for his alleged ignorance of the *Man'yōshū* and other matters of antiquarian interest like the historical use of the *kana* syllabary. [54]

Azumamaro's focus on the *Man'yōshū* was consistent with the growing interest in the anthology during the Tokugawa period. The locus of *Man'yōshū* scholarship during his lifetime remained in the Kansai metropolises of Osaka and Kyoto, though, in the early eighteenth century, the *Man'yōshū* was also being studied in Edo by such figures as Kitamura Kigin and Toda Mosui (1629–1706). [55] Azumamaro claimed that what made the ancient verses so valuable was their expression of sincerity *(makoto)* and concern with the here and now. "Ancient poems," he wrote, "are all about the actual, and none of them are abstract." [56] This high regard for the *Man'yōshū* and his reasons for it figure prominently in the writings and thought of Kamo no Mabuchi in particular.

In other respects, however, Azumamaro's views on verse were trite, even by the highly conservative traditions of Japanese poetics. He described poetry as "an expression of the truth *(makoto)* of human emotions" [57] and spoke of poetry as a Way that "rejects vulgar

---

[52] *Man'yōshū dōjimon*, in *KZ*, I, 481.
[53] Miyake Kiyoshi, pp. 303–304.
[54] *Ise monogatari dōjimon*, in *KZ*, I, 315. See also Miyake Kiyoshi, pp. 551–555.
[55] See my "*Man'yōshū* Studies in Tokugawa Japan."
[56] *Man'yōshū hekian shō*, in *KZ*, I, 336.
[57] *Ise monogatari dōjimon*, in *KZ*, I, 89.

common words and favors elegant emotions."[58] He believed that
"what makes a poem a poem is the linkages *(tsuzukegara)* between
the words"[59] and rejected the notion that simply having the correct
number of syllables was a sufficient rule of prosody. He insisted
that poems are constructed of words that have both phonetic and
semantic associations which link the constitutent words into a unit.
"In this way," he wrote, "a poem becomes a poem—by seeking
words that have connections."[60] Yet, as much as this represents
Azumamaro's small contribution to the history of poetic criticism,
his emphasis on the elegant and the refined in verse ran counter to
the prevailing sentiments of those engaged in the rediscovery of the
Man'yōshū, who tended to find within its verses a simple freshness
and directness they regarded as superior to the (for them) excessively
elegant poetry of the Heian and medieval periods.[61]

From Azumamaro's writings on Shinto and literature, one constructs an image of him intellectually as a figure with one foot in
the old and another in the new—an image of him as the transitional
figure that he was. As much as he sought to ground his Shinto
theology in a singular text, he remained in large measure a prisoner,
as it were, of contemporary rival theologies and his own preconceptions; despite his efforts to give the study of ancient literature, especially verse, priority within his curriculum, there was little that
was new in his criticism; and for all his efforts to attract the attention of prominent individuals to his antiquarian researches, he remained throughout his life a figure on the periphery.

His contributions to the formation and development of nativist
scholarship in Japan are found, ultimately, in the tone and vision
that he set, the methodology that he espoused, the institutional
setting of the private academy that he founded, and the advances of

---

[58] *Man'yōshū hekian shō,* in *KZ,* I, 366.
[59] From his *Man'yō mondō,* quoted in Miyake Kiyoshi, p. 306.
[60] *Man'yōshū dōmō shō,* in *KZ,* III, 259.
[61] This view was shared by both Kinoshita Chōshōshi (1569–1649) and Shimokōbe Chōryū (1624–1686), the pioneers of Tokugawa-period *Man'yō* scholarship. See Nosco, "*Man'-yōshū* Studies in Tokugawa Japan," pp. 114–115.

the students whom he taught. It is to these matters that we now turn.

Azumamaro's "Petition to Found a School" is a remarkable document. It contains the most concise statement of Azumamaro's academic and institutional goals and aspirations, and the most articulate definition of the new field of National Learning as he envisioned it. It is a bold and moving document with revolutionary implications, and yet it is in every way consistent with the otherwise rather conservative formulations of its purported author. It also has a complex history, and doubts have repeatedly surfaced as to its authenticity.

The "Petition" was at best a little-known document during Azumamaro's lifetime. There are no references to it by either his students and contemporaries or by his immediate successors in nativist pursuits. The document's existence might not be known today were it not that, in 1798, Kada Nobusato (1740–1800) appended the "Petition" to a collection of Azumamaro's poems being published for the first time. Within two decades, the "Petition" attracted the attention of Hirate Atsutane who cited it as the reason why Azumamaro merits recognition as the first of National Learning's outstanding figures.[62] It was not until the late-nineteenth century, however, that the first doubts concerning the "Petition's" authenticity were raised by Inoue Yorikuni, an early authority on Azumamaro.[63] These doubts were reinforced by the publication in 1942 of Miyake Kiyoshi's magnum opus on Azumamaro's life and thought, which argued that the weight of the evidence supports the conclusion that the "Petition" was a late-eighteenth-century forgery by one or more members of the Kada School.[64] More recently, however, the "Petition" has found new supporters, and the majority of scholars have accepted the view presented by Ōkubo Tadashi in 1963 that, unless definitive evidence surfaces to the contrary, the

[62] See above, p. 72, for a summary of the hagiography of National Learning's "Great Men."
[63] See Miyake Kiyoshi, p. 473.
[64] Ibid., p. 539.

"Petition" in its current form merits acceptance as an authentic product of Azumamaro's brush dating from his later years.[65] Despite its controversial transmission and history, the "Petition to Found a School" remains the single document most closely identified with Kada no Azumamaro and is almost invariably described as his primary contribution to the development of eighteenth-century nativism.

To proceed under this assumption of authenticity, it is believed that the "Petition" was written by Azumamaro and entrusted to his adopted son and intellectual heir, Kada Arimaro, for delivery to the shogun, Yoshimune. Azumamaro was in failing health at this time, and Yoshimune, despite the influence of the orthodox Neo-Confucian Muro Kyūsō, was showing an interest in the Confucian Ancient Learning of Ogyū Sorai and a tolerance of such previously proscribed materials as foreign books. The text of the "Petition" is in exquisite classical Chinese, replete with allusions to the Chinese classics, and its requests are couched in abjectly humble language, exceeding the formality of language found in most shogunal petitions. One cannot escape the irony that, for all its later concern for the purity of the Japanese language and its belief in the influence of language upon thought, the tradition of National Learning located a genesis of sorts in a document written entirely in classical Chinese.[66]

The "Petition" opens with words of praise for the 1st Tokugawa shogun, Ieyasu, who is credited with having brought peace to the land, a peace that allowed learning to flourish. It proceeds to praise the current shogun, Yoshimune, for the soundness of his policies, his respect for ancient studies, and his interest in acquiring rare books of antiquarian interest from throughout the land. As Azumamaro wrote directly to his intended audience, "Because his [Yoshimune's] policies are perfected and he has leisure for other pursuits, he has turned his mind to ancient studies."

---

[65] Ōkubo Tadashi, *Edo jidai no kokugaku,* p. 83.

[66] For a nearly complete translation of the Petition, see Tsunoda, et al., II, 5–9. Unless otherwise noted, all quotations from the Petition are from this translation. For a complete text of the Petition, with commentary and transcription into classical Japanese, see *KSRZK,* pp. 330–337.

Azumamaro next described how, when he was in Edo as a young man, he took joy in working with old texts and even then entertained the idea of founding a school of National Learning but hesitated at the time to raise the subject because of his youth and obscurity. However, now in his sixtieth year, he has been unexpectedly struck by illness, and so, fearing that upon his death his ancient studies might not be continued, he makes bold to petition the shogun as an expression of his concern. He lamented the profusion of Buddhist and Confucian studies, which he believed were pursued at the expense of Japanese studies; he accused his contemporaries who lectured on Shinto or verse of having been seduced by the theories of T'ang and Sung dynasty Confucianism and Buddhism; he excoriated their writings as unfaithful representations of what the men of old thought and taught, and declared: "The teachings of our divine emperors are steadily melting away, each year more conspicuously than the last. Japanese learning is falling into ruin and is a bare tenth of what it once was."

For these reasons, Azumamaro explained, he has devoted himself to the retrieval and revival of the ancient Way of Japan and felt compelled to solicit the shogun's aid: "Prostrate, I here make my humble request: that I be given a quiet tract of land in Kyoto where I can open a school for studies of the Imperial Land," with Fushimi proposed by Azumamaro as one possible site. The school, as he envisioned it, was to house his collection of old books and rare manuscripts relevant to the study of ancient Japan and was to serve as a kind of research center and library, lending texts throughout the land and providing a forum for the exchange of ideas on ancient studies. It was Azumamaro's expressed hope that, through such activities, there might come about a reawakening of interest in Shinto and Waka verse.

It was, however, as he surveyed the history of Chinese studies in Japan, that Azumamaro became his most aggressive:

Alas, how ignorant the Confucian scholars were of the past, not knowing a single thing about the imperial Japanese learning. How painful, the stupidity of later scholars—who cannot bewail the destruction of the ancient learning? This is why foreign teachings have prevailed, and one meets them in street conversations and corner gossip. This is why too our teachings have so declined. False doctrines are rampant, taking advantage of our weakness.

In view of the fact that the 5th, 6th, 7th, and regnant 8th Tokugawa shogun all either showed an active interest in the promotion of Confucian scholarship or solicited Confucian counsel on matters of social policy, Azumamaro's disdain for his Sinological counterparts is extraordinary.

He followed this attack on the Confucians and vilification of foreign teachings with a carefully phrased statement of his methodology, using the terminology of those same Confucian schools he so vigorously castigated:

> If the old words are not understood, the old meanings will not be clear. If the old meanings are not clear, the old learning will not revive. The Way of the former kings is disappearing; the ideas of the wise men of antiquity have almost been abandoned. The loss will not be a slight one if we fail now to teach philology.

The notion expressed here of a Way of the former kings being part of an ancient learning which, in turn, is encoded in the ancient meanings of old words is, in fact, a pastiche of the terminology and methodology of the leading schools of Confucian ancient studies contemporary with Azumamaro. Both "ancient meaning" *(kogi)* and "ancient learning" are identified with Itō Jinsai who called his school the Hall of Ancient Meaning (Kogidō). The Way of the former kings was also a key term in the writings of Ogyū Sorai, who died in the year the "Petition" is believed to have been delivered and whose thought was just entering its period of greatest popularity and widest acceptance.[67]

Azumamaro, of course, committed no sin by seeking to communicate the aims of his "Petition" in the scholarly idiom of his day—an idiom with which the shogun was undoubtedly familiar—but his wholesale appropriation of the terminology and methodology of

[67] According to Maruyama's *Studies in the Intellectual History of Tokugawa Japan* (p. 136), "the golden age of the Sorai school began after Sorai died," reaching its peak during the 1740s.

the Confucian classicism of his age, while denouncing the proponents of such studies in no uncertain language, is one of several
seemingly contradictory features of the "Petition." Another is his
disparagement of contemporary Shinto. "Those who now treat
Shinto," he wrote, "all follow theories of Yin-yang or of the Five
Elements," apparently unconscious of the applicability of this assertion to his own Shinto formulations. In the same manner, the "Petition's" emphasis on philology is curious, since there is no evidence
that Azumamaro used philology in order to glean new insights from
ancient texts, and, as demonstrated above, he appears to have used
philological research largely to validate his preconceived notions.

Nowhere in the "Petition" did Azumamaro present a coherent
exposition of what he meant by the words "ancient Way." He wrote
of the "ancient Way of our country" and those familiar with his
writings would have understood this to refer to the Way of the gods
(Shinto) or the Way of the gods of heaven and earth (*jingidō;* his
own Shinto theology) but, in view of the vehemence with which he
denounced the Sinological counterparts to the ancient learning his
"Petition" proposed, his relative silence on the "ancient Way of our
country" is peculiar.

Some scholars have also questioned whether Azumamaro used the
word *kokugaku* (National Learning) or *Wagaku* (Japanese Learning)
is the original manuscript of the "Petition," since several variant
texts are extant. They have suggested that, in 1728, the date of the
"Petition," the word *kokugaku* was not yet in use to refer to nativist
scholarship and that the presence of the word is evidence of at least
the tampering with, if not the forgery of, the "Petition" by later
generations of nativists.[68] This allegation, however, is refuted by
the fact that, as early as 1719, the Shinto popularizer Masuho Zankō
used *kokugaku* in a vilification of "stinking Confucian half-wits who
know nothing at all about *kokugaku*." [69]

---

[68] The word *kokugaku* was originally used in eighth-century Japan in much the same way
in T'ang-dynasty China, i.e., to distinguish provincial academies (*kokugaku,* or the "studies in the *kuni"*) from the "university" (*daigaku*) in the capital. It was not until the
eighteenth century that the word came to be used in Japan to refer to nativist pursuits.
[69] From his *Shinro no tebikigusa,* in *KSRZK,* p. 222.

The persistence of these various controversies reflects the dispro-
portionate attention given to the "Petition" in most scholarship on
National Learning; for, despite several remarkable features of the
document, it is ultimately more significant for the aspirations it
reveals than the goals it achieved. Azumamaro never received the
gift of land or the patronage he sought. Nonetheless, his school had
enrolled some 30 identifiable students by the time of his death, of
whom one-half came from the same province of Musashi in which
the Inari Shrine was situated.[70] Of these students, the two most
important in terms of their later careers as nativists were his adopted
son, Kada Arimaro (1706–1751), and Kamo no Mabuchi (1697–
1769).

After Azumamaro's death in 1736, the direction of his school
was assumed by Kada Arimaro who, despite his relative youth, had
already served for nearly a decade as Azumamaro's representative in
Edo and played a key role in the transmission of the "Petition" to
the bakufu. Arimaro was especially gifted in his literary criticism
and had a broad knowledge of such antiquarian matters as ancient
manners, customs, and practices. If not more familiar, then he was
certainly more comfortable than his stepfather with the application
of avant-garde critical approaches to nativist topics. He continued
Azumamaro's interest in cultivating associations among the bakufu
elite and won a position in the service of Tayasu Munetake (1715–
1771), son of the shogun Yoshimune.

Kamo no Mabuchi was several years older than Arimaro and was
a relative newcomer to Azumamaro's school, having enrolled formally perhaps as early as 1728 but not having begun his studies in
residence at Fushimi until 1733. Nonetheless, Mabuchi was well
acquainted with Azumamaro's teachings, since he was an intimate
in his native Hamamatsu of several of Azumamaro's students and
was taught to read by Azumamaro's niece. As we shall see in the
next chapter, in many ways Mabuchi's scholarship proved closer
than Arimaro's to the concept of National Learning as Azumamaro
had envisioned it. Though the two were rivals of sorts during roughly

[70] Haga Noboru, *Kokugaku no hitobito—sono kōdō to shisō,* pp. 274–275.

the decade following Azumamaro's death, Kamo no Mabuchi emerged unchallenged as the premier nativist in Japan at the mid-point of the eighteenth century following Arimaro's death in 1751.

Like most transitional figures who are neither the proverbial fish nor fowl, Azumamaro defies precise categorization or assessment, and yet this is precisely what makes such figures so interesting and forces one to regard and accept them on their own terms. As we have seen, there was little of distinctive novelty in Azumamaro's Shinto theology, literary criticism, or antiquarian researches. Intellectually and ideologically, he fits in well with his contemporaries: he shared the classicist orientation of much early-eighteenth century Confucian thought; he participated in both the rediscovery of the *Man'yōshū* and the resurgence of interest in Waka verse, which were prominent features of eighteenth-century literature; and he continued a long and distinguished, albeit rather staid, tradition of antiquarian researches into the material culture, customs, and practices of the imperial court.

His significance in the history of nativist thought is in many ways more symbolic than real and lies rather in the concept of National Learning as he envisioned it and the conjunction he represents of several contemporary developments that figure prominently in the thought and careers of his major successors. Azumamaro believed that Japan had a Way in ancient times, a Way that he called the "Way of the gods [of heaven and earth]," and that this Way had suffered as a result of what he perceived to be an excess of attention to the originally non-native Ways of Buddhism and Confucianism. Since the fifteenth century, leading Shinto theologians had sought to distinguish their creed from the Buddhist cosmological assumptions that had accrued to it, but the disparagement of Confucianism by Shinto theologians was generally something new in the eighteenth century, though it was not exclusively Azumamaro's.

Applying the methodology of over half a century's development of Confucian Ancient Learning, Azumamaro sought to apply philological analysis to selected ancient texts, to glean thereby the original messages of those texts without the obfuscating encumbrance of later commentary, and to garner support for such efforts from official circles. Since nativist philology had been pioneered by Keichū in the late-seventeenth century under the sponsorship of Tokugawa Mitsukuni, there was again nothing distinctively novel about Azumamaro's efforts other than the fact that, unlike Keichū, who was distinguished by having his talents solicited, Azumamaro remains better known for his exertions in the solicitation of support.

What ultimately distinguishes Azumamaro from his contemporaries like Masuho Zankō or Toda Mosui is the manner in which one can find represented within his career and thought those themes that figure so prominently in the later development of the ancient Way thought of National Learning. He believed in the existence of a native and ancient Way which he identified with Shinto. He believed that this Way had been overshadowed over a period of a thousand years by the foreign creeds and doctrines of Buddhism and Confucianism, with potentially deleterious effect to at least the polity if not the individual, and he thereby posited an adversarial relationship between nativism and non-native creeds. He argued for the importance of preserving ancient texts and traditions that might otherwise be forever lost, and that philological method was of critical value to the reconstruction of the native Way and its distillation from non-native accretions. And, he asserted the importance of such endeavors as a national imperative, soliciting the support of both the government and individuals for the expansion of his private academy.

There is, thus, a certain appropriateness for the tendency among nineteenth-century nativists to perceive in Kada no Azumamaro a kind of genesis for their endeavors, since one finds in Azumamaro's writings—just as they did—the first immature articulations of those nostalgic and patriotic themes that characterize the next century of National Learning thought. This appropriateness becomes more apparent when one examines the career and thought of his student and major successor, Kamo no Mabuchi, the second of National Learning's "Great Men."

FIVE

Entering the Past: Kamo no Mabuchi

(1697–1769)

The city of Hamamatsu has for centuries benefited from its location on the Tōkaidō highway near the midpoint between Kyoto and Edo. During the Tokugawa period, the castle town derived economic advantage from the constant passage to and fro of that steady stream of official travelers (daimyo and their retinue), as well as less official wayfarers (merchants, sojourners, religious pilgrims, and so on) which daily passed through the city. It will be recalled that this is the same route on which the European observer and physician Engelbert Kaempfer found "scarce credible" the number of daily travelers and proclaimed the route to be "on some days more crowded than the public streets in any of the most populous towns of Europe."[1] Even today, when the city is best known for its production of motorcycles and pianos and the local delicacy of *unagi* (eel), the city is a train stop on the Shinkansen Kodama route—the contemporary counterpart of the Tōkaidō in the Tokugawa period—and remains very much betwixt Japan's ancient and modern capitals.

Hamamatsu's best-known native son is Kamo no Mabuchi, born in the village of Iba, known today as the Higashi Iba district of Hamamatsu, in the 10th year of the Genroku era, 1697.[2] He was

---

[1] Quoted in Sansom, III, 136.
[2] Hamamatsu is better known as the birthplace of Kamo no Mabuchi than for the fact that

the son of Okabe Masanobu (1654–1732), who in turn was descended from the Kamo family who had served as hereditary wardens of the Kamo Shrine in Kyoto. The Okabe family was itself divided into three main lines: one styled the Naka Okabe (Central Okabe, considered the main branch) worked either as shrine administrators or agriculturalists; a second styled the Nishi Okabe (Western Okabe) tended toward vocations either as Shinto priests or as lower-ranking samurai; and a third known as Higashi Okabe (Eastern Okabe) were primarily agriculturalists. Mabuchi's father was born into the Nishi Okabe line but was later adopted by the Higashi Okabe, and thus it is believed that he made his living principally by working the soil, though the family's intimate connections with Shinto made them far from rural rustics.[3]

Mabuchi's given name at birth was Sōshi, which means "three-four" and is believed to refer to the date of his birth on the 4th day of the 3rd month.[4] Whether or not this demonstrates a sense of humor on the part of his father, as some have suggested, the evidence is strong that both his parents were found of learning and took special interest in Waka verse. In his diary, the *Okabe nikki,* Mabuchi remembered his mother as a woman who "had always revered the gods and buddhas, . . .and had compassion for the lonely and wretched. If she heard of a beggar coming to ask for food, she would take her own things and go to feed him."[5] His father is said to have been a robust and spirited man—"uncommonly obese" in Mabuchi's words—who died in his seventy-eighth year after a life of hard work and financial difficulty.[6] Mabuchi was his parents' only surviving son, and by all accounts the relationship between parents and son was close and affectionate. Japanese studies of Mabuchi's life invariably suggest that his parents were instrumental in instill-

---

Tokugawa Hidetada, the second Tokugawa shogun (r. 1616–1623) was born in the local castle.
[3] Inoue Minoru, *Kamo no Mabuchi no gakumon,* pp. 8–10.
[4] Terada Yasumasa, *Kamo no Mabuchi—shōgai to gyōseki,* p. 5.
[5] Quoted in Saigusa Yasutaka, *Kamo no Mabuchi,* p. 20.
[6] Mabuchi described his father in a letter found in Yamamoto Yutaka, comp., *KKMZ:SH,* II, 1314.

ing in their son both that love of verse which characterized his entire life and a measure of pride in his ancestry, especially the samurai Okabe Masasada (1545–1619), who distinguished himself during the years of warfare that culminated in the Tokugawa unification.

Much, indeed, has been made of Mabuchi's early education and cultural environment. From 1707 on, he received early instruction in reading from Sugiura Masako, the niece of Kada no Azumamaro, who had married Sugiura Kuniakira in 1704. Both Sugiura Kuniakira (1678–1740) and Mori Terumasa (1685–1752), Shinto priests respectively at the Suwa and Gosha Shrines in Hamamatsu, studied under Kada no Azumamaro. Sugiura Kuniakira's association with Azumamaro began as early as 1701, when he had journeyed to Edo and was introduced to the still relatively young Azumamaro, who had himself only recently arrived in the metropolis. Some two years later, in 1703, Kuniakira became one of Azumamaro's first students, but the honor may have been as much Azumamaro's as Kuniakira's; Kuniakira had already by that time *twice* met the regnant shogun, Tsunayoshi, the first time in 1691 when he was invited to Edo castle to witness a performance of Nō by Tsunayoshi himself, and the second in 1695 when he was again invited to the castle to hear Tsunayoshi lecture on the *Book of Changes (I ching)*.[7] In 1704, the year of Kuniakira's marriage to Masako, Mori Terumasa likewise made the journey to Edo in order to enroll in Azumamaro's school.

The intellectual world in which Mabuchi lived during the first twenty-five years of his life thus appears to have been oriented toward Shinto on the one hand and poetry on the other, and in both spheres Kada no Azumamaro was a much-respected figure. Just as Mabuchi's own family, the Okabe, was identified with the local Kamo Shrine, his closest associations during these years were with the members of the Sugiura and Mori households, whose lives were similarly intertwined with the operations of the two other major Shinto shrines in Hamamatsu. Sugiura Kuniakira, at whose home Mabuchi learned to read and write and who was related to Azuma-

---

[7] On Sugiura Kuniakira, see Uchida Asahi's "Sugiura Kuniakira no shōgai."

maro by both marriage and studies, lectured on nativist topics in Hamamatsu to a small group of students drawn largely from the ranks of the Shinto clergy, and, as early as 1705, he began to host gatherings to discuss Waka—meetings that became monthly from 1720 and that Mabuchi regularly attended from the time of their formal inception.

Kada no Azumamaro stopped in Hamamatsu on his journeys back and forth from Edo and Fushimi. In the late spring of 1713, when Azumamaro was en route to Edo, he stayed briefly in Hamamatsu, visiting his students and niece and participating in at least one poetry gathering. He stayed for fully two months, in 1722 when he was again en route in what was to prove his last trip to Edo, and it is believed that at that time an introduction was arranged for him to meet Kamo no Mabuchi.[8] Azumamaro's final visit to Hamamatsu came the next year when he was returning to Fushimi from Edo, and he stayed for thirteen days.

In addition to his first meeting with Azumamaro, the 1720s mark a complex period in Mabuchi's life. When he was still just a boy not more than 5 or 6 years old, Mabuchi had been formally adopted by his cousin and elder sister's husband, Okabe Masamori of the Western Okabe line. The adoption period lasted less than one year, however, and Mabuchi soon returned to his biological parents when Masamori and his bride produced a son of their own, though Masamori was formally adopted by Mabuchi's father as his legal heir. Masamori's line, it will be recalled, at times contained samurai, and Masamori served as such in the retinue of the lord of Hamamatsu castle, Matsudaira Sukekuni.

In 1723, the Western Okabe line lacked a male heir, and so it was arranged for Mabuchi to be adopted into the household through marriage to the daughter of Masamori's brother, Okabe Masanaga.[9] While the marriage bore all the outward marks of an arranged affair, evidence suggests that Mabuchi fell deeply in love with his

[8] Saigusa, *Kamo no Mabuchi*, pp. 87–88.
[9] To add to the complexity of this, the father of the biological brothers Okabe Masamori and Masanaga (i.e., the brother of Okabe Masanobu, Mabuchi's father), is also named Okabe Masanage.

young bride, some eleven years his junior, [10] and numerous authorities have suggested that Mabuchi's marriage to her marked the
happiest interval of his life. This made her death the next year all
the more traumatic—in his diary, *Okabe nikki,* Mabuchi recalled
her death years later as his first experience with grief. It has been
suggested (first by Hirata Atsutane) that Mabuchi was moved by
the tragedy to join the Shingon priesthood, apparently in emulation
of the career of Keichū, but that his parents refused to grant him
permission. [11] His grief is apparent in the following verse composed
shortly after her death: [12]

How much too much grief	Kanashisa no
I felt by loving so;	amarite omou
In restless sleep my dreams	utatane no
Go on, allowing no escape—	yume ni mo tsuge yo
Death's parting mountain path.	shide no yamamichi.

That, years later, her memory still haunted Mabuchi is suggested
by the fact that in 1759 he adopted Okabe Masanaga's granddaugh-
ter, Oshima, and arranged for her marriage to Nakane Sadao whom
Mabuchi adopted as his heir. [13]

One year after his bride's death, a marriage was arranged for
Mabuchi to the daughter of Umeya Katayoshi, a prominent figure
in Hamamatsu, who managed the lodging facilities for daimyo and
courtiers en route through the town. [14] In 1727, this marriage resulted in the birth of a son named Mashige, who carried on his
grandfather's work at the lodge. The marriage appears to have brought
little satisfaction to Mabuchi, who soon left both wife and son.

Despite the suggestion of emotional turmoil inherent in these
events, these were fruitful years for Mabuchi in terms of his intellectual associations. In 1724, he met Watanabe Mōan (1687–1776),
a prominent local Sinologist and physician in service to the lord of

---

[10] Saigusa, *Kamo no Mabuchi,* pp. 97–100.
[11] See Terada, pp. 53–55; and Araki Yoshio, *Kamo no Mabuchi no hito to shisō,* p. 70.
[12] Quoted in Saigusa, *Kamo no Mabuchi,* p. 103.
[13] Oshima was the daughter of Masanaga's eldest son, Okabe Masaie.
[14] Mabuchi's second wife has been variously named. Terada calls her "Iso" (p. 56), though
other authorities have suggested both "Oyo" and "Umeko" for her given name.

Hamamatsu castle, when Mōan attended a poetry gathering hosted by Sugiura Kuniakira. Mōan had studied medicine and Chinese studies in the Kansai, where one of his fellow students was Dazai Shundai (1680–1747), under whose influence and tutelage Mōan learned the *kobunjigaku* (study of ancient words and phrases) methodology of Ogyū Sorai. Mōan also had direct contact with Hattori Nankaku (1683–1759), another of Sorai's leading students, who, together with Shundai, is thought to have shaped Mōan's perspectives on things Chinese.[15]

Kamo no Mabuchi studied under Mōan for approximately six months about the time of his first marriage. It is believed that he was encouraged in this by Okabe Masamori and Masanaga, that is, his wife's father and uncle, who themselves had an interest in Mōan's researches, as well as by Sugiura Kuniakira, whose son, Tomomasa, was one of Watanabe Mōan's first students in Hamamatsu.[16] Mōan had established a reputation as an authority on not just Chinese verse but also the writings of the major Taoists, Lao Tzu and Chuang Tzu, and it has often been suggested that the strongly Taoist coloration of Mabuchi's later views on the ancient Way in Japan may be due, at least in part, to the influence of Watanabe Mōan's teachings.[17]

Thus, one observes a variety of contacts and possible influences on Mabuchi's intellectual development during the first three decades of his life in Hamamatsu. First, while Mabuchi's "world" was not the sectarian yet cosmopolitan world of the Fushimi Inari Shrine, such as that in which Kada no Azumamaro had been reared, it was still a world—both through family and acquaintance—in which Shinto personages and concerns were prominent. Second, Mabuchi appears to have had, from an early age, a genuine fondness, perhaps even passion, for Waka verse, and this interest was nurtured through his regular participation in local poetry gatherings. Third, though nativism was still a not fully articulated concept at the time, Ma-

[15] Terada, pp. 41–46.
[16] Saigusa, *Kamo no Mabuchi,* pp. 93–94, 129.
[17] See Sasaki Nobutsuna, *Zōtei Kamo no Mabuchi to Motoori Norinaga,* pp. 17–18.

buchi's closest circle of intellectual associates included several students and one teacher of the new concept of National Learning. And, fourth, he had been exposed to the methodology of Confucian Ancient Learning, its literary theory, and, in the form taught by Watanabe Mōan, its application to the study of the texts of classical Taoism.

In Hamamatsu, neither Edo nor Kyoto were "remote" by virtue of the town's location on the Tōkaidō and the daily passage of travelers to and from Japan's major metropolises. Mabuchi may not, through his second wife, have been the personal acquaintance of the ranks of distinguished persons who lodged in Hamamatsu, and yet he was no stranger to them. The power of the Tokugawa was likewise close at hand, symbolized by Hamamatsu castle which, during Mabuchi's years in Hamamatsu, was under the lordship of members of the Matsudaira family. Mabuchi was also part of a family more closely knit than one generally encounters in the biographies of Tokugawa-period intellectuals—a family of diverse vocations, traditions, and lines, which took pride in its ancestry and yet seems to have found no shame in financially reduced circumstances, a family with no particular intellectual heritage which nonetheless appears to have encouraged a genuine fondness for learning among its members.

In view of the fact that Kada no Azumamaro figured so prominently in Mabuchi's intellectual world, and considering the recent disappointments he had experienced in his personal life, Mabuchi's decision, in 1728, to proceed to Fushimi in order to register in Azumamaro's school has a certain "logic" to it.[18] Azumamaro at this time—it was the year of his "Petition"—was in failing health but still active in his school. Mabuchi, however, did not move to Fushimi for full-time study until 1733, the year after his biological father's death in Hamamatsu. Perhaps Mabuchi felt that his own life had brought him to a certain crossroad, for the move seems to

---

[18] Controversy has surrounded the precise dating of Mabuchi's move to Fushimi and enrollment in Azumamaro's school. The current consensus, as presented above, has the enrollment taking place in approximately 1728 and the actual move to Fushimi in 1733.

represent, in a physical sense, Mabuchi's emotional severance of those ties that bound him to the environs of his birthplace and marks the start of a new and altogether different life.

Our first evidence of Mabuchi's life in Fushimi dates from the 3rd month of 1733, when Mabuchi participated with more than a dozen of Azumamaro's students in a Waka gathering at Azumamaro's home. The nature of the gathering suggests that Mabuchi was receiving instruction from Azumamaro and participating actively with his fellow students in the life of the school. That the verses of Kada no Azumamaro and several others of his students at this occasion were recorded in the *Man'yōgana* transcription method shows that Mabuchi was now, perhaps for the first time, exposed to the intricacies of the poetry anthology that figured most prominently in his later thought and career.[19]

It also appears that Mabuchi was in contact with the rival Dōjō circle of poets who enjoyed the privilege of personal attendance on the emperor.[20] Since Kada no Azumamaro's poetics were critical of Fujiwara Teika, the prime exemplar of the Dōjō school of verse, Mabuchi's contacts with Dōjō poets suggest that he may initially have been straddling the divisions between these rival camps; his later disdain of Teika's verses is often traced back to his contact with Azumamaro.

That his allegiances were not suspect within Azumamaro's school is attested to by Mabuchi's continued participation in poetry gatherings through 1734 and 1735 and, more significantly, by his beginning, in 1735, a series of lectures on the *Hyakunin isshu* in Azumamaro's home. Mabuchi was somewhat practiced in this anthology of verse, since he had already lectured on it some seven years earlier at Sugiura Kuniakira's home in Hamamatsu. Still, it is an important indication of his growing stature in Azumamaro's school, where, with Kada Arimaro and Kada Nobuna already resident in Edo, Mabuchi may well have been the leading resident student.

---

[19] Terada, pp. 72–73.
[20] Saigusa, *Kamo no Mabuchi,* pp. 170–171.

Through the years 1733–1735, Mabuchi returned annually for brief visits to his mother in Hamamatsu, where he also participated in poetry gatherings; one begins at this time to find evidence of his own interest in the *Man'yōshū*. Four of the verses he composed and read in Hamamatsu in 1735 are included in his *Agatai shokan* (Notes from the field, 1767) and are grouped under the title "Year-End Poems" *(Saibanka)*. One of these verses is in the *chōka* (long-poem) style of the *Man'yōshū*, demonstrating that Mabuchi had begun to experiment with the composition of verse in ancient modes, a practice he continued the rest of his days. Yet another indication of this interest is Mabuchi's reference in the *Agatai shokan* to having read Keichū's the *Stand-in's Chronicle* "some thirty years ago." [21] Kada no Azumamaro was well acquainted with Keichū's commentaries on the *Man'yōshū* and *Tales of Ise,* and it appears that Mabuchi read these as well as Keichū's commentary on the *Hyakunin isshu* near the end of his time in Azumamaro's school. [22]

In the 4th month of 1736, while en route to Hamamatsu from Fushimi, Mabuchi wrote a short work titled "Tabi no nagusa" (The consolations of traveling), the earliest of his extant prose works. [23] In the essay, Mabuchi discussed the local legends and histories of various famous sites, interspersing his own comments with references to such works as the *Kojiki, Nihon shoki, Engi shiki, Man'yōshū, Kokinshū, Gosenshū, Shuishū, Tales of Ise, Tale of Genji, Uji shūi monogatari,* and *Mumyōshō.* [24] Despite its brevity, the work attests to the remarkable broadening of Mabuchi's intellectual horizons during his years in Fushimi and affirms the impression one gains of him at this time as a newly confirmed nativist.

---

[21] Quoted in ibid., p. 175

[22] See above pp. 82–83, 88 for Azumamaro's indebtedness to Keichū's scholarship on the *Man'yōshū* and *Tales of Ise;* and Terada, pp. 88–89, for Mabuchi's familiarity with Keichū's commentary, the *Hyakunin isshu kaikanshō.*

[23] According to Terada, pp. 18–20, Mabuchi's earliest extant poem dates from 1720.

[24] The *Kokinshū, Gosenshū,* and *Shuishū* are collectively referred to as the *Sandaishū* (Anthologies of three eras) by virtue of being the first three poetry anthologies compiled by imperial command; for *Uji shūi monogatari,* see Douglas Mills, *A Collection of Tales from Uji: A Study and Translation of Uji shūi monogatari*; the *Mumyōshō* is a book of poetics attributed to Kamo no Chōmei (1155–1216).

The growth Mabuchi experienced in Azumamaro's school and the identity he vicariously gleaned from it ended, however, in the 7th month of 1736 with the death of Kada no Azumamaro after a decade-long bout with disease. The next month, a memorial service was held in Fushimi, attended by most of Azumamaro's students from Hamamatsu, including Mabuchi. It appears that Azumamaro's dream of establishing an enduring academy in Fushimi for the study of National Learning was soon abandoned, and, by the spring, Mabuchi found himself in Edo where he joined Kada Arimaro (1706–1751) and Azumamaro's younger brother, Kada Nobuna (1685–1751).

With Arimaro, Nobuna, and Mabuchi in Edo, Japan's political center became for the first time its center for nativist studies. This represents, in fact, just one facet of a broad cultural shift during the reign of the 8th Tokugawa shogun, Yoshimune (r. 1716–1745), from the Kansai metropolises of Kyoto and Osaka to the Kantō. With its greater population and wealth and as a communications and transportation nexus, Edo had acquired a superior infrastructure for the support of a self-sustaining popular culture; by the 1740s, nativism was on the verge of assuming a more prominent position within that culture.[25]

Upon arriving in Edo, Mabuchi lodged with Nobuna and Arimaro in the Hongō Yushima section of present-day Bunkyō ward, just a short walk from what today is the main campus of the University of Tokyo and at the time was the estate of the daimyo of Mito. Kada Nobuna attempted to continue the teachings of his late brother on Shinto, philology, and poetry, while Arimaro had established a reputation as an authority on ancient history, legal codes, and other aspects of antiquarian researches.[26] Arimaro was the more gifted and original of the two, and, though his stepfather had failed to win the shogun Yoshimune's sponsorship of a nativist academy, Arimaro had, since the mid-1730s, been employed in the service of

---

[25] I discuss these issues in "*Man'yōshū* Studies in Tokugawa Japan."
[26] Saigusa, *Kamo no Mabuchi*, pp. 182–183.

Yoshimune's second son, Tayasu Munetake (1715–1771), as tutor in Japanese studies.

Mabuchi now began a series of steps that slowly established his reputation as an authority on classical literature from the native tradition. One month after arriving in Edo, Mabuchi led a four-month-long seminar on the *Hyakunin isshu* in the Kada home and, in 1738, he inaugurated a year-long series of lectures on the *Man'-yōshū*. Since he had lectured on these same works at Azumamaro's school in Fushimi, these talks were familiar territory for Mabuchi. Furthermore, with Kada Nobuna's compilation in 1738 of the *Man'yōshū satsuki*—which presented the views of Mabuchi, Nobuna, and the late Azumamaro in dialogue form—Mabuchi's views on literature were, for the first time, available in written form. It was also in 1738 that Kamo no Mabuchi acquired his first formal student, Ono Furumichi.[27] Then, in 1740, he started what was for him a new series of lectures on the *Tale of Genji* at the home of Nemoto Harutane, a former student of Azumamaro who resided in the Nihonbashi section of Edo.[28] Clearly, the heirs to Azumamaro's teachings were making their presence felt in the intellectual world of Edo, and Mabuchi was at the forefront of their endeavors.

It was at this time that Kada Arimaro became embroiled in a sequence of events that generated considerable controversy. In 1738, while he was in the service of Tayasu Munetake, Arimaro was commissioned by the bakufu to write a description of the Daijōe (Great Thanksgiving) banquet at the court of Emperor Sakuramachi (r. 1735–1747).[29] Arimaro wrote two versions of the occasion, one presented to the bakufu, the other retained for use with his students. It was his publication of this latter version in 1739 under the title *Daijōe*

---

[27] Ono was a physician from present-day Shizuoka who had a particular interest in Japanese studies. He went blind as an adult. Sources differ as to his year of birth, one suggesting 1715 (Inoue Minoru, p. 311) and another 1697 (*Waka bungaku daijiten*).

[28] Mabuchi was residing with Nemoto at the time. Mabuchi lodged from 1738 to 1740 with not fewer than five households. See Ōyama Tadashi, *Kamo no Mabuchi den*, p. 305.

[29] A composite description of the traditional ceremony can be found in Herschel Webb, *The Japanese Imperial Institution in the Tokugawa Period*, pp. 108–110. Note that the Daijōe is the banquet that accompanies the Daijōsai ceremonies described by Webb.

benmō (Great Thanksgiving primer) that precipitated the crisis. Apparently, it was not so much the contents of the work as the fact that he published it without securing the court's permission, which aroused the Dōjō circles and resulted in a bakufu order to confiscate the printer's blocks and to place Arimaro under house arrest for several months.[30] Despite his lese majesty, however, Arimaro appears to have remained within the good graces of Tayasu Munetake, at least for several more years.

It was also in the late 1730s that Kamo no Mabuchi first came into contact with the Murata family in Edo. Murata Harumichi was a well-to-do merchant whose wealth came from, among other ventures, a wholesale trade in dried sardines. Harumichi had an interest in Shinto matters, and, while in Edo, Kada no Azumamaro had at times lodged at the Murata home in the Nihonbashi section of town. It is believed that Mabuchi was introduced to Harumichi by Kada Arimaro and Nobuna, and that Mabuchi was hired by Harumichi as a tutor. Murata Harumichi's two sons, Harumi and Harusato, both became students of Kamo no Mabuchi and formed part of the core of what came to be known as the "Edo group" within Mabuchi's school.[31]

Mabuchi was forming other associations that also figured prominently in his later career. Through Murata Harumichi, he was introduced to the Matsusaka samurai Katō Enao, an afficionado of Japanese studies who held the rank of *yoriki* in the office of the Edo City Commissioners (Machi Bugyō). Enao took an interest in Mabuchi's work, loaned Mabuchi a house next-door to his own, and later entrusted the education of his son, Katō Chikage (1735–1808), to Mabuchi.[32] Like his father, Katō Chikage also served in the office of the Edo City Commissioners and later reached the exceptionally high position of attendant to Tanuma Okitsugu, virtual civil dictator from 1767 to 1786.[33] Together with the Murata sons, Chikage was also part of the core "Edo group" within Mabuchi's school

---

[30] See Nakamura Yukihiko's "Kaisetsu" in his (ed.) *Kinsei bungakuron shū*, p. 111.
[31] Ōyama, pp. 306 ff.
[32] Katō Chikage is also known as Tachibana Chikage.
[33] Hisamatsu, *Biographical Dictionary of Japanese Literature*, p. 237.

and, after Mabuchi's death, continued his teacher's work on the *Man'yōshū*.[34]

Within five years of his arrival in Edo, Mabuchi had become surprisingly well established—his students grew each year in number, and their prominence was exceptional—and he even found time to advance his writing. In 1742, he wrote the first study of the *Man'yōshū* that was solely his own, the *Man'yōshū Tōtōmi uta kō* (On the Tōtōmi verses of the *Man'yōshū*), a study of 18 poems from the *Man'yōshū* composed in or by poets from Tōtōmi.[35] In the same year, he also completed a study of the *Kokinshū* commissioned by Tayasu Munetake, and moved, for the first time, into his own house in the Kayabachō section of Edo.[36] However, 1742 proved to be an altogether fateful year for Mabuchi in yet another way.

As Mabuchi recalled the circumstances several months after the fact, "In the early autumn, Kongokun [Lord Tayasu Munetake] ordered Arimaro to write about the Way of poetry. Arimaro replied that, even though from a very young age he had been raised by Azumamaro, his stepfather had only rarely discussed verse, since he had concentrated on antiquarian matters." Munetake, however, was apparently intent upon securing Arimaro's own views and is said to have insisted: "Then, just set aside Azumamaro's views and give me your own opinions on the matter." Arimaro apparently understood that, at this point, it would indeed have been "difficult to decline" and "within just three days wrote the *Kokka hachiron* (Eight essays on Japanese poetry)."[37]

As innocuous as this exchange may sound, it actually placed Kada Arimaro in an impossible position. Tayasu Munetake was a remark-

---

[34] See my "*Man'yōshū* Studies in Tokugawa Japan," pp. 134–135.
[35] The work also refers to the so-called "Azuma uta" or poems from Japan's (at that time) more remote eastern provinces. It will be recalled that the *Man'yōshū satsuki* by Kada Nobuna contained views on the anthology by Mabuchi, Azumamaro, and Nobuna, but the *Man'yōshū Tōtōmi uta kō* was Mabuchi's first study of the anthology as a solo author.
[36] The study was titled *Kokinshū sachū ron;* whether Mabuchi's maiden work on the *Man'-yōshū* was likewise commissioned by Munetake is uncertain. The *Kokinshū sachūron ron* was presented by Mabuchi to Kada no Arimaro, who, in turn, presented it to Tayasu Munetake. It was mistakenly presumed to be a work by Arimaro and is thus found in the *Kada zenshū*. See Terada, pp. 117–119, 125.
[37] *Kokkaron okusetsu,* in *KKMZ:SH,* 1, 22.

ably learned man in his own right, and, as a boy, had been tutored by Dohi Motonari, himself a former student of Arai Hakuseki. As his writings on the subject demonstrate, Munetake had a thoroughly traditional Confucian perspective on the normative value of verse. Arimaro, however, had an altogether different perspective, which expressed an appreciation for poetry as an art but nothing else—a view consistent with the avant garde poetics of Ogyū Sorai's Ken'en school.[38] Arimaro's alternatives were either to misrepresent his own views to please his lord, or to express his views accurately and risk possible dismissal. To his credit but also to his undoing, Arimaro chose the latter course in his *Eight Essays*.[39]

Arimaro's work so disturbed him that Munetake quickly brushed a rebuttal to it titled "My Views on the Eight Essays on Japanese Poetry" ("Kokka hachiron yogon"), and, perhaps to add fuel to the emerging controversy, Munetake solicited Kamo no Mabuchi's views on the matter. Exactly three months after Arimaro had presented the "Eight Essays," Mabuchi presented to Munetake his work titled *Gleanings on My Views of the Eight Essays (Kokka hachiron yogon shūi)*.[40] In this fashion, the rebuttals continued in rapid succession for four years; the controversy and the issues it raised actually continued to flare up in sporadic fashion decades after the initial exchange.[41]

The controversy that arose as a result of Arimaro's *Eight Essays* has been described as "the most celebrated controversy over the nature of the Waka" in Tokugawa Japan,[42] though the "debate" was no less political and philosophical than literary. Arimaro's single most inflammatory assertion in the *Eight Essays* was that, "since

---

[38] In this analysis, I disagree with Nakamura (pp. 414–415), who argues that Arimaro's position in the controversy is closest to that of Itō Jinsai and that Mabuchi's is closer to that of Ogyū Sorai. (Nakamura and I do, however, agree on our interpretation of Munetake's positions.) See also n. 39 below.

[39] I discuss the ensuing controversy more fully in my "Nature, Invention, and National Learning."

[40] Mabuchi revised this work the following year and retitled it *Conjectures on the Essays on Japanese Poetry (Kokka ron okusetsu)*.

[41] For example, Motoori Norinaga, Fujiwara Korenari, and Arakida Hisaoi renewed the "battle" in the late 1760s.

[42] Donald Keene, *World Within Walls: Japanese Literature of the Pre-Modern Era, 1600–1867*, p. 314.

versification is not one of the Six Accomplishments, it has never been of benefit to the administration of the country, nor is it of help in one's daily ordinary activities," and he insisted that Japanese poetry was "nothing more than a celebration of what is purely our own."[43] From this, the rest of his theory flowed quite logically. By denying the possibility of didactic or normative value to poetry, there remained only the criterion of artistic merit to value verse, and, accordingly, Arimaro extolled the sophisticated poetics of the *Shin kokinshū* (1205) over such anthologies as the *Kokinshū* or *Man'-yōshū*. He acknowledged that the *Man'yōshū* did have a special place in the history of Japanese poetry; since it is "the oldest of all Japanese poetry anthologies, one cannot claim to have studied poetry without studying it,"[44] but his preference for the verse of later ages was unambiguous, and he described as "ignorant" and "unworthy of refutation" the notion that poetry constitutes a Way.[45] As Arimaro summarized his position in a later work written during the height of the fray, the feeling one gets from a good poem is neither more nor less than "the amusement one gets from playing a game of *go* or chess *(shōgi)*."[46]

Tayasu Munetake's positions in the controversy differed on almost every point from those of Arimaro. He insisted that versification was indeed one of the Confucian Six Accomplishments (under the category of "etiquette"), that it partook of those same natural principles *(ri* or *kotowari)* which governed that delicate balance at the heart of both man and the cosmos, and that, as a result, verse was of intrinsic value to the national morality. Poetry that reflected artistic excellence at the expense of moral principles, he claimed, was not only of no value to the nation but was potentially of great danger to the national weal. He concluded that, by virtue of its

---

[43] *Kokka hachiron,* in Nakamura, pp. 52–53. The Confucian Six Accomplishments *(rikugei)* were etiquette *(rei),* music *(gaku),* archery *(sha),* riding *(gyō),* calligraphy *(sho),* and mathematics *(sū).*

[44] Ibid., p. 64.

[45] Ibid., p. 53–54.

[46] From his *Kokka hachiron sairon,* quoted in Shigematsu Nobuhiro, *Kinsei kokugaku no bungaku kenkyū,* p. 217.

antiquity, the poems of the *Man'yōshū* reflected a primordial and unadorned linkage with ancient natural principles and were thus particularly worthy of esteem. Furthermore, Munetake maintained that the *Man'yōshū* was compiled using the *Book of Songs (Shih ching)* as its model, and hence, like its Chinese classical prototype, its compilers had moral edification and rectification as their intended goals.[47]

Mabuchi's various positions in the controversy were closer to Tayasu Munetake's than to his erstwhile colleague's in National Learning. For example, concerning the value of verse, Mabuchi proclaimed that "poems might appear to be useless, but they calm the heart and bring a man to peace, and who could possibly not realize that they can be of broad use as an aid to government?"[48] In other words, while Arimaro denied a normative function for verse and Munetake regarded verse as an instrument of moral edification, Mabuchi esteemed verse for what he regarded as its potential for the pacification of an otherwise turbulent heart. Here, as elsewhere, by comparison with Kada Arimaro, Mabuchi's views were closer to but not replications of Tayasu Munetake's.

The issue of a possible relationship between verse and natural moral principles again demonstrates the differences among the three. Where Arimaro (like Ogyū Sorai)[49] saw no relationship between verse and cosmic moral principles and Munetake (like orthodox Neo-Confucians) did, Mabuchi (like Itō Jinsai)[50] regarded principle(s) to be insufficient either as an explanation of human character or as an instrument of governance:

> In general, while principle is the underlying principle of the world, principle alone is not enough to govern the world. When a poem relates a human truth, can one suppose that all true emotions are included within

---

[47] Ibid., pp. 217–218.

[48] *Kokka ron okusetsu,* in *KKMZ:SH,* I, 35.

[49] In his *Keijishi yōran,* Sorai wrote, "Chinese poems are the same as Japanese poems. They are not meant to expound the Way, to discipline oneself, and to govern others, nor are they meant to show how to maintain order in the state and peace in the world." Quoted in Maruyama Masao, *Studies in the Intellectual History of Tokugawa Japan,* pp. 108–109.

[50] In his *Dōjimon,* Itō Jinsai proclaimed that "one cannot hope to explain away everything in the world with the one word 'principle.' " In *Nihon rinri iheu,* V, p. 113.

principle? Principle is just principle, and when one expresses those irrepressible thoughts that are over and above principle, we call those in Japanese "undiluted yearnings" *(warinaki negai)* . . . If one simply expresses
this undiluted spirit, who would not be moved by it? If the words one
sings are easy and one's voice is moving, there is a sensation of human
emotion that transcends principle.[51]

In other words, the notion that natural principles exist and underlie
human affairs was acceptable to Mabuchi in the early 1740s, but he
believed that neither the world as a whole nor the richness of human
emotion were reducible to this one cosmological element. Good
government, according to Mabuchi, requires emotional accord, and
this emotional accord is facilitated when the irrepressible "undiluted yearnings" of the human heart are ventilated through a medium such as the composition of verse. "The poems of ancient man,"
he concluded, "were spontaneous *(onozukara)* expressions of human
concerns in which a person sang about his feelings whenever they
arose. Moreover, it was in this very manner that the age was naturally *(onozukara)* governed."[52]

Yet another example of the conflict among Arimaro, Munetake,
and Mabuchi is found in their differences on the origins of poetry.
Adopting variations of those views most widely held in their day,
Arimaro found the origins of verse in ancient songs,[53] while Munetake felt that poems evolved from the early ancient epithets *(kanji)*
attached to place names in the earliest chronicles.[54] By contrast,
Mabuchi found the hand of the divine in the origins of poetry and
invoked no less an authority that the Preface to the *Kokinshū:* "The
Preface to the *Kokin Waka shū {Kokinshū}* has the words, 'Poems
date from the time of the separation of heaven and earth' written in
it. This is a reference to the *Kojiki* where the god Izanagi said to the
goddess Izanami, 'Oh, what a lovely maiden' and she replied, 'Oh,
what a handsome man.' "[55] By adopting this position, Mabuchi

---

[51] *Saihōtō Kongokun,* in *KKMZ:SH,* I, pp. 64–65.
[52] Ibid., p. 52.
[53] *Kokka hachiron,* in Nakamura, pp. 47–48.
[54] For example, "eight-cloud-rising Izumo" *(yakumo tatsu Izumo),* etc.
[55] *Kokka ron okusetsu,* in *KKMZ:SH,* I, 23.

reinforced that area of agreement between himself and Munetake whereby both found cosmic significance in verse; but, where Munetake articulated this significance in terms of metaphysical principles, Mabuchi presented it in the theological terms of divine origins.

It is remarkable that, throughout the controversy surrounding the original *Eight Essays,* each of the principals' positions so closely represented the application of one or another of the diverse Confucian and Neo-Confucian stances on Chinese versification to verse from the native tradition. For example, Mabuchi asserted that, "when those above enjoy poetry, those below will follow suit . . ."; if this sounds Confucian, that is because it *is* Confucian, and only the continuation of the quotation—"if those above make use of the ancient spirit and words, those below will likewise return to the ways of antiquity"—reveals the nostalgic posture of a mid-eighteenth-century nativist.[56]

If one were to summarize in the most general terms the respective positions of Kada Arimaro, Tayasu Munetake, and Kamo no Mabuchi in the *Eight Essays* controversy, it would be as follows: Arimaro esteemed art for art's sake; Munetake believed in art's value to the nation; and Mabuchi valued art for the sake of the individual. Arimaro's position represented the application of the avant garde poetics of the Ken'en school to verse from the native tradition; he rejected utterly the medieval conviction that art was intended to "praise the good and blame the evil" *(kanzen chōaku)* and thereby to fulfill a normative function in society; and his various positions in the controversy have, accordingly, a refreshingly "modern" quality. The positions of Munetake, in turn, reflect the application to Japanese verse of those poetic principles reflected in orthodox Neo-Confucianism: He believed that the poems of the *Man'yōshū,* like those of the *Shih ching,* contained a "mother lode" of those same natural moral principles which in matrix-fashion governed the cos-

---

[56] Ibid., p. 35. In the *Analects* (12:19), Confucius is quoted as telling the ruler Chi K'ang Tzu, "If you desire what is good, the people will be good. The character of a ruler is like wind and that of the people is like grass. In whatever direction the wind blows, the grass always bends." From Wing-tsit Chan, tr. and comp., *A Source Book in Chinese Philosophy,* p. 40.

mos; and that the anthologies reflected their compilers' didactic intention to gather together verses of normative value to the *moralitat* of the realm and in this way to contribute to national administration, moral rectification, and individual pacification. Kamo no Mabuchi, by contrast, regarded ancient verse as having been divinely created for the direct purpose of tranquilizing the individual, thereby contributing indirectly to the social well-being of the polity; that is to say, he believed the ancient song-poems performed the function of venting powerful human emotions which, if left unchanneled, might prove disruptive to national harmony.

Munetake was impressed by Mabuchi's synthesis of Confucian and nativist ideals; upon the resignation of Kada Arimaro, in 1746, Munetake appointed Kamo no Mabuchi as his tutor in Japanese studies *(Wagaku goyō)*, a position Mabuchi held until his own voluntary retirement in 1760. The timing was propitious, since, in the same month in which Mabuchi took up the appointment, his house in Kayabachō was destroyed in a major conflagration that consumed much of Edo. Since his mother had died in Hamamatsu in the previous year, 1746, like 1733 when he left Hamamatsu for Fushimi, stands out as a kind of watershed in the development of Mabuchi's thought and career. Never before in his adult life had Mabuchi been as professionally or financially secure; for his thought it marks the commencement of a new level of ideological nativism.

It is customary for Japanese scholarship on Mabuchi to divide the last twenty-three years of his life—his most productive years as an author and teacher—into two phases: his years of service to Tayasu Munetake (1746–1760), and his years as the self-styled "old man of the fields" *(agatai no ushi)*. Though it might be argued that one's life is a garment without seams, this division has considerable utility for an understanding of the development of Mabuchi's thought and is reflected in the analysis that follows.

His entry into Munetake's service marked the first time in his professional life that Mabuchi was financially secure. In 1747, he was given a "five-man stipend" *(gonin fuchi)*, which was doubled in 1751 after five years of service, and tripled one year later. This stipend was over and above the tuition income he received from his growing number of private students. Furthermore, with the deaths of both Kada Arimaro and Nobuna in 1751, Kamo no Mabuchi emerged as not only the sole surviving heir to the mantle of Kada no Azumamaro's scholarship, but also the premier nativist in Japan at the midpoint of the eighteenth century.

Changes were also evident in the government. Tokugawa Yoshimune, Munetake's father, had stepped down as shogun in 1745 and was succeeded by his frail eldest son (Munetake's brother), Ieshige, who ruled as the 9th Tokugawa shogun from 1745 until his death in 1760. Historians have been less than flattering in their descriptions of Ieshige—George Sansom has referred to him as "feeble and incompetent, . . . dissipated and erratic"[57]—and he was known during his lifetime as the "peeing shogun"*(shōben kubō),* a reference to his habit of bed-wetting. He was handicapped in his execution of the office by a stammer, which made him virtually unintelligible to all except his personal attendant and eventual chamberlain *(so-bayōnin),* Ōoka Tadamitsu (d. 1760). This enabled Tadamitsu to serve as the solitary spokesman for the shogun and marks the start of several decades during which the chamberlain exercised at least as much power as the shogun himself—a change suggestive of not only the decline of shogunal authority but also the eventual decline of the whole bakufu.

The first work Munetake commissioned Mabuchi to write after entering his service was the *Explication of Shinto Liturgies in the Engishiki (Engishiki norito kai),* completed in the 9th month of 1746. The liturgies were transcribed in an exceedingly complex language which used Chinese characters at times phonetically and at times for semantic meaning, distinguishing between these usages by the size of the written characters. Mabuchi made explicit in his study of the work that his own teacher, Azumamaro, had not instructed him in these matters and that the *Explication* was entirely Mabuchi's own work. The excellence of Mabuchi's analysis is attested to by

---

[57] Sansom, III, 173.

the fact that even modern scholarship on the *Engishiki* refers to his *Explication* as the starting point for serious study of the work.[58]

Mabuchi's Preface (*jo*) to the work also provides an excellent introduction to his ancient Way thought at this still early stage of its development. In this Preface, Mabuchi for the first time explicitly idealized the ancient past and, developing further certain themes evident in the *Eight Essays* controversy, articulated a relationship between superior government and superior literature:

> From the time when the [imperial] court was at Ōtsu in Ōmi through the period of the Fujiwara court at Yamato, grand august government filled the heavens and reached to every nook and cranny of the earth; and, thanks to this glorious tranquillity, literary expression was blessed with both beauty and elegance.[59]

Historically, the period to which Mabuchi referred is roughly the fourth through seventh centuries. Within this four-hundred-year interval, the period he singled out for special praise corresponds to the years 690 to 710, when, he claimed, "grand and august government reached perfection and declined somewhat in the Nara period [710–793], together with the true heart (*magokoro*)."[60] This idealization of the pre-Nara past of Japan—and the attendant derogation of the Nara period—was utterly new in the nativist tradition; it also marks Mabuchi's first use of the term *true heart*—a seminal term in his later thought—in a prose work.

Mabuchi linked both the pre-Nara excellence and the Nara decline in "grand and august government" to literature, especially verse. He postulated a relationship between the decline in government and the decline in fashion of composition of verse in the *chōka* mode and proclaimed that "what is truly astonishing is that the beauty of literature was part and parcel of the tranquility of govern-

---

[58] See Takeda Yukichi, ed., *Norito*, p. 381; and Terada, pp. 133–135.
[59] *Engishiki norito kai jo*, in *KKMZ:SH*, I, 446.
[60] Ibid., I, 447. Mabuchi here refers to the Fujiwara court, which spanned the reigns of Emperors Jitō (r. 690–697), Monmu (r. 697–707), and Genmei (r. 707–715) up to the founding of Japan's first "permanent" capital at Nara.

ment."[61] Though he did not here further articulate his premises concerning this relationship, it may be assumed from his writings in the *Eight Essays* controversy—writings with which Munetake, the solitary intended audience for the *Explication,* was certainly familiar—that Mabuchi was referring to what he believed to be poetry's capacity to pacify the individual and thereby to contribute to social well-being.

Two other ways in which Mabuchi demonstrated his independence from the scholarship of Azumamaro and established what became a framework for the later work of himself and his principal eighteenth-century nativist successors were his precise periodization of Japanese history and his reevaluation of the earliest chronicles. Mabuchi divided Japanese history into five major stages: high antiquity (*jōko*), earliest times through 628; the ancient period (*jōsei*), 629–793; the middle period (*chūsei*), 794–930; the later period (*gesei*), 931–1072; and the final period (*kosei*), 1087 to his present. Mabuchi further specified certain subdivisions for these stages like "middle-ancient period" (*jōsei no chū*), "late-middle period" (*chūsei no ge*), and so on, representing a sophisticated nativist alternative to the periodization recommended by the Confucian Arai Hakuseki in his *Lessons from History* (*Tokushi yoron,* c. 1723).[62]

Mabuchi's reevaluation of the relative priority he accorded the two most ancient extant histories was likewise novel. Where Azumamaro and other nativists had given priority to the *Nihon shoki* over the *Kojiki,* Mabuchi reversed this ranking and justified this preference by means of a linguistic argument:

> The *Nihon shoki* was compiled from various writings of high antiquity . . . but, since its Confucian compiler was obsessed with writing in Chinese, it often deviates from the true essence of high antiquity. The *Kojiki* is the quintessential national history. Since it is written in Japanese, no other work approaches its usefulness for observing ancient customs or learning ancient words.[63]

---

[61] Ibid.

[62] For Mabuchi's periodization, see ibid., I, 442. For Hakuseki's periodization, see Joyce Ackroyd, *Lessons from History: The Tokushi yoron by Arai Hakuseki,* pp. xxi-xxiii.

[63] *Engishiki norito kai jo,* in *KKMZ:SH,* I, 442.

This argument, resting as it does upon the premise that only the Japanese language can communicate truths about Japan, became a cornerstone of Mabuchi's later scholarship as well as that of Motoori Norinaga later in the eighteenth century. It is an argument Kada no Azumamaro had proclaimed but had not himself followed, and therein lies perhaps the single most important difference between Azumamaro's work and Mabuchi's.

Kamo no Mabuchi believed that certain truths were untranslatable—that the medium was indeed inseparable from the message—and that the key to understanding the ancient past in Japan rested upon a sound understanding of the earliest language in Japan.[64] It was an argument that in Confucian studies had reached its most sophisticated articulation in the writings of Ogyū Sorai, whose teachings at this time had just reached their peak of popularity, signifying Confucianism's slow decline and relinquishment of its vanguard role in the intellectual world of Tokugawa Japan. The school of thought that appropriated that argument and moved to fill the vacuum created by Confucianism's decline was National Learning with Kamo no Mabuchi at its forefront.[65]

Mabuchi produced several other works during the first five years of his service to Munetake. In 1747, he wrote *Explication of Poetic Epithets (Kanji kai)*, a preliminary study of *makura kotoba*, and, in 1749, he completed both *On Antiques (Koki kō)*, a work on antiquarian objects commissioned by Munetake, and *Explication of the Man'yōshū (Man'yo kai)*, a general study of the anthology, which Mabuchi wrote within ten days of its commissioning by Prince Kan'-eiji and which is said to have been shown to the abdicated Emperor Sakuramachi.[66] The latter work concentrates on such various topics as the anthology's poets, placenames, manuscript editions, the order of the various fascicles *(kan)*, technical linguistic matters, and so on. It also includes an early articulation of Mabuchi's methodology, which, at this stage of its development, contained numer-

[64] This relationship between medium and message is, of course, adapted from Marshal McLuhan, *Understanding Media*.
[65] See Maruyama Masao, *Studies in the Intellectual History of Tokugawa Japan*, p. 143.
[66] The full title of the work is *Man'yō kai tsūshaku narabi ni shakurei*.

ous echoes of Keichū. Like Keichū's *Man'yō daishōki*, Mabuchi's *Man'yō kai* advised that "those who live in the present age *(kosei)* should forget the lessons of our age when we read ancient works and approach them with an open mind"; it recommended that one use the comparative study of near-contemporary texts like the Taihō codes, *Kojiki*, *Nihon shoki*, *Engi shiki*, and *Wamyōshō* in order to elucidate difficult words; and then, once one has mastered the vocabulary and style of ancient texts and the annotated editions have become a distraction rather than an aid, Mabuchi recommended that one return to the *Man'yōshū*, for "nothing compares with learning the human feelings and national customs, deciphering the ancient words, or understanding the ancient literature."[67]

These early essays provide indications of both Munetake's expectations from Mabuchi and Mabuchi's thought on a variety of matters relevant to an understanding of his ancient Way thought. One finds Mabuchi involved with the philological study of a number of ancient texts but with a concentration on the *Man'yōshū* and an emphasis on the capacity of ancient Japanese (as opposed to Chinese) words to communicate truths about the Japanese past; he depicted the society and government of the pre-Nara past in idealized terms; and he postulated a relationship between the idealized conditions of the past and the literature of those times. In later years, Mabuchi revised and expanded several of these less well known early essays into some of his most famous works.[68]

During the 1750s, Mabuchi wrote commentaries on both the *Tales of Ise* and *Tale of Genji*,[69] annotation for the *Kojiki*,[70] and several essays on philological or poetic topics,[71] but his most important

[67] *Man'yō kai*, in *KKMZ:SH*, I, 203–204. Keichū had likewise counseled that readers of the anthology should "try to forget the spirit of their own age and become part of the spirit of ancient man." For Keichū's remarks, see above (Ch. 3, p. 59).

[68] The *Kanji kai* served as the base for *Kanji kō* (1757); material from *Engishiki norito kai* was included in *Norito kō* (1768); and the *Mam'yō kai* contains material that later appeared in *Man'yō kō* (1768).

[69] The *Ise monogatari koi* (1753) and *Genji monogatari shinshaku* (1758).

[70] *Kojiki kashiragaki* (1757).

[71] Of these, the most important were the *Sandaishū sosetsu* (1752), *Man'yōshū shinsai hyakku kai* (1752), and *Kanji kō* (1757).

project during these years was his work on his magnum opus, the *Man'yō kō (On the Man'yōshū)*. Though Mabuchi had probably contemplated the production of a full commentary on the *Man'yōshū* for several years, the project was not commissioned by Munetake until 1756. Mabuchi worked quickly on a first draft, but then continued the slow process of revision for more than a decade before declaring the work complete in 1768. All the Prefaces, however, which contain his most explicit statements on the ancient Way, as well as nearly half the commentary were finished prior to Mabuchi's resignation from his service to Tayasu Munetake in the 11th month of 1760.

There is no more concise statement of Mabuchi's ancient Way thought at this time than his Preface to the commentary on Book Six of the *Man'yōshū*, which includes the following statement of purpose and method:

> In revering the august and awe-inspiring emperor, one thinks of spreading order throughout the realm. By so thinking, one especially reveres those imperial reigns of the ancient past. From this reverence of the past, one proceeds to examine ancient writings, and, when one reads them, one thinks of unraveling the words and spirit *(kokoro)* of the past. From this one moves directly to reciting ancient poetry, and to do so one turns to the *Man'yōshū*. Now one learns the words and spirit of the past, and next one learns of the sincerity *(makoto)*, directness, vitality, manliness *(ooshiku shite)*, and elegance of the hearts of ancient men. It is precisely by learning these things that one's understanding of the ancient past becomes clear. [12]

Mabuchi's words represent a virtual curriculum for the transformation of a Japanese into a nativist embarked upon the nostalgic quest, and we shall examine this quotation in detail by making reference to other writings by Mabuchi and events contemporary with it.

The first step in the transformation is reverence for the emperor—a reverence Mabuchi described in the religious terms of awe in the presence of what one perceives to be the divine, what Rudolph Otto has called the *mysterium tremendum*. [73] This reverence, in

---

[72] *Man'yō kō maki roku no jo*, in *KKMZ:SH*, I, p. 176.
[73] See Rudolph Otto's *The Idea of the Holy*.

turn, was linked by Mabuchi to the normative goal of spreading order throughout the realm—a linkage that, while not altogether new within Japanese thought, was one on which nativists had remained conspicuously silent prior to the late 1750s. Significantly, it was during these years that the imperial institution reentered the area of political discourse with effects that were not felt fully until a century later.

Two figures, Takenouchi Shikibu (1712–1767) and Yamagata Daini (1725–1767)—perhaps no more than "isolated malcontents" in the context of their times[74]—achieved a measure of notoriety for their activities on behalf of the imperial institution. Shikibu, a student of the Confucian and Shinto theories of Yamazaki Ansai, operated a school in Kyoto attended by courtiers *(kuge)* as well as commoners to whom he lectured on both ancient chronicles like the *Nihon shoki* and theories of imperial loyalism. Shikibu taught that the emperor was more to be revered than the shogun and that the reason the emperor was not appropriately honored stemmed from deficiencies in the training of those in personal attendance upon the emperor. Correct these deficiencies, claimed Shikibu, and the country as a whole will without hesitation submit to imperial rule. When, in 1755, the imperial regent *(kanpaku)*, Ichijō Michiyoshi, learned that younger courtiers were honing their skills in fencing and archery for what was suspected to be an anti-bakufu action, he investigated the matter, and the bakufu's deputy *(shoshidai)* in Kyoto likewise interviewed Shikibu. Their conclusion was that Shikibu's teachings, while not subversive, were nonetheless inappropriate, and his preferred textbooks were banned from the court. Further lapses in discipline among Shikibu's students resulted in 1758 in their dismissal from office and house arrest as well as an interrogation of Shikibu by the Kyoto City Commissioner *(machi bugyō)*. During the questioning, Shikibu is said to have responded as follows to a query on his teaching that the country was facing a major crisis: "When the country is in possession of the Way, rites, music, and punishments proceed from the sovereign. When the country lacks the Way,

---

[74] See Webb, pp. 249–253.

they proceed from the feudal lords. When they proceed from the feudal lords, it is rare that these do not lose their power in ten generations."[75] His inquisitors, of course, did not miss his allusion to the fact that the Tokugawa bakufu was at the time headed by the 9th shogun. When Shikibu elaborated upon his remarks by suggesting that the bakufu should consult imperial opinion on policy matters of substance, he was ordered expelled from Kyoto, ostensibly on the less offensive charge of having publicly fraternized with courtiers at a drinking party.

Yamagata Daini, by contrast, started a school for samurai in Edo, where he taught martial arts and Confucianism. In 1759, he wrote a work in which he accused Japan's succession of military governments of having improperly assumed a variety of prerogatives that belonged to the imperial court and of having confused the correct distinction between the civil *(bun)* and the military *(bu)*:

> The principle of ancient and modern times for achieving good government is that the civil order should defend the country in ordinary circumstances and the military order should attend to occasions of crisis. In the present government there is no distinction between civil and military affairs. Those who attend to times of crisis also defend the country in ordinary times.[76]

The bakufu was justified in regarding the work as subversive of its rule, and Yamagata Daini was executed some years later in 1767 for his active involvement in an anti-bakufu plot. At the same time, Takenouchi Shikibu was exiled to Hachijō (where he died shortly after) as punishment for his knowledge of the plot and failure to report it to the authorities; and Fujii Umon, a student of Daini's, was imprisoned for having used violent language in a public denunciation of the bakufu.[77]

These proponents of imperial loyalism *(sonnō ron)* from the late 1750s shared the notion that the times were disordered and out of harmony with historically demonstrable principles of sound gover-

---

[75] Quoted ibid., pp. 249–250.
[76] Quoted ibid., p. 251.
[77] Based on Webb, pp. 248–252; Sansom, III, 178–179; and Maruyama Masao, *Studies in the Intellectual History of Tokugawa Japan*, pp. 276–280.

nance. Takenouchi Shikibu's response to his inquisitor that "I sincerely believe that society is in a precarious state" and Yamagata Daini's assertion that "I find nothing worthwhile in the government of the east since the 1180s" were unambiguous challenges to the legitimacy of bakufu rule and were couched within the context of a discourse on the imperial court.

These pronouncements on the decline of the times received a measure of seeming verification when, after more than a decade of feeble rule, the shogun, Ieshige, and his chamberlain, Ōoka Tadamitsu, both died in 1760. While, under other circumstances, this conjunction might have paved the way for a renewal of shogunal authority, in this instance Ieshige was succeeded by the 10th Tokugawa shogun, his 40-year-old son, Ieharu, whom George Sansom has characterized as "slovenly in his person, lazy, and untidy"[78] and whose favorite by this time was the notoriously ambitious and corrupt Tanuma Okitsugu.

His fourteen years of service in Edo to Ieshige's brother, Tayasu Munetake, make it certain that Kamo no Mabuchi was aware of both the facts and the nuances of these various ideological issues and political developments, and one observes in this a richly patterned context for Mabuchi's attention to the imperial institution in his own writings of this time. Mabuchi was, in fact, in interesting intellectual company when he linked revering the emperor with thinking of spreading order through the realm, and, though the bakufu is not explicitly mentioned in his Preface to Book Six of the *Man'yō kō,* it is nonetheless present if only by unstated comparison.

Mabuchi explained that, "by so thinking," that is, by thinking about spreading order in conjunction with revering the emperor, one reveres especially those imperial reigns of the ancient past, since, as Mabuchi declared elsewhere, "The emperors of ancient ages inwardly worshiped their ancestral imperial gods and outwardly exercised strict authority, and thereby they brought order to unruly lands and pacified mighty men. They governed in a manner in accord with heaven and earth and that constituted a magnificent and

---

[78] Sansom, III, 174.

unblemished Way."[79] Mabuchi maintained that these ancient emperors, whose rule conformed to natural cosmic principles, delegated administrative matters to loyal ministers who, "since they served with a manly true heart *(ooshiki magokoro)*, governed the land ruled by our emperors in a manner as broad and far-reaching as the earth and coeval with heaven itself."[80]

Mabuchi, of course, wrote of the imperial prerogative in terms of the divine attributes of the institution itself and made reference to the heavenly sun succession *(amatsu hitsugi)* whereby the imperial line was believed to descend in an inviolate chain from the heavenly divine ancestor *(amatsu kamurogi)*. However, though the attributes of imperial rule were believed to have remained the same in his own day as in the remote past, Mabuchi recommended that one turn one's attention to the study of more ancient reigns, since it was only then that imperial rule constituted that "magnificent and unblemished Way" which conformed to the beneficent principles of the natural order, a Way whereby divine emperors were decisive in the exercise of their authority and reverent to their imperial ancestors. Furthermore, Mabuchi felt that, in his own age, these various aspects of the divine imperial sovereignty had become "as remote as the sound of the wind," since, when "people in later ages" discoursed upon these matters, their discussion were based more upon their own "prejudices and misconceptions" than on a sound understanding of the historical development of the imperial institution.[81]

As for what had changed in the political order between then and his own times, Mabuchi maintained, for the most part, a discreet silence, stating elsewhere only that "grand and august" imperial government had "declined somewhat during the Nara period,"[82] for the change, as he envisioned it, had nothing to do with the attributes of the imperial institution per se—attributes he believed to be eternal and unalterable—but rather hinged, as we shall see, upon a fundamental change in the human heart. By articulating his

---

[79] *Man'yōshū taikō,* in *KKMZ:SH,* I, 147.
[80] Ibid., I, 148.
[81] Ibid., I, 146.
[82] *Engi shiki norito kai jo,* in *KKMZ:SH,* I, 447.

position in this manner, and by referring to the imperial institution's successful delegation of administrative authority to loyal ministers—prototypes, as it were, for shogunal rule—Mabuchi was able not only to express reverence for the imperial institution of his own day, but also to encourage his followers to study the reigns of the past without presenting his arguments and exhortations in terms that could be construed as specifically subversive to the ideological foundations of contemporary bakufu government.

Mabuchi believed that one's interest in the imperial reigns of the past would lead to the study of ancient writings, and that consonant with this study was an interest in "unraveling the words and spirit *(kokoro)* of the past." At one level, Mabuchi's quest was scarcely different from that of a modern intellectual historian—substitute the word *discourse* for *spirit,* for example, and Mabuchi begins to sound not unlike Michel Foucault—since the scholarly aspect of Mabuchi's quest was to move beyond the chronicled facts of an age and to glean from the texts themselves that very élan vital with which the age was infused. As we have seen, the prose texts he favored included the legal codes of the Taihō era (701–704), which, Mabuchi believed, despite having been written in Chinese and patterned after the legal codes of T'ang China, "often differed in their spirit and thus are often most useful in an examination of high antiquity," and the *Kojiki, Engi shiki,* and *Wamyōshō* dictionary.[83]

Yet, it was above all poetry, according to Mabuchi, that expressed those "undiluted yearnings" of the human heart and was thus most valuable for the reconstruction of the "spirit" of an age. "It is especially the poems of ancient ages," he wrote, that embody the words and spirit of ancient man," and, of all ancient verses, of course, Mabuchi most esteemed those of the *Man'yōshū,* for it was those verses that contained "a singular spirit comprised of ancient things elegantly described and a correct *(naoki)* heart."[84] Mabuchi recognized that the study of such ancient verses posed distinctive challenges—that "ancient poems," in his words, "appear unwieldy"

---

[83] *Man'yō kai,* in *KKMZ:SH,* I, 203.
[84] *Man'yōshū taikō, KKMZ:SH,* I, 146.

or "pointless and base"—but he felt that upon closer examination, one finds them to be "elegant . . . noble and true"; the poems of later ages, by contrast, might initially appear to be "soothing" and "sensible," but, when one looks closer, they are discovered to be "distressing . . . false and shallow."[85] The reason for this, according to Mabuchi, is that ancient verses communicate the unaffected true heart (*magokoro*) of ancient man, while those of later ages reflect an excessive concern with technique and "artifice" (*shiwaza*) and are thus, quite literally, artificial expressions of unfelt sentiments.[86] Thus, the superiority of ancient verses is threefold: They are the finest medium for a reconstruction of the spirit of the ancient past; they are artistically superior to later verses by virtue of their spontaneous expression of intense emotion; and they are of normative value by virtue of their capacity to communicate the values of the true and correct "heart" of ancient man.

The verses of the *Man'yōshū,* of course, had all these attributes, according to Mabuchi, but the one he most emphasized was their normative value—they were replete, he claimed, with moral lessons one might claim as one's own but only after philological study and recitation. It will be recalled that the question of a possible normative value for verse was a key issue in the "Eight Essays" controversy, and, in a possible disparaging allusion to Kada Arimaro, Mabuchi asserted that "a man who was ignorant of all the ways in which China and the imperial land [of Japan] differ once said that there are no moral teachings in the *Man'yōshū* and that it is nothing more than an amusement, but this is just proof of his foolishness concerning our land."[87] To learn these moral teachings, according to Mabuchi, one had to master the anthology, and to do so required the philological study of even such relatively arcane matters as ancient poetic epithets (*makura kotoba*).[88]

---

[85] Ibid., I, 151.

[86] Ibid., I, 148.

[87] Ibid., I, 151.

[88] In a reference to the system of ceremonial cap ranks worn at the imperial court, Mabuchi wrote that, "if you encounter a man wearing a cap, you learn his rank; if you look at his clothing, you learn his demeanor." He claimed that *makura kotoba* in the same manner

In a passage that makes explicit the nature of the nostalgic quest and the anthology's role in it, Mabuchi explained that, if one is diligent in one's study and advances to the recitation of ancient verses, one cannot remain unaffected by this exercise. "Unconsciously *(onozukara)*," he claimed, "the verses will color one's heart and may even enter and become part of one's speech," until one reaches the point where "only one's body is left behind in this later age as one's heart and speech return to the distant past."[89] In other words, as one enters the remote past through the medium of ancient verse, one unconsciously disengages oneself from the realms of the immediate and engages the spirit of a world removed in time but not in space; in this process, one encounters a host of ancient virtues.

The virtues Mabuchi identified with the ancient past—truthfulness or sincerity *(makoto)*, directness or straightforwardness in speech *(kotoba naoku)*, vitality *(ikioi)*, manliness *(ooshiku shite)*, and elegance *(miyabitaru koto)*—represented for him attributes of the ancient heart and are helpful to our enquiry into his ancient Way thought in two respects: On the one hand, they contribute to our understanding of Mabuchi's enchanted vision of the past, and, on the other, they provide us with indications of his disenchanted perspective on his own age. Before attempting to analyze Mabuchi's disaffection with the present in terms of these virtues, let us turn first to a more comprehensive examination of his beliefs concerning ancient society.

Mabuchi described ancient man in terms of near perfection. According to Mabuchi, ancient men "worshiped the imperial deities, had no foulness *(kitanaki)* in their hearts, venerated their emperors, and committed no transgressions *(tsumi)*."[90] They were, in short, both perfect political subjects and perfect religious supplicants. Their possession of true hearts bound them to an unconscious conformity to the natural principles that governed heaven and earth and thereby

---

contributed to one's understanding of a verse as well as the spirit of the age which infused it. See *Kanji kō,* in *KKMZ:SH,* II, 713.

[89] *Man'yōshū taikō,* in *KKMZ:SH,* I, 146.

[90] Ibid., I, 147.

eliminated contention as a socially disharmonizing activity. As Mabuchi put it, "In ancient times men's hearts were correct, and so words were few."[91] In short, life in ancient times was simple, natural, and characterized by an untutored moral perfection. It was not that Mabuchi's ancient man lacked emotions or concerns or feelings, but rather that mechanisms existed within the society to attend to such needs before they might prove disruptive to the archaic harmony.

According to Mabuchi, and again representing a further development of themes first evident in the *Eight Essays* controversy, this ancient harmony among individuals socially and within the body politic rested upon the power of versification. "In their hearts," he wrote, "men felt happiness and sadness, love and hate. When they were unable to repress these feeling, the feelings came out in verse, and the verses were in lines of 5 and 7 syllables. This was the natural rhythm of heaven and earth."[92] Thus, versification was not only an outlet for intense emotional experience, as Mabuchi had described it a decade earlier, but it also, by its very prosody, conformed to and replicated the rhythms of the cosmos. As described earlier, Mabuchi regarded the beauty of this ancient verse as "part and parcel of the tranquility of government," that same government by ancient emperors that accorded with and filled heaven and earth, and constituted a "magnificent and unblemished Way." In this sense, then, the ancient perfection in versification, government, and individual behavior was a singular entity contingent upon the mutual reinforcement of its constituent elements in conformity with natural cosmic principles. The quest for and attainment of this ancient perfection and the spirit that underlay it, encrypted as they were within the verses of the *Man'yōshū*, represented for Mabuchi an incomparable joy.

Because of the interdependence Mabuchi postulated for the three realms of ancient government, behavior, and versification, it stood to reason that the disruption of any one of these elements would

---

[91] *Kanji kō jo,* in *KKMZ:SH,* II, 710.
[92] Ibid.

result in the collapse of the entire edifice; this is how Mabuchi explained the transition between the ancient perfection and the fallen present. In his earlier writings, he had identified the beginnings of this transition with the Nara period when that "grand and august" imperial government "declined somewhat together with the true heart," but, in his writings near the end of the period of his service to Munetake, he wrote of this as a more gradual process which did not come to an end until the Engi (901–923) and Jōhei (931–938) eras. It was during those centuries, he claimed, that "men's hearts became increasingly shallow, and no one thought about the ancient values of our imperial land,"[93] and "men's hearts turned to wickedness and telling lies."[94] This Fall from what was tantamount to a natural state of grace began, according to Mabuchi, when "some people adopted the Chinese language altogether, while others used Chinese words mixed with their own until the result was neither Chinese nor Japanese but rather some odd mixture of the two."[95] He explained that, as people increasingly used the Chinese language, they not surprisingly developed an interest in Chinese literary and philosophic works, so that "it came about that many people recited only Chinese texts to the point where they were no longer able to understand our august Way, which conforms to heaven and earth."[96] Mabuchi claimed that, with this attraction to Chinese writings, people became "thoughtless in everything" and "forgot the customs of heaven and earth in this country, preferring things Chinese."[97]

Thus, according to Mabuchi, the triune perfection of ancient government, behavior, and verse was disrupted by what was at first a fascination and later an infatuation with the Chinese language and works written in it. By immersing himself in such works, ancient man quite literally fell out of tune with the natural rhythms of heaven and earth, and lost the true heart that encompassed the host

[93] Ibid., II, 716.
[94] *Tatsu no kimie Kamo no Mabuchi toikotae*, in *KKMZ:SH*, II, 1027.
[95] *Bun'i kō*, in *KKMZ:SH*, I, 595.
[96] Ibid., I, 594.
[97] *Tatsu no kimie Kamo no Mabuchi toikotae*, in *KKMZ:SH*, II, 1002.

of ancient virtues. At this stage of his writings, Mabuchi spoke only of reentering that ancient past and the spirit that infused it—in his later writings, he described how one might reassimilate those virtues by reanimating the dormant true heart.

The exercise of using Mabuchi's highly subjective pseudo-historical portrait of the ancient past in order to glean insights on his possible attitudes toward his contemporary society is, of course, an oblique one, and yet the inverse correspondences are so striking that they demand comment. In an age governed by a shogun recognized by twentieth-century historians to have been "feeble and incompetent," Mabuchi extolled the "grand and august" government of ancient divine emperors. Where the administration of the bakufu was conducted in his age through the intermediary of a chamberlain alleged to interpret the garbled and incomprehensible speech of the shogun, Mabuchi commented upon the "straightforwardness" and "directness" of words in ancient times. In a political arena known for its duplicity and cunning, Mabuchi remarked upon both the sincerity and truthfulness of the ancient heart, which made unnecessary an excess of words. And, at a time in Japanese history when the samurai class as a whole showed indications of effeteness and enervation in an age of enduring peace, Mabuchi wrote of the virility and vitality of ancient man. Japanese scholarship on Mabuchi has been unanimous in its conviction that his thought was utterly apolitical, and, if he had been—like most Japanese of his age—far removed from the locus of political activity, one might be inclined to agree. Yet, his position within the household of the former shogun's brother and at the very threshold of the bakufu gave him an incomparable vantage point to view contemporary political issues and activities; it is, therefore, impossible to ignore the possibility of interpreting his depiction of the ancient past as an oblique criticism of the present.

In many ways, Mabuchi swam against the academic mainstream of his age. At a point in Japanese intellectual history where scholarly discourse had been dominated for over a century by largely Confucian and Neo-Confucian speculation, Mabuchi wrote of the deleterious effects upon the human heart of an immersion in Chinese writings. And, at that point in the history of Japanese literature when poets were rediscovering the Waka of the classical and medieval periods, Mabuchi extolled the most archaic native verses precisely because of what he assumed to be the relative disregard of artifice and technique in their composition. Nonetheless, his application of the methodology and many of the assumptions of Confucian ancient learning to verse from the native tradition proved to be a marvelously attractive new field of scholarship and placed him within the classicism that characterizes mid-eighteenth-century scholarly discourse in Japan. His focus on the *Man'yōshū* was likewise much in tune with the renewed interest in the anthology which had begun a century earlier, an interest that had been slowly gathering momentum with Mabuchi now at its forefront.

It appears that, during his years in Edo, Mabuchi had become somewhat estranged from his biological son, Mashige, who showed little interest in his father's work and who himself had developed a secure livelihood in Hamamatsu working for the Umeya lodge. Accordingly, in order to fix matters of succession and in probable anticipation of his own retirement, Mabuchi, in 1759, adopted a daughter named Oshima, who was born the daughter of Okabe Masaie, Mabuchi's beloved first wife's brother. The next year, he arranged for Oshima's marriage to Nakane Sadao, whom Mabuchi adopted as heir and who assumed Mabuchi's position in the service of the Tayasu household upon Mabuchi's retirement in the 11th month of 1760. In a sense, Mabuchi was now beholden to no one as he embarked on his final most productive decade.

After his formal retirement from Munetake's service, Mabuchi continued to draw a pension from Munetake in the form of a five-man stipend, and their association continued on an informal basis as Mabuchi occasionally lent his services to his former lord. In 1763, Munetake presented Mabuchi with the gift of a five-month tour of Japan on which Mabuchi—now in his late sixties—was accompanied by half a dozen or so students and attendants, including the brothers Murata Harusato and Harumi (sons of Murata Harumichi). On the trip, Mabuchi visited such famous sites as Mt. Fuji, Nara, and the Ise Shrines, often encountering younger students interested in the field of National Learning. Shortly after his return to Edo, his adopted daughter Oshima died, and a student named Motoori Norinaga, whom Mabuchi had met on his travels, enrolled in Mabuchi's school.

As early as 1755, Mabuchi had remodeled his home using antique furnishings and styles, suggesting a desire to recreate a physical environment more consistent with the archaic realm in which he dwelled psychologically. In 1764, he took this a step farther and moved to the Hama section of Edo, where he adopted the sobriquet "old man of the fields" *(agatai no ushi)*. It was here that Mabuchi spent the rest of his days, writing and lecturing to students who crowded onto the broad veranda of his small home.

A contemporary description of Mabuchi by his student Katō Chikage confirms an impression of him at this time as something of a free-spirited eccentric:

> He was very different in appearance from ordinary men. From his looks, he might be taken to be a person of small acuteness and slow thinking, but sometimes the true heart of a Japanese burst forth in his language, which was then distinguished by the most perfect eloquence. . . . His house and furniture were both formed upon ancient models, and he neither lent ear to nor bestowed attention to anything modern. In this way his mind naturally acquired an old-fashioned mould, and all its productions, whether written or verbal, were pervaded by the same tint.[98]

It seems that, aside from his students, Mabuchi lived in relative seclusion, and, despite occasional bouts with illness, this combination of freedom and independence, on the one hand, and the isolated contemplative life, on the other, appear to have contributed to a remarkable burst of scholarly activity during his last five years.

In some respects, Mabuchi's ancient Way thought during this period represents a continuation and development of themes he first articulated during his years of service to Tayasu Munetake. His reverence for the imperial reigns of the past and present, for example, as well as his love of ancient verse or his vision of ancient

---

[98] Quoted in Satow, p. 175.

life as blissfully perfect yet morally untutored remained unchanged during later years.[99] At times he selected new metaphors to express earlier concerns. For example, in 1765, he wrote on the unchanging imperial order; "The emperor is the sun and moon, and his subjects the stars. . . . Just as the sun, moon and stars have always been in heaven, so too our imperial sun and moon with stars as vassals have existed without change from ancient days and have ruled the world fairly."[100] But, his fundamental perspective on the imperial court remained unaltered. The analysis that follows focuses on only those aspects of his ancient Way thought that changed or developed significantly during his final years.[101] These include his concept of the Way of heaven and earth, his nostalgia for an idealized past, his enumeration of ancient virtues and their relationship to the true heart, his explanation for the Fall from the state of ancient natural grace, and his articulation of national superiority.

Prior to his retirement from Munetake's service, Mabuchi had postulated the existence in ancient Japan of a Way that conformed to heaven and earth, an imperial Way that accorded with the natural principles of the cosmos. In his later works, Mabuchi renamed this the "Way of heaven and earth" (*ame tsuchi no michi*) and described it as the Way that unconsciously brought man into harmony with the forces of nature that surrounded him, endowed him naturally with an inclination toward socially constructive behavior, and obviated thereby the need for moral instruction. According to Ma-

---

[99] For Mabuchi's views at this stage on ancient verse and his belief that, in ancient times, men's words and affairs were straightforward and few, see *Kai kō, KKMZ:SH*, I, 106; *Niimanabi, KKMZ:SH*, II, 919–920; and *Kokui kō, KKMZ:SH*, II, 1104. In the *Goi kō* (*KKMZ:SH* II, 796), he wrote, "In this land of the rising sun, since people's hearts were straightforward, their affairs were few, and their words, accordingly, were also few. If both your affairs and words are few, there is no misunderstanding and you never forget what you hear."

[100] From his *Kokui kō*, in Tsunoda, et al., II, 15. On emperors, see also Mabuchi's *Shoi kō*, in *KKMZ:SH*, I, 689.

[101] In terms of his ancient Way thought, Mabuchi's most important writings during his "old-man-of-the-fields" years included the following: *Kai kō* (On the concept of poetry, 1764); *Niimanabi* (Primary learning, 1765); *Manabi no agetsurai* (Discussion of learning, 1766); *Norito kō* (On Shinto liturgy, 1768); *Goi kō* (On the concept of words, 1769); and *Shoi kō* (On the concept of writings, 1769).

buchi, it was a Way that was entirely natural in its genesis, reflecting neither divine nor human intervention in its construction.

Mabuchi contrasted the Way of heaven and earth with what he regarded as the inferior "invented" Ways that had been imported from China, like Buddhism and especially Confucianism. Buddhism, he felt, was not a "major evil," since it only "makes men stupid," but Confucianism was another matter altogether. [102] "Chinese Confucianism," declared Mabuchi, "is a human invention that reduces the spirit of heaven and earth to something exceedingly trivial." [103] He dismissed the Chinese ideal of the sage as "another tiresome drone of those who study Chinese things," [104] and insisted that the Chinese attempt "to explain the principles of the world" with their Confucian Way was nothing less than arrogant. [105] He branded as an "ignorant notion" the Confucian aspiration to "establish a single system for the people to follow for the rest of time," [106] and he was unsparing in his criticism of those in Japan who recommend the study of things Chinese, calling them "stupid people addicted to pleasures who have no idea where they are going." [107] As for those Japanese in his eyes foolish enough to follow Chinese Ways, Mabuchi declared that he "had yet to encounter a single one who was truly a decent person." [108]

What Mabuchi found most objectionable about the Confucian Way was that, on the one hand, its alleged benefits were not historically demonstrable, and, on the other, it represented a doctrine created and fashioned through the exertions of the human intellect. From Mabuchi's point of view, this made the Confucian Way fallible, since, in his words, "there are many mistakes in products of the human mind," and "when we look at the writings of noble and learned men, we see that the ages that used their Ways did not

---

[102] *Kokui kō, KKMZ:SH*, II, 1086–1087.
[103] Ibid., II, 1083.
[104] *Shoi kō, KKMZ:SH*, I, 689.
[105] *Kokui kō, KKMZ:SH*, II, 1085–1086.
[106] Ibid., II, 1099.
[107] *Manabi no agetsurai, KKMZ:SH*, II, 893.
[108] Ibid. Mabuchi likened them to people born in Shinto families who convert to Buddhism and then seek to destroy their Shinto families.

benefit by them, since they were not in accord with the spirit of heaven and earth." [109] To take the myriad phenomena of the world and to attempt to account for them with a concept like Neo-Confucian principle was, according to Mabuchi, tantamount to destroying their very vitality, since "it is precisely those things that are naturally brought about in tandem with heaven and earth that are fully alive and functioning," and, "while it is not bad to have a broad and general knowledge about things, it is nonetheless a weakness of man's spirit when he inclines toward such knowledge." [110] Mabuchi thus recognized the understandable propensity for seeking explanations of the world one inhabits, but, from his point of view, the problem lay in the coventionally available answers, for "what people call teachings are not really teachings at all." [111]

In Mabuchi's thought, this ancient Way thus represents, by virtue of its very naturalness, the antithesis of the invented Confucian Way. Comparing the origins of the Way in Japan to the process whereby roads and paths are naturally created when people reside in uncultivated woodlands, Mabuchi wrote that "so too the Way of the divine age spontaneously took hold in Japan." [112] Mabuchi acknowledged the possibility that the teachings of a few "good men" might have existed in ancient Japan without deleterious effect, because, "as long as a few teachings were carefully observed, the country was well off without special instruction," and "the teachings were practiced in accordance with heaven and earth." [113] Furthermore, since those ancient teachings "were always so hard to master, as time went by people learned an easier Way," that is to say, the Way of heaven and earth. [114]

One aspect, according to Mabuchi, of the life lived in conformity to this Way was that ancient man lived in a state of perfect harmony

[109] *Kokui kō, KKMZ:SH*, II, 1092–1093.
[110] Ibid., II, 1087.
[111] *Manabi no agetsurai, KKMZ:SH*, II, 894–895.
[112] *Kokui Kō*, in Tsunoda, et al., II, 12.
[113] Ibid., II, 14–15.
[114] *Niimanabi, KKMZ:SH*, II, 919–920.

with birds, beasts, and the forces of nature. He claimed that the
Chinese propensity to regard man as the highest of all creatures was
just another of their "bad habits" and stated that, in the eyes of
heaven and earth, "there is no distinction between men, beasts,
birds, or insects." [115] Mabuchi went so far as to suggest that, since
humans, of all creatures that existed in the divine age, had changed
the most, then man might actually be inferior to the birds and
beasts unless he learned afresh the natural Way of heaven and earth. [116]

Mabuchi's depiction of the natural Way of heaven and earth contains several points of agreement with the eighteenth-century Shinto
theologians, Yoshimi Yukikazu (1673–1761) and Matsuoka Yūen
(1701–1783). Both Yukikazu and Yūen had studied Shinto theology under Tamaki Masahide (1672–1736), a contemporary of Kada
no Azumamaro and one of the heirs to the esoteric traditions of
Suika Shinto which had arisen after Yamazaki Ansai's death; and
both had drifted away from Suika teachings, Yūen through actual
expulsion from the school for his divergent views.

Yoshimi Yukikazu, who lived in Nagoya, regarded the aims of
National Learning as virtually identical to those of Shinto theology.
As early as 1743, he was reported to have taught that "the clarification of what has existed since the divine age should be called
National Learning; however it should also be regarded as Shinto
theology." He defined Shinto as "nothing other than a completely
natural Way . . . of how things ought to be which was bequeathed
by the sun goddess in the divine age and was only later termed
Shinto"; and he advised against using the "Ways of foreign lands." [117]
Yukikazu, however, regarded these matters as more within the pur-
view of Shinto theology than National Learning, which he felt should
restrict itself to such antiquarian matters as (1) the manner in which
"divine sages" governed Japan; (2) the Way of lords and vassals; (3)

---

[115] *Kokui kō, KKMZ:SH*, II, 1097.
[116] *Koku kō*, in Tsunoda, et al., II, 13.
[117] As reported by Fujitsuka Tomonao, *Kyoken sensei shokaiki*, in *KSRZK*, pp. 237, 246.
Fujitsuka Tomonao was Yukikazu's major disciple and recorded his master's teachings in
his work in 1743.

correct performance of ceremonial affairs and administration; and
(4) the use of official chronicles to determine historical truth.[118]

Matsuoka Yūen also articulated a number of themes identified
with National Learning without himself being regarded as a major
kokugakusha. His critique of the Chinese concept of the sage, for
example, was as virulent as any written during the eighteenth century. In *Shintōgaku sunawachi Yamato damashii* (Shinto theology means
the Japanese spirit) he wrote that "a man might be called a sage,
but, when looked at from the perspective of the Japanese spirit, all
sages are bastions of treacherous villainy"; and he used the familiar
seventeenth-century Shinto argument that the Japanese polity was
superior to that of the Chinese by virtue of the fact that Japan
historically enjoyed lord-vassal relationships with a higher degree of
fidelity.[119]

Though there is no conclusive evidence to demonstrate that Mabuchi was familiar with the writings of either Yoshimi Yukikazu or
Matsuoka Yūen, their general agreement on a variety of issues demonstrates that, during the middle decades of the eighteenth century,
there was a measure of nativist consensus on such matters as the
ancient Way in Japan, the Chinese sage, and the alleged danger of
foreign Ways. This consensus, in turn, suggests that National
Learning and Shinto theology were still in the process of articulating themselves vis-à-vis each other as competing discourses, with
the primary distinction between the two being the relative priority
given to the philological study of ancient texts within National
Learning. This emphasis on philology, in turn, represents National
Learning's ongoing participation in the classicist discourse pioneered by Confucian Ancient Learning with which National Learning likewise shared certain methodological and historical assumptions.

Mabuchi's depiction of the Chinese Confucian Way as a product

[118] Ibid., p. 236.
[119] In *KSRZK*, p. 260. On the seventeenth-century Shinto arguments, see my *Confucianism and Tokugawa Culture*, pp. 172–178.

of human invention represents a significant point of agreement with the teachings of Ogyū Sorai. Mabuchi's adult years in Hamamatsu and Fushimi, as well as his early years in Edo, overlap with the period of greatest scholarly acceptance of Sorai's Ken'en school teachings on a variety of issues. Mabuchi is believed to have studied Sorai's thought under Watanabe Mōan in Hamamatsu, and, during his early years in Edo, he appears to have had a cordial association with Hattori Nankaku (1683–1759), one of Sorai's leading students, from whom Mabuchi is said to have learned Chinese poetry and to whom Mabuchi in turn taught National Learning.[120]

The relationship between Mabuchi's ancient Way thought and that of the Sorai school was, in fact a close one, but it was a relationship based on Mabuchi's repeated rejection of several of the Ken'en school's most basic assumptions as well as Mabuchi's transformation of certain Ken'en school assumptions into anti-Confucian arguments. As early as his involvement in the *Eight Essays* controversy, Mabuchi expressed his objections to the avant garde view that verse was devoid of normative value—a view that followed from Sorai's explanation of the Way—and, while Mabuchi shared Sorai's assumption that Confucianism was a Way invented by sages, it was precisely this quality of invention to which Mabuchi objected most strongly in his vilification of Confucianism. Mabuchi claimed that, since the Confucian Way was a product of human ingenuity and cleverness, it was sui generis incompatible with the "truths" of the natural Way of heaven and earth.

Mabuchi was equally harsh with other Japanese Confucian scholars. He condemned Kaibara Ekken and "others like him" for their "ignorance about ancient Japan."[121] The only eighteenth-century Confucian to whom Mabuchi in his writings accorded a measure of respect was Arai Hakuseki, whom Mabuchi referred to with the honorific *sensei* and who, he acknowledged, understood ancient

---

[120] According to Shimizu Hamaomi (1776–1824), quoted in Maruyama Masao, *Studies in the Intellectual History of Tokugawa Japan*, p. 146. Mabuchi chose to be buried in the same temple graveyard where Nankaku was interred.

[121] *Tatsu no kimie Kamo no Mabuchi toikotae*, KKMZ:SH, II, 1013.

learning: "There are often good points made in his writings."[122] It may be, however, that Mabuchi's respect for Hakuseki was not unrelated to the fact that Hakuseki's only disciple, Dohi Motonari, had served Tayasu Munetake first as Confucian tutor and later as personal chamberlain *(yōnin)*.

Of all Chinese modes of thought, however, it is perhaps most obvious that Mabuchi's depiction of the ancient natural Way bears a close resemblance to the writings of philosophical Taoism as represented by Lao Tzu and Chuang Tzu. Lao Tzu's *Tao te ching* was the only Chinese text Mabuchi designated a "correct work,"[123] and he acknowledged that there were "numerous points of agreement between Lao Tzu and our own ancient thought."[124] Concerning Lao Tzu himself, Mabuchi admitted that his sayings "did accord with the Way of the world," that there "is wisdom in what he wrote," and that Lao Tzu had "hoped for something like the customs and practices of our own country's past."[125] Claiming historical validation for Lao Tzu's teachings, Mabuchi declared that the only time in China's long history that the country had been well governed and prosperous was during the reign of Emperor Wen-ti (r. 179–156 B.C.) when Mabuchi believed Lao Tzu's teachings were put into practice.[126]

Perhaps, however, the similarities of his own ancient Way teachings with Taoist thought were too strong for Mabuchi's comfort, for he cautioned his students that, while Taoist teachings "may be of some small help, one should not be drawn to them."[127] In addition to the similarities between Mabuchi's and Lao Tzu's views

---

[122] Ibid., II, 1012–1013, 1045. Mabuchi especailly admired Hakuseki's work titled *Tōga* (Eastern elegance).

[123] *Goi kō, KKMZ:SH*, II, 826.

[124] *Manabi no agetsurai, KKMZ:SH*, II, 892.

[125] *Kokui kō, KKMZ:SH*, II, 1093; and *Goi kō, KKMZ:SH*, II, 826.

[126] *Manabi no agetsurai, KKMZ:SH*, II, 895. Mabuchi, however, appears to have had a somewhat distorted view of Wen-ti whom Herrlee G. Creel referred to as "a genuine paragon of Confucian virtue." See his *Chinese Thought from Confucius to Mao Tse-tung*, p. 166.

[127] *Tatsu no kimie Kamo no Mabuchi toikotae, KKMZ:SH*, I, 1044–1045.

concerning an ancient natural Way, Mabuchi also shared another assumption with the ancient Taoists—that a primordial natural state of grace was disrupted and eventually lost by the introduction of moral teachings.[128] It is to Mabuchi's views on ancient virtues and their loss to which this analysis now turns.

In the writings of his last years, just as during his time in service to Munetake, Mabuchi continued to describe life in ancient Japan as beatific because of its conformity to natural rather than human laws. While he acknowledged that ancient man was not morally perfect and was capable of minor acts of wickedness, Mabuchi insisted that, since such acts "could not be hidden, they could not develop into anything serious and remained nothing more than a moment's aberration."[129] According to Mabuchi, it was those qualities of directness and straightforwardness that made it impossible for ancient man to conceal his wrongdoings. As a result of this naive simplicity, ancient man's words and affairs were few, and, since "there were no ponderous affairs in the world, men understood the foolishness of vanity and neither strove for gain nor engaged in willfulness."[130]

In addition to this host of ancient virtues, however—virtues that were in a sense "traditional" to nativist depictions of the past—Mabuchi in his last years attributed the entire arsenal of Confucian cardinal virtues to ancient man as part of a rebuttal of claims to the contrary by Dazai Shundai (1680–1747), another of Ogyū Sorai's students. Shundai had asserted that the proof that the Way had not existed in Japan prior to the introduction of Chinese learning "lay in the fact that there were no Japanese words for benevolence, righteousness, propriety, music, filial piety, and so on."[131] Mabuchi, in his *Kokui kō* (On the concept of the nation) rebuttal to Shundai, insisted that the so-called Confucian virtues had existed "throughout the world like the movement of the four seasons" and rejected

---

[128] See *Tao te ching*, Ch. 18; and *Chuang Tzu*, Ch. 9.
[129] *Kokui kō*, in Tsuonda, et al., II, 12; and *KKMZ:SH*, II, 1088–1089.
[130] *Kai kō*, *KKMZ:SH*, I, 109.
[131] From his *Bendōsho*, quoted in Saigusa, *Kamo no Mabushi*, p. 228.

the notion that these virtues were of Chinese origin and could be acquired only through the study of Confucianism.[132] Mabuchi acknowledged that those virtues might not have existed in name in ancient Japan, but he insisted that they existed in fact and that "people were automatically *(onozukara)* endowed with benevolence, righteousness, and propriety."[133] These repudiations of Shundai's position by Mabuchi were, in fact, among not fewer than thirty such attacks on the Sorai school written during the years 1750 to 1790.[134]

The other manner in which Mabuchi expanded his depiction of ancient virtues was through the greater emphasis he placed upon the masculinity he attributed to all persons from that age. "The Yamato state," he wrote, "was a manly *(masurao)* state, and in ancient times everyone partook of this masculinity."[135] Mabuchi acknowledged that ancient women in Japan retained a measure of femininity relative to their male counterparts, but he insisted that both men and women possessed the true heart and were thus equipped equally with those virtues that devolved from it. With respect to ancient verse, for example, Mabuchi claimed that "the poems by women in the *Man'yōshū* do not differ greatly from those by men" and that, when one "examines the poems by women, it is completely understandable that they should have their own natural softness to them."[136] Likewise with battle, Mabuchi claimed that, in times of war, "when men led their battalions, their wives led their own battalions and faced the enemy." Mabuchi accordingly dismissed the notion that "women were in any way deficient in their Japanese spirit *(Yamato damashii)*."[137]

---

[132] *Kokui kō, KKMZ:SH,* II, p. 1095.
[133] *Manabi no agetsurai, KKMZ:SH,* II, 813.
[134] Maruyama Masao, *Studies in the Intellectual History of Tokugawa Japan,* pp. 136–137. Mabuchi's principal attack on Shundai, his *Kokui kō* (1765), in turn, received numerous posthumous attacks and defenses including Numada Jungi's *Kokui kō benmō* (1784); Yakotai's *Doku Kamo no Mabuchi kokui kō* (1785); Ohori Morio's *Kokui kō benmō ben* (1793); and Hashimoto Inahiko's *Bendoku kokui kō* (1806). See Saigusa, *Kamo no Mabuchi,* pp. 290–291.
[135] *Niimanabi, KKMZ:SH,* II, 915.
[136] Ibid., II, 917.
[137] Ibid., II, 919.

Mabuchi especially emphasized woman's role as instructor and a nurturer of children: "Even more important is the role of the wife as an instructor, something we should never forget. In the ancient imperial court, the mother was respected in countless ways. From the very first, the mother is charged with the raising of children because her skill is greater than the father's." [138] Seeking a measure of cross-cultural validation for his claims in this regard, Mabuchi added as a note to the quotation above that conditions in ancient pre-Chou-dynasty China were much the same, but that later "everything was changed by force" and that "this was man's law and not the spirit of heaven and earth." [139]

If, within the context of his times, Mabuchi's stance on these matters suggests what might today be styled as "feminist," this may not be unrelated to the fact that nearly one-third of his students at the end of his life were women—a figure among the highest of any major private academy in Tokugawa Japan, even that of Motoori Norinaga, who extolled what he styled the femininity *(taoyameburi)* of the classical tradition. In fact, there were more women students in Mabuchi's school than merchants and agriculturalists combined, and more than twice as many women as samurai. [140]

Mabuchi's idealized depiction of the ancient past and his attempt through the medium of ancient verse to reenter that past and reclaim its attendant virtues conform closely to what Mircea Eliade has described as a "nostalgia for paradise." Mabuchi's idealized ancient state, of course, was neither the paradise of a perfect bliss nor the paradise of an afterlife, but it was the idealized realm of that human condition *in illo tempore* when men and women lived in a world of naive and innocent harmony with each other and all other creations of nature. This realm, according to Mabuchi's depiction of it, was removed from his own environment in time but not in

---

[138] *Niimanabi, KKMZ:SH,* II, 919.

[139] Ibid., II, 929.

[140] Motoori Norinaga had 488 students, of whom just 22 (5%) were women, and the nineteenth-century nativist Hirata Atsutane had just 4 women registered among his 650 students. See Itō Tasaburō, *Kokugaku no shiteki kōsatsu,* p. 324; and Haga Noboru, *Bakumatsu kokugaku no tenkai,* p. 292.

place, and his thought included an exhortation for a return to it: "If even the Chinese," he asked rhetorically, "long for a return of all things to antiquity, then shall we, governed by the imperial sun succession, not return to the lofty ways of the past established by our ancestors, and shall we cling to the present, an age that has descended like a river down from the mountains?"[141] The answer, of course, was no, and thus, to the extent that Mabuchi directed attention to this idealized depiction of the past in an attempt (in Eliade's words) to "rise above the present condition of man—that of man corrupted—and to reenter the state of primordial man," Mabuchi's ancient Way thought represents a nostalgia for a terrestrial paradise.[142]

It is the nature of earthly paradises that they do not endure, since they are posited upon the notion of a contradiction between civilization and nature. Whether by human disobedience, divine disgust or indifference, or unconscious civilizational development, human participation in the cosmic hierophany is by and large terminated. The events or process that result in this termination represent the Fall, and it is in the character of fallen persons that they carry within themselves an indistinct memory of that time before time. The optimism of the nostalgic quest, however, devolves from the assumption that the primordial state of grace is recoverable—that fallen man may become risen man, reclaiming the paradisiac condition of his ancestors—and one finds a comparable optimism in the thought of Mabuchi.

In his writings during his years of service to Munetake, Mabuchi had described a gradual disruption to the delicate and mutually supportive harmony he postulated between ancient versification, government, and human nature, and he attributed the loss of this trinity to the allegedly corrosive effects of exposure to Chinese language and writings. In the writings of his last years, however, Mabuchi recast this process as a sudden loss of the true heart in each succeeding generation as Japanese persons were led astray from con-

---

[141] *Kai kō, KKMZ:SH,* I, 107–108.
[142] Mircea Eliade, *Myths, Dreams, Mysteries,* p. 59.

formity to the Way of heaven and earth by the pernicious doctrines of Confucianism. Furthermore, while, in his earlier writings, Mabuchi had proclaimed that the ancient virtues were rediscoverable through the medium of ancient verse, in his last years, he wrote of the transformative power of those ancient verses as their spirit enabled one to reanimate the dormant true heart.

Mabuchi, now in the last years of his life, described the initial disruption of the idealized ancient past in language that partook of both the nostalgic lament and the xenophobic diatribe:

> Ancient Japan was governed well in accordance with the spirit of heaven and earth, and there was none of this petty sophistry; but then, suddenly, when these convincing theories were imported from China, ancient men in their straightforward fashion took these theories as truth, and the theories spread far and wide. From high antiquity and for countless-ages, Japan had enjoyed a measure of prosperity, but, no sooner were these theories introduced . . . than tremendous chaos erupted. Later, in the Nara court, dress and procedures and so on were all Sinified, and, while outwardly all was elegant, men's hearts turned to wickedness. Since Confucianism made men crafty, men became excessively reverent by aggrandizing their lords until the entire country acquired the heart of a servant.[143]

In other words, according to Mabuchi, ancient Japan was governed well in conformity to the Way of heaven and earth, but this virtual perfection in government was suddenly disputed by the introduction of Confucianism from China. In his naiveté, ancient man in Japan was so drawn to and "beguiled by Chinese Ways that he forgot his own roots."[144] Mabuchi employed a variety of medical metaphors to describe the consequences. He compared the effect of these doctrines on ancient man to that of "giving a healthy person too strong a dose of medicine," that made the patient sick instead of well.[145] The problem with the medicine, he declared, was that it was a foreign and unnatural remedy: "A physician may study Chinese texts, but, when it comes to curing illnesses, his successes are few; in our country, it is precisely those seemingly useless and

---

[143] *Kokui kō, KKMZ:SH*, II, 1086.
[144] *Kai Kō, KKMZ:SH*, I, 108.
[145] *Manabi no agetsurai, KKMZ:SH*, II, 813.

impractical medicines that have been transmitted naturally that invariably cure the ailment." [146]

Again seeking a measure of historical validation for his pronouncements, Mabuchi declared that those same doctrines and nostrums which had "repeatedly thrown China into disorder" had "the same effect in Japan." [147] No sooner were they introduced, he claimed, than great chaos erupted, [148] followed by the relentless Sinification of Japanese imperial ceremony and practice from the Nara period onward; and, while in all outward appearances a facade of elegance was maintained, inwardly, inside the Japanese heart, the spirit of Confucian craftiness (*sakashira*) took hold, turning man toward disobedience, cunning, and other manifestations of evil.

Likewise, according to Mabuchi, men—like the age in which they lived—lost their masculinity. He wrote that, as a consequence of having accepted Chinese styles, "the people abandoned the manly Way and adopted national fashions that prized femininity." [149] Using poetry to demonstrate this, Mabuchi contrasted what he regarded as the masculinity of the *Man'yōshū* with the femininity of the *Kokinshū*, claiming that "men composed poems in the same style as women and lost all distinction from them." [150] Accordingly, Mabuchi criticized the entire Heian period as a time when "even the old manliness became feminine." [151]

Of all the respects in which Mabuchi's ancient Way thought changed during his years as the "old man of the fields," none was more significant than his assertion that the loss of the true heart was not simply an event that had occurred once in the remote but historical past, but rather was repeated in each generation, an assertion that stemmed from his conviction that the proclivity toward an untutored behavioral perfection was not simply an attribute of an-

[146] *Kokui kō, KKMZ:SH,* II, 1088.
[147] Ibid., I, 1087.
[148] An apparent reference to the succession disputes and conflicts between the Nakatomi and Soga clans which preceded the accession to the throne of Emperor Tenmu (r. 673–686).
[149] *Niimanabi, KKMZ:SH,* II, 916.
[150] *Kai kō, KKMZ:SH,* I, 114.
[151] *Niimanabi, KKMZ:SH,* II, 915.

cient man in general but rather was a genetic prerogative of being Japanese. "Those born in this country," wrote Mabuchi, "have straightforward hearts and will spontaneously behave in a righteous manner." [152] According to this interpretation, a Japanese of any era is equipped at birth with all the seeds of perfection his forebears had enjoyed *in illo tempore,* but, upon exposure to Chinese modes of thought, a Japanese loses that natural and inherent rectitude that represents his birthright.

Mabuchi claimed, however, that, with effort, the inheritance was recoverable. Recognizing the difficulty of the task, Mabuchi described the individual who has been seduced by the Chinese spirit of logic and cleverness as follows: "He is a person whose heart has been set, and, since he has lost his original Japanese spirit *(Yamato damashii)* . . . he will not find it easy to embark on that pure and straightforward thousand-generation-old ancient Way." [153] The road back, according to Mabuchi, lay in the study and recitation of the verses from the *Man'yōshū* in order to acquire and internalize their spirit, for, "when one acquires the spirit of ancient verse, one transcends logic, and, by using its pacifying aspects, the age will be well governed and men will be at rest." [154] In other words, the nostalgic quest is completed for a Japanese by using ancient verse from the native tradition as the medium whereby to reclaim and reanimate one's original disposition and thereby to conform oneself effortlessly to the natural dictates of the cosmos; by doing so, the age as a whole, in turn, will revert to that ancient order reminiscent of its primordial perfection.

Mabuchi's claims regarding a distinctive Japanese heart and spirit were just one aspect of a vigorous argument for national and racial superiority in the writings of his last years. Such patriotic arguments, of course, were not altogether new in National Learning, since Kada no Azumamaro had vigorously argued along similar lines, as had other nativists. However, the fact that this line of argument

---

[152] *Norito kō jo, KKMZ:SH*, I, 450.
[153] Kai kō, *KKMZ:SH*, I, 110–111.
[154] *Kokui kō, KKMZ:SH*, II, 1104.

does not appear in Mabuchi's writings during his years of service to Tayasu Munetake suggests that Mabuchi may have deliberately and discreetly restrained himself during that period of his life when he was closest to the center of Japanese political authority.

Superiority, of course, is a relative matter, and, for Mabuchi, the principal point of reference was vis-à-vis China. Like Azumamaro, Mabuchi used the ahistorical argument that Japan, unlike China, did not change its masters. He regarded Chinese history as a relentless tale of contention and vying for power by individuals who by birth had no legitimate claim to authority, and an equally dismal record of subordination to these same upstarts by those newly subordinate to them. Referring to China, Mabuchi wrote that, "whenever some vulgar fellow sprang up, slew the ruler, and proclaimed himself the new emperor, everyone bowed before him and served him faithfully." [155] He ridiculed the Confucian practice of citing the idealized government of the ancient past instead of searching for more recent examples of virtuous rule, and branded Chinese claims of ancient sage rulers as nothing more than "specious legends." [156] In this regard, Mabuchi wrote that "neither [the sage rulers] Yao and Shun nor the Hsia, Yin, and Chou dynasties were as good as the legends made them out to be, and there were probably many evils in them." [157]

Mabuchi's argument, as we have seen, also drew on the assumption—originally and ironically shared by both Taoists and Confucians alike—that force was an unsatisfactory instrument for governing others. [158] Mabuchi insisted that it was because those who had power wished to maintain it that the Chinese had resorted in vain to the invention of doctrines like Confucianism; but, "since China is a country of wickedness, no amount of profound instruction could keep the innate evil from overwhelming the country." [159] Japanese history, by contrast, was believed by Mabuchi to demonstrate that

---

[155] Ibid., I, 1085.
[156] *Kokui kō*, in Tsunoda, et al., *Sources of Japanese Tradition*, II, 10.
[157] *Kokui kō*, *KKMZ:SH*, II, 1098.
[158] See Lao Tzu's *Tao te ching*, Ch. 17, 30; and Confucius's *Analects*, 2:1, 2:3, and 15:4.
[159] *Kokui kō*, in Tsunoda, et al., II, 14–15.

only heaven and earth, acting through the instrument of imperial rule by divine emperors, were capable of achieving and sustaining a stable polity.[160]

It was customary for seventeenth-century articulations of Japanese superiority to be framed in relation to China. In the eighteenth century, such formulations were often expanded to include reference to India, those of the Shinto popularizer Masuho Zankō during the years 1716 to 1719 being among the earliest.[161] In his last year, Mabuchi asserted the superiority of Japan in relation to China and India:

> If you think of the three countries of India, China, and Japan, our country where the sun rises represents man's youth, and so, with truth as the rule, the age is well governed. India is the land where the sun sets and corresponds to man's old age, and thus men's hearts there are pure and noble. China as the land where the sun is at its apogee corresponds to man's middle age, when his heart is evil, and thus their land is not well governed—men overthrow their masters, appoint themselves, and ultimately are overthrown by others. Thus, in every respect, our country should be the most highly valued.[162]

In language reminiscent of Renaissance Europe's depictions of the Golden Age, in which youthful innocence was often metaphorically associated with the verdure of springtime and the spontaneity of childhood, Mabuchi proclaimed Japan's superiority "in every respect" because it was well governed and truthful and represented man at his youthful and most innocent best.[163] According to Mabuchi, Japan was a land whose people did not need moral codes or ethical pronouncements to guide their behavior, since they possessed the true heart and instinctively followed the natural Way of heaven and earth. The evidence for this superiority lay, he believed, in the historical record of the inviolate succession of divine em-

---

[160] *Manabi no agetsurai*, KKMZ:SH, II, 895.

[161] To my knowledge, no seventeenth- or eighteenth-century Japanese writer claimed Japan's superiority to Korea, which may indicate that such superiority was taken for granted. See my essay on Zankō in *Confucianism and Tokugawa Culture*, pp. 182–183.

[162] *Goi kō*, KKMZ:SH, II, 795.

[163] On this characterization of Renaissance Europe, see Levin, p. 4.

perors; and all the blessings enjoyed in the primordially distant past were resurrectable for the Japanese through the medium of the verses of the *Man'yōshū*.

There is, in Mabuchi's life and thought, ample evidence to suggest that he was, at least in part, estranged from his immediate environment. He lived the last years of his life in relative seclusion as something of an antiquarian eccentric and as the self-styled "old man of the fields"—an ironic sobriquet for someone who chose to live on the outskirts of what was at the time the world's most populous city. His writings advised the reader to dissociate himself from the immediate and to associate only with what was temporally remote—to disengage from the present, "an age which has descended like a river down from the mountains," and to engage the spirit of the ancient past. Mabuchi's idealization of that archaic society in near-paradisal terms represents at least an unconscious critique of the society in which he lived.

In that, a century later, Japan dismantled the bakufu and reverted to imperial rule, Mabuchi's exhalted depiction of the blessings to be gained from rule by divine emperors—the so-called natural Way of heaven and earth—appears to be fraught with political significance; yet the political significance of his writings within the actual context of his times is a far more complex problematik. Because conformity to the Way was a natural and spontaneous matter for Mabuchi, and deviation from that Way by implication an unnatural distortion, National Learning ideology, as represented by Mabuchi, undermined the kind of concerted purposive action that makes politics "political." As Matsumoto Sannosuke, the leading authority on the political thought of National Learning, described this phenomenon, "It is precisely the assertion of the Way as an actuality, or paradoxically the non-normative 'normativeness' and the apolitical 'politicalness' that constitute the involuted political character of National Learning." [164] A corollary to this might be that it is easier at times to describe what Kamo no Mabuchi's political thought was not than to describe what it was.

---

[164] Matsumoto Sannosuke, *Kokugaku seiji shisō no kenkyū*, p. 63

There is no ambiguity about the fact that Mabuchi regarded his times (with some justification) as a fallen age. During the last few years of his life, anti-corvée tax protests were joined in 1764 by over 200,000 disgruntled peasants along the road linking Edo to Nikkō, site of Tokugawa Ieyasu's mausoleum, in the largest civil disturbance in Japan in over a century. In 1767, the pro-imperial loyalist Yamagata Daini was executed for his suspected involvement in an anti-bakufu plot. And, in the same year, Tanuma Okitsugu further consolidated his hold over the indifferent shogun Ieharu by rising to the post of chamberlain. During these last five years of his life, Mabuchi repeatedly referred to the present times as a "final age" (*sue no yo*), a phrase his readers would immediately have identified (by the use of identical *Kanji,* or Chinese characters) with the Buddhist concept of *masse,* the terminal degenerative age in which mankind would witness the final destruction of the cosmic law (*mappō*).

Mabuchi, however, never referred in his writings to specific contemporary events of a political character—to do so would have been hazardous, to say the least—and his references to the Tokugawa house appear to contain contradictions. For example, what seems to be Mabuchi's harshest denunciation of the shogunal family was couched in a discussion of the Buddhist concept of karmic retribution. The Buddhists, Mabuchi explained, teach that there is a fundamental law of the universe ensuring retribution for one's sins; they also teach that killing is of all crimes the most heinous. Using the historical record in a stinging refutation of this Buddhist "law," Mabuchi wrote:

> Some time ago, in an earlier age, there were widespread political disturbances, and for years men became soldiers and killed each other. In those days, if you killed one person, you were an ordinary man. If you killed a few persons, you became a samurai. Those who killed a few more became today's daimyo, and those who killed even more became the heads of entire provinces. But those who killed countless numbers of people became the supreme leaders of the nation and prospered for generation upon generation.[165]

---

[165] *Kokui kō, KKMZ:SH,* II, 1100.

The reference, of course, is to Japan's Warring States (Sengoku, 1482–1588) period and the wars of unification that preceded the formation of the Tokugawa order; the "supreme leaders" can only be the Tokugawa house. Where, asked Mabuchi, is there evidence of karmic retribution in this? But, in asking this rhetorical question, he offered a description of the successive Tokugawa shogun as the descendants of a virtual mass murderer, Tokugawa Ieyasu.

It is not possible to determine conclusively whether this passage from Mabuchi's *On the Concept of the Nation* (1765) represents simply a historical rebuttal to a Buddhist truth or something more, for just one year later Mabuchi referred to Ieyasu's achievements in the most glowing terms:

> The eastern illuminating avatar [Tōshōgū, Ieyasu's posthumous honorific] brought Kyoto, Osaka, and all the four directions under his sway and established regulations for the daimyo and Tokugawa vassals—something no other government had achieved and something impossible during our middle ages—and in doing so he demonstrated the boundless and immortal nature of his heart, comparable to that of a god or sage.[166]

The statement is so excessive in its praise and so extraneous to its context that it invites a measure of skepticism, particularly since referring to someone either as avatar (Buddhist saint) or sage was not for Mabuchi exactly a compliment, though others were likely to interpret it as such. At the very least, however, it did afford Mabuchi a measure of protection against any insinuation of disloyalty at a time when the bakufu was on the verge of demonstrating a renewed willingness to move decisively against even the slightest threat of insurrection.

It is significant that, despite Mabuchi's repeated emphasis on the natural and spontaneous pre-moral archaic order, Mabuchi himself appears to have accepted the political realities of his age to a degree that made politics, or at least a political interpretation of his writings, all but impossible for his immediate followers. In a continuation of the quotation above, Mabuchi concluded his eulogistic

---

[166] *Manabi no agetsurai, KKMZ:SH*, II, 896.

references to Ieyasu by proclaiming, in terms suggestive of his European contemporary Voltaire (1694–1778), that "people today need only revere this ruler [Ieyasu] and keep their homes in order."[167] The ramifications of Mabuchi's ancient Way thought were restricted to the realm of the individual consciousness, and thus, while Mabuchi exhorted his contemporaries to return to the spirit of the ancient past, the transformation was ultimately to be more personal than political—it was to take place within the psyche as persons reclaimed the true heart and the blessings thereof which they enjoyed as their birthright.

Kamo no Mabuchi died in the 12th month of 1769. One year before his death, he saw the first publication of his work—Books One and Two and the Appendix of his magnum opus, the *Man'yō kō*—and the number of his students demonstrated the viability of the private nativist academy in eighteenth-century Japan.[168] If analyzed by class, the largest group among these students were samurai, followed closely by merchants, then Shinto clergy. Furthermore, his students represented a far greater geographical distribution than Kada no Azumamaro's students, suggesting that National Learning was advancing significantly as a national field of study.[169]

In view of Mabuchi's long teaching career and the breadth of his interests, it is understandable that divisions among his students were evident. The students who were most prominent in the life of his school were known as the "Four Deva Kings" and included Katori Nahiko, Kawazu Umaki, Katō Chikage, and Murata Harumi. These students, however, had diverse specialties and interests, and it is customary to speak of three main factions within Mabuchi's school: the *Man'yō* group, Edo group, and *Shin kokin* group.

The most prominent students in the *Man'yō* group were Tayasu Munetake, Katori Nahiko (b. 1723), Kawazu Umaki (d. 1777), Arakida Hisaoi (1746–1804), Awata Hijimaro, and the Buddhist

---

[167] Ibid.
[168] Haga (*Kokugaku no hitobito*, p. 43) claims as many as 303 students for Mabuchi.
[169] Ibid., pp. 274–275.

priest Kairyo. As their name suggests, this group stressed the study of *Man'yō* poetics. Most of its members had become Mabuchi's students during his years of service to Munetake, and they tended to be somewhat older than members of the other groups. Within this group, Arakida Hisaoi, a priest at the Ise Shrines, established a reputation as an authority on both the *Man'yōshū* and the *Nihon shoki* and, in later years, participated in a lively and occasionally bitter series of exchanges with the leader of the *Shin kokin* group in Mabuchi's school. Katori Nahiko continued his teacher's philological work on the *Man'yōshū* and is believed to have had over 200 students of his own. Kawazu Umaki, in turn, is perhaps best known, not for his work on the *Tosa nikki* and *Kojiki,* but rather for the fact that Ueda Akinari (1734)–1809), the celebrated author of gothic tales, was at one time his student.

The Edo group, by contrast, had as its major figures Katō Enao and his son Chikage (1735–1808), Murata Harumichi and his son Harumi (1746–1811), and the posthumous disciple, Shimizu Hamaomi (1776–1824). This somewhat younger group tended to identify itself with Mabuchi's "old-man-in-the-fields" years, though they differed with their teacher in their expressed preference for the verses of the *Kokinshū* poetry anthology, which Mabuchi had criticised for its "feminine spirit." Murata Harumi was known both as an extravagant bon vivant and as a superb Waka poet, though his scholarly contributions include work on historical phonology and the discovery of a ninth-century Sino-Japanese dictionary, the *Shinsen jikyō.* Harumi's student, Shimizu Hamaomi, enjoyed the patronage of the most important political figure of his age, Tayasu Munetake's son Matsudaira Sadanobu (1758–1829), and worked to publicize the scholarship of Mabuchi's school. Katō Chikage's most important scholarly work was the *Man'yōshū ryakuge* commentary, though he enjoyed a reputation as something of a renaissance man, gifted in poetic criticism and composition, painting and calligraphy, equally at ease in the bakufu, the imperial court, or the salon.[170]

---

[170] Based on ibid., pp. 43–49; Miyake Yasutaka, pp. 294–302; and Hisamatsu, *Biographical Dictionary of Japanese Literature.*

The leading figure in the *Shin kokin* group was Motoori Norinaga from Matsusaka. The group took its name from the *Shin kokinshū* poetry anthology, compiled in 1205, and, in its poetics, the farthest removed from Mabuchi's teachings on verse. Motoori Norinaga had read a copy of Mabuchi's *Kanji kō* (On poetic epithets), in which Mabuchi explained his linguistic reasons for preferring the *Kojiki* to the more frequently cited *Nihon shoki*,[171] and, years later, Norinaga described how, after one reading, he found the work sufficiently compelling to merit rereading, and, after reading it several more times, he found himself in complete agreement with Mabuchi's ideas and wished to learn more about the spirit of ancient Japan.[172] The opportunity to meet Mabuchi arose when Mabuchi, en route in his 1763 journey around Japan, stayed at the Shinjōya Inn in Matsusaka after spending the day touring the Ise Shrines. It was the only meeting between the two nativists, but the next year Norinaga journeyed to Edo, enrolled in Mabuchi's school, and began work on a three-decade-long project in the form of a complete commentary on the *Kojiki*. In the process, Norinaga emerged not only as Mabuchi's leading student, but also as the premier National Learning scholar in the second half of the eighteenth century.

---

[171] In the work Mabuchi wrote (*KKMZ:SH*, II, 718): "When the same subject is referred to in both the *Kojiki* and *Nihongi*, I use the *Kojiki*. The *Kojiki* is the true book."

[172] Norinaga describes this in his "Ono ga manabi no arishi yō" in the *Tamakatsuma* in *MNZ*, I, p. 85–86.

SIX

Resurrecting the Past: Motoori Norinaga

(Through 1771)

"The lament for a golden age is only a lament for golden men"
HENRY DAVID THOREAU

Among the major eighteenth-century nativists, Motoori Norinaga (1730–1801) was a true celebrity. His achievements were impressive and diverse. He brought the level of literary criticism on Japan's greatest classic, *The Tale of Genji*, to a new level of sophistication. His magnum opus, the *Kojiki den* commentary on Japan's oldest extant history, represents the most ambitious philological exercise ever undertaken in Japan. He had over 500 students by the time of his death, less than half of whom came from his immediate environs. His scholarship was studied at the imperial court, and daimyo solicited his views on political, economic, and social concerns. His may well have been the finest intellect active in Japan during the second half of the eighteenth century. And, just as his researches on the *Genji* and *Kojiki* remain today the starting point for much serious work on those classics, he too remains an object of fascination with more book-length studies of his life and thought published than those of all other nativists combined.

Numerous distinguished scholars who were not themselves Norinaga's biographers have seen in his career and thought the fulfill-

ment of the intellectual aspirations of National Learning.[1] Indeed,
if one regards National Learning, as Hisamatsu Sen'ichi did,[2] as the
gleaning of an ancient Way from one's philological examination of
certain archaic native texts, the argument can be made both that
Norinaga was the greatest Tokugawa period nativist and that the
scholarly tasks of National Learning were essentially complete by
the time of Norinaga's death in 1801, since Kada no Azumamaro's
work on the *Nihon shoki,* the work of Keichū and Kamo no Mabuchi
on the *Man'yōshū,* and Norinaga's own studies of the *Kojiki* had left
no philological stones unturned.[3]

Norinaga owed much to his teacher, Mabuchi, but, unlike previous studies of Norinaga, this chapter focuses more on their differences than their points of agreement. Where, for Mabuchi, the literary and nostalgic ideals were inseparable, one observes a certain
bifurcation in Norinaga's thought which brought him, in his literary criticism, to extol for their technical artistry such masterpieces
as the *Shin kokinshū* anthology of verse and *The Tale of Genji;* his
ancient Way thought, however, rested almost exclusively on his
understanding of the *Kojiki.* Where Kamo no Mabuchi was a classicist who sought to enter into and recapture the spirit of the ancient past through the medium of ancient *Man'yō* verse, Motoori
Norinaga was a fundamentalist who attributed to the even older
Kojiki the literal authority of scripture and sought to resurrect in
the present the ancient Way whose essentials he believed to be encoded within the text. And, where Mabuchi's thought represents a
kind of naturalism intended to enable man to conform spontaneously to the dictates of a natural Way of heaven and earth, No-

---

[1] A partial list would include Saigo Nobutsuna's *Kokugaku no hihan*; Miyake Yasutaka's
Kokugaku no undō; Shigematsu Nobuhiro's *Kinsei kokugaku no bungaku kenkyū*; Ōkubo Tadashi's *Edo jidai no kokugaku*; and Hirano Kimihiro's "Kokugaku: kokugakusha ni okeru
bungaku ishiki." This attitude is also discernible in Maruyama Masao's *Studies in the Intellectual History of Tokugawa Japan* and Matsumoto Sannosuke's *Kokugaku seiji shisō no kenkyū.*
[2] Hisamatsu, *Keichū den,* p. 227.
[3] The major drawback of such a perspective is that it devalues the contribution of Hirata
Atsutane (1776–1843), Norinaga's most celebrated successor and the last (and self-proclaimed) of National Learning's "great men," who preached and thereby popularized the
ancient Way themes of National Learning thought.

rinaga's thought was more religious, requiring faith in the Way of the gods, a Way created and sustained through the mysterious workings of the divine.

The discussion of Norinaga that follows in this chapter and the next concentrates principally on his ancient Way thought and examines aspects of his literary criticism only to the extent that they shed light on the development of his thought as a whole or contribute to an understanding of his perspectives on the ancient Way.[4] Norinaga's work on the *Kojiki* and his depiction of life in the divine age led him to exalt the beatific virtues of an era hundreds of years more ancient than that in which he found his literary ideals. In fact, many of the qualities he attributed to the divine age represent the very antithesis of the complexity and sophistication intrinsic to the works he so admired in his literary criticism. One contention of the analysis that follows is that there is no wholly satisfactory manner in which to reconcile these apparently contradictory preferences other than to recognize them as complementary and opposing facets of his remarkable intellect and erudition.

Norinaga's ancient Way thought embraced deeply religious convictions and, in some respects, was tantamount to a contemporary religion: Norinaga believed that the ultimate responsibility for all thought, action, creativity, and production lay with the gods, and that all aspects of life were fundamentally wondrous and mysterious; he regarded the workings of the gods as being of a transcendental nature which made them all but incomprehensible to the limited resources of the human intellect; he felt that the more profound questions of human existence and experience were essentially unanswerable, except to the extent that the scriptural authority of the *Kojiki* or divine revelation shed light on such matters; and he argued that Japan's superiority to other lands was grounded in the fact that Japan was the home of those same gods who created, sustained, and succored the earth itself. His depiction of the ancient Way, in short,

---

[4] For an extended and highly suggestive discussion of the political implications of Norinaga's poetics, see Watanabe Hiroshi, "*Michi* to *miyabi*—Norinagagaku to *kagakuha* kokugaku no seiji shisōshiteki kenkyū."

required faith—awe before, love of and trust in the operation and presence of the divine in the human realm—but the promise it held forth was one of full participation in a sacred hierophany with a host of attendant blessings. This chapter examines these issues and themes as Norinaga developed them through the year 1771, when he completed his first comprehensive statement of his ancient Way theology, *The Rectifying Spirit;* the next chapter carries the discussion through the final three decades of Norinaga's life.

Motoori Norinaga was born in the town of Matsusaka in Ise province in the 5th month of the year 1730.[5] His surname at birth was Ozu, and his family—relatively prosperous cotton wholesalers— took pride in their samurai ancestors, who, during the fifteenth and sixteenth centuries, had carried the surname of Motoori in service as retainers to the provincial governor of Ise, a post that was hereditary among the descendants of the celebrated fourteenth-century scholar-courtier, Kitabatake Chikafusa. After the Kitabatake were crushed by the forces of Oda Nobunaga, the Motoori became *rōnin* and moved to Matsusaka, where they entered the service of the Gamō family. Of particular interest to the family was their ancestor Motoori Takehide, who was said to have died a valiant death in battle in 1591. His widow, at the time pregnant with Takehide's child, settled in the village of Ozu—hence the surname—and remarried one Aburaya Gen'uemon, who ran a local lantern-oil shop. After giving birth to the late Takehide's son, she and her new husband moved back to Matsusaka where, having previously renounced all claims to samurai status, they established themselves locally as manufacturers of cotton and lived the life of successful, though socially inferior, merchants in an area renowned for its commercial successes.[6]

Norinaga's grandfather, Ozu Shōa (d. 1729), raised the family's

---

[5] All biographical information on Motoori Norinaga in this chapter comes from Muraoka Tsunetsugu's *Motoori Norinaga;* Jōfuju Isamu's *Motoori Norinaga;* and Shigeru Matsumoto's *Motoori Norinaga, 1730–1801.*

[6] The Ozu family lived near the home of another prominent Matsusaka merchant family, the Mitsui. See John G. Roberts, *Mitsui: Three Centuries of Japanese Business.*

fortune to its highest by opening a number of cotton-goods and other shops in Edo. Shōa's sons, however, died prematurely, and so, in order to continue his line of the family, he arranged for his daughter Kiyo to marry his nephew Sadatoshi (1695–1740). This was Kiyo's second marriage; from her first she already had a son named Sadaharu (1711–1751), whom Sadatoshi adopted as heir. Following Kiyo's untimely death in 1729, Sadatoshi married Murata Okatsu (1705–1768), and their first son was Norinaga. Upon the birth of Norinaga, Sadaharu graciously offered to relinquish his position as heir, since his stepfather and stepmother had a child of their own. Sadatoshi, however, declined the offer, and Sadaharu was dispatched to Edo in the late 1730s to manage the Ozu family's shops. Sadaharu may have been a gallant stepson but his skills as a manager were questionable; by 1740, trade at the Ozu cotton shops had declined so precipitously that Sadatoshi felt obliged to make an inspection trip there in the spring. Sadatoshi died later that same year, and the family property was bequeathed to Sadaharu, who sold the Edo shops and invested the proceeds—the still handsome sum of 400 *ryō*—so that his family in Matsusaka might live off the interest.

The young Norinaga was denied the privilege of legal heirship, and was likewise sheltered from its responsiblities. Since his stepbrother lived with his own family in Edo, Norinaga appears to have enjoyed all the doting affection customary for a first-born son. After the death of her husband in 1740, Okatsu, in order to reduce expenses, moved her family of four children to a different dwelling in Matsusaka, and, from this point on, Norinaga was raised entirely by his mother. His early education suggests that no expense was spared: His lessons in reading and writing began when he was 7; by the time he was 11, his studies included the Confucian classics and the recitation of Nō texts; at 16 he studied archery, one of the martial arts, and, at 18, he became practiced in the art of the tea ceremony; at 19, he received advanced training in Confucianism, and it appears that, from his early teens on, he showed a strong interest in Waka verse and the literary classics of the native tradition.

His religious upbringing was in the Buddhist Pure Land (Jōdo) denomination of his pious parents. Pure Land Buddhists believed that, in the present "latter ages" *(masse),* known also as *mappō* (the [age of the] end of the law), humans were unable to attain salvation through good works and were dependent upon the saving grace of the Amida Buddha who, in fulfillment of a vow, offered blissful rebirth in the "pure land" of the Western Paradise to all who would but invoke his name in the recitation of a formulaic phrase known as the *nenbutsu.* Norinaga's father, grandfather, and great-grandfather were all said to have been particularly pious devotees of the *nenbutsu* practice; and, on his mother's side of the family, Norinaga's mother, aunt, and uncle all took the Buddhist tonsure, as did both of Norinaga's sisters and his younger only brother, most of them in their advanced years. Even in an age when the Pure Land was the most popular of all Buddhist denominations, this piety was extraordinary, and one finds echoes of certain key Pure Land assumptions—that the present represents a fallen age, and that faith in divine benificence is the instrument for a better life—in Norinaga's ancient Way thought.

Nonetheless, in a fashion as common then as now, even pious Buddhists like Norinaga and his family reverenced the native deities of Shinto, and, in this regard, his parents attached special significance to his birth. Norinaga's parents regarded their first-born son as a *mōshigo,* a child born in answer to prayers to a deity, in this case the Shinto *kami* Mikumari, enshrined in Yoshino in Yamato province and believed to be a provider and protector of children. As part of their prayer, his parents vowed to express their thanksgiving for the still-hoped-for child by taking him to the shrine in his thirteenth year, a vow Norinaga kept for his parents in 1742, two years after the death of his father, by making the journey himself, leaving his mother and younger siblings at home in Matsusaka. Norinaga seems also to have shared a particular local fascination with the workings of the nearby Ise Shrines, believed in Shinto to represent the abode of the sun goddess Amaterasu and the god of the five grains Toyouke. It is thus clear that, while the Pure Land traditions of his ancestors represent Norinaga's primary religious orientation during his teens, he also had a less pronounced but nonetheless demonstrable interest in Shinto.

In the autumn of 1748, Norinaga was adopted as heir by the Imaida family of paper manufacturers, who lived in Yamada in the immediate vicinity of the Ise Shrines. At about the same time as the adoption, Norinaga received the "fivefold instruction" (*gojū sō-den*) at his family temple, an advanced catechistical form of Pure Land Buddhist instruction which confirmed his status as an adult within this church. For reasons that remain unclear—the most common explanation is that his temperament was too bookish for the life of a merchant—Norinaga grew dissatisfied with the arrangements of his adoption and made frequent visits to Matsusaka until he finally dissolved the adoption after just over two years. One feature of this interlude is that Norinaga recorded in his diary that he visited the nearby Ise Shrines at least once a month and, in 1749, observed there the unusual *sengū* ceremony in which Amaterasu was reinstalled in her shrine following the completion of its reconstruction, an event that occurs at 20-year intervals [7]

In 1751, just a few months after the dissolution of the adoption, Norinaga's stepbrother, Sadaharu, passed away in Edo, and Norinaga was abruptly thrust into the position of family head. Norinaga journeyed to Edo to settle Sadaharu's estate and then returned promptly to Matsusaka. His mother may have realized that he had neither the inclination nor the disposition to be a successful merchant, for she encouraged Norinaga instead to go to Kyoto to study medicine. Thus, in the 3rd month of 1752, Norinaga departed for Kyoto and shortly thereafter changed his surname to Motoori, the name of his samurai ancestors.

While the presumed purpose of his residence in Kyoto was to study medicine, it appears that Norinaga was in no hurry to find a teacher of this subject, and it was approximately a year and a half before he began his medical training, first under Hori Genkō (1686–1754), then under the pediatrician Takegawa Kōjun (1725–1780). By contrast, it took only a few days after his arrival in Kyoto for

---

[7] Matsumoto, *Motoori Norinaga, 1730–1801*, p. 20.

Norinaga to enroll in the school of Hori Keizan (1689–1757), a Confucian scholar well versed in the Japanese literary and poetic classics as well as in both the orthodox Neo-Confucian teachings of Chu Hsi and the avant garde theories of Ogyū Sorai. For the next two years and seven months, or roughly one-half his stay in Kyoto, Norinaga lodged in the home of Hori Keizan.

Norinaga's biographers are unanimous in regarding his years in Kyoto from 1752 to 1757 as a highly formative interval in the development of his thought. Norinaga was certainly diligent in his studies: He composed over 2000 Waka, purchased at least 40 books, and hand-copied not fewer than 15 others during his years in Kyoto; both his study under Keizan's tutelage and his training in the traditional medical arts imparted to Norinaga a remarkably broad understanding of the texts of classical Sinology as taught in eighteenth-century Japan. His perspectives on Chinese and Japanese verse are believed to have been influenced by the poetics of the Sorai school; he also studied versification under both Morikawa Akitada of the Reizei school and Ariga Chosen, a follower of the poetic theories of Matsunaga Teitoku. Through his acquaintance in Kyoto with Higuchi Munetake, a former student of Keichū's disciple Imai Jikan, Norinaga read Keichū's commentary on the *Hyakunin isshu,* and, through the notes of Hori Keizan, he also became familiar with Keichū's studies of other works, including the *Stand-in's Chronicle of the Man'yōshū.* He read the *Nihon shoki tsūsho,* a study of the *Nihon shoki* by Tanikawa Kotosuga (1709–1776), a Shinto scholar from Tsu in Ise province, who argued that the native Way of Japan is Shinto. Norinaga also made copies of Andō Tameakira's *Shika shichiron,* a study of *The Tale of Genji,* and numerous other works he found in Hori Keizan's library. And, in late-1757, shortly after returning to Matsusaka from Kyoto, Norinaga read his first work by Kamo no Mabuchi, the *Kanji kō* study of poetic epithets Mabuchi had completed just a few months earlier, in which he explained his preference for the *Kojiki* over the more commonly cited *Nihon shoki.*

It is also apparent, though his biographers have tended to overlook this, that Norinaga enjoyed himself in much the manner one might expect of a brilliant student in his twenties in Japan's ancient capital. His teacher, Hori Keizan, enjoyed the company of students in general and Norinaga in particular and took them on excursions to visit famous Kyoto temples like the Chion'in and the gardens of imperial princes, to view cherry blossoms in the spring in Yoshino and the Higashiyama district, and so on. On such occasions, it was customary for Keizan and his students to compose verses appropriate to the occasion and to end the day's festivities at a local teahouse. Norinaga, on his own, developed a fondness for the Nō and popular theaters, sumo, Shinto and Buddhist festivals, horseback riding, samisen performances, and medieval ballads. He also cultivated a taste for tobacco, and his heavy drinking prompted his mother in 1756 to write to him concerning the matter. Norinaga's expenses in Kyoto were creating serious financial concerns for his mother in Matsusaka, and she was forced on several occasions to borrow money in order to meet her son's obligations.[8] Perhaps in response to these concerns, but more likely as a direct consequence of Hori Keizan's death in the 9th month of 1757, Norinaga returned in the 10th month to Matsusaka where he opened a medical practice.

In his first important work, *A Small Boat Amidst the Reeds (Ashiwake obune)*, completed around 1757, it is possible to discern three themes that figure prominently in Norinaga's later writings: an idealized depiction of the ancient past and a regard for Shinto as the "great Way" of both ancient and contemporary Japan; a theory of poetics that esteemed verse more for its artistic merits than its presumed value to self and society; and a perception of life's ineffably "wondrous" qualities. When analyzed in conjunction with letters Norinaga wrote at the time, the *Small Boat* provides the clearest indication of Norinaga's thought at the end of his Kyoto years.[9]

---

[8] Jōfuku, pp. 43–52.

[9] The "Small Boat" is an undated manuscript. Jōfuku Isamu accepts 1758 or 1759 as probable dates of completion. Sasaki Nobutsuna, by contrast, has suggested that a draft of the work was complete as early as 1755 ("Kyōto ryūgaku no kinenhi," in *MNZ*, Vol. II). Motoyama Yukihiko *(Motoori Norinaga)* and Haga Noboru *(Motoori Norinaga: kinsei kokugaku no seiritsu)* both accept 1756 as the probable date for the work, while Muraoka Tsunetsugu *(Motoori Norinaga)* and Shigeru Matsumoto *(Motoori Norinaga, 1730–1801)*

Norinaga referred to his Shinto as "natural Shinto" *(shizen no Shintō)*. He wrote that "it is quite different from what contemporary Shinto scholars refer to when they speak of Shinto," and defined it as the "Way that has existed ever since the creation of heaven and earth and the divine age."[10] Though Norinaga may have selected the term *natural Shinto* to distinguish his theological understanding of Shinto from others', contemporary Shinto opinion clearly favored a regard for Shinto as a natural Way indigenous to Japan. Watarai Nobuyoshi, the leading seventeenth-century exponent of Ise Shinto (of all Shinto theologies the one with which Norinaga was most likely to have been familiar), had referred to Shinto as the "natural Way of heaven and earth,"[11] and Yoshimi Yukikazu, a leading eighteenth-century Shinto theologian and authority on the *Nihon shoki,* called Shinto "a completely natural Way . . . which was bequeathed by the sun goddess in the divine age and only later termed Shinto."[12]

A letter written at this time by Norinaga to Shimizu Kichitarō, a fellow student in Hori Keizan's school, whom Norinaga criticized for his excessive love of Confucianism, sheds further light on Norinaga's understanding of "natural Shinto":

> In ancient times, both the lord and the people [of our country] dedicated themselves to natural Shinto, in accordance with which they were moral without personal cultivation and the land was at peace without government. Propriety and righteousness existed naturally; there was no need to depend upon the Way of the Sages. Later, however, in medieval times,

---

prefer 1757.

The matter is endlessly debatable. All of Norinaga's biographers do agree that the *Small Boat* is representative of Norinaga's thought at the end of his Kyoto years. From my point of view, the more interesting (and unresolvable) question is whether the *Small Boat* was completed prior to Norinaga's first exposure to the writings of Kamo no Mabuchi. The points of agreement between the *Small Boat* and Kamo no Mabuchi's writings at that time are extraordinary, but, as I seek to demonstrate in the analysis of the work, other scholars with whom Norinaga was familiar from his readings in Kyoto had argued on individual points along similar lines, and so it is impossible to determine the sequence.

[10] *Ashiwake obune,* in MNZ, II, 45.

[11] From his *Yōfukuki,* in KSRZK, p. 87.

[12] As recorded by his disciple, Fujitsuka Tomonao, in the *Kyoken sensei shokaiki,* in ibid., p. 237.

customs gradually changed, and the people became deceitful; disloyal subjects disordered the land and corrupted morals. Then it became necessary to rule the land and to maintain morals by borrowing the Way of the Sages from an alien country. This was an unavoidable matter. [13]

In other words, Norinaga regarded "natural Shinto" as a native and primordial way, coeval with heaven and earth and possessing the capacity to enable ancient man to be moral without morality, to be governed without government, and to practice Confucian virtues without Confucian teachings. He regarded this Way as the "great Way of our country," not confining its potential blessings to the ancient past but perceiving its relevance to the present. [14] This Way, however, presumably declined, since persons at some point after the divine age became "deceitful" and their behavior "disordered," and it was in response to these problems that the Chinese Confucian Way was adopted as one possible solution. Thus, as early as 1757, Norinaga's depiction of the native Way in the ancient past was, in all respects save two, consistent with the views of National Learning as articulated at that time by Kamo no Mabuchi. The two exceptions were that Norinaga dated the loss of natural untutored morality as a medieval phenomenon, and that Norinaga described Confucianism as a solution to the problem of moral decline rather than its cause. In later writings, Norinaga changed his position on these two points, but he retained the general portrait of antiquity and Shinto as depicted in 1757.

A second major topic in Norinaga's *Small Boat* and again one that figures prominently and largely unmodified in his later thought is his theory of poetry. It will be recalled that a major controversy in nativist circles during the 1740s and 1750s concerned the relevance of verse to the well-being of both the individual and the polity. Kamo no Mabuchi's view that verse, and particularly ancient verse, was of normative value had prevailed—at least in Tayasu Munetake's eyes—against the more progressive view of Kada Arimaro

---

[13] Quoted in Matsumoto Shigeru, *Motoori Norinaga, 1730–1801*, pp. 63–64. On Shimizu, see ibid., p. 36.
[14] *Ashiwake obune*, in MNZ, II, 45.

that the value of verse was exclusively aesthetic, a perspective consistent with the poetics of the Sorai school. Through an ingenious and subtle argument, Norinaga managed to straddle the otherwise opposing views of those who regarded verse as an amusing pastime and those who perceived the composition and study of verse as fundamental to the maintenance of social order and the well-being of the individual.

Norinaga distinguished between what he called the "essence" *(hontai)* of poetry and its "potential" *(mochiyuru tokoro).* He wrote that the essence of poetry is "nothing more than an expression of what one feels in one's heart," and that it is "of no use as an aid to governing the country nor can it be used to regulate the individual."[15] In this respect, Norinaga's poetics were consistent with those of Sorai and Arimaro, who argued that verse was an appropriate amusement, like a game of *go* or chess, but that it was of no value to the complex tasks of governing the realm or ordering men's lives. Norinaga also argued, however, that poetry has a "potential," which makes it of indirect value in these matters. He claimed that, since poetry expresses the distilled core of human feelings and emotions, men in ancient times found verse useful in terms of bettering their understanding of each other. By thus knowing one another's most intimate thoughts as well as those of their subjects, rulers were able to formulate policy on a more informed basis, and in this way poetry contributed indirectly to the betterment of government.[16]

Norinaga's opinion that verse is a superior medium for the expression of emotion resembles Kamo no Mabuchi's concept of poetry's capacity to express man's "undiluted yearnings," and the overall tone of Norinaga's poetics is consistent with what others have called the "emotionalism" of National Learning, that is, the unrestrained affirmation of the affective dimensions of human experience. Norinaga acknowledged that Waka may be spoken of as *a* great Way "if by this one means the manner in which Waka can sweep away melancholy, express a thought, or depict the moods of

---

[15] Ibid, II, 3.
[16] Ibid., II, 49.

the four seasons," but he insisted that it should not be regarded as *the* great Way of Japan which, of course, he felt to be natural Shinto. [17] During the rest of his career, in which he produced some of the finest literary criticism ever written in Japan, Norinaga never deviated from this basic perspective on verse, and, unlike Kamo no Mabuchi, he never fully reconciled his poetics with the cosmological constructions of his ancient Way thought.

The third enduring theme expressed in Norinaga's *Small Boat* is his nascent concept of the wondrous qualities of life, both as recorded in the chronicles of the past and in terms of what one can observe in the present. Norinaga's arguments in this regard were linked to his belief in the literal truth of matters and events recorded in ancient texts and were directed against the skeptical rationalism of such Neo-Confucian thinkers as Arai Hakuseki who regarded early myth as historical allegory. Norinaga wrote:

> It is a great misconception for one to believe that, if something does not exist in the present, then it did not exist in the past. The only way for us to learn about things in ancient times is through books. When something is mentioned in these books, then it is clear that this thing existed in ancient times. If one claims that it is stupid to believe everything one reads . . . then there is no way to learn about the past. It is those straight-laced stinking Confucians who insist that anything wondrous must be false and cannot exist, and this way of thinking is extremely narrow-minded. . . . There are things in the world that are beyond the ability of the mind of the ordinary man to comprehend. . . . One should look at the divine age chapters of the *Nihon shoki*. [18]

Thus, according to Norinaga, the world is infused with wondrous and rationally inexplicable phenomena, and it is a delusion to pretend that they do not exist. Wondrous phenomena in the present are merely contemporary manifestations of those wondrous phenomena in the past which ancient man chronicled for posterity. It is, accordingly, no less foolish for man to disbelieve the ancient records than it is to attempt to rationalize the miraculous and super-

---

[17] Ibid., II, 45.
[18] Ibid., II, 25.

natural aspects of life in the present. Norinaga singled out the "stinking" Confucians in this regard—an extraordinary declaration in light of his studies under Hori Keizan—for their persistent conviction that the world and all its inexplicable phenomena are reducible to rational explanation, and he recommended that one read the divine age, that is, mythological, chapters of the *Nihon shoki* for insight into the true nature of reality.

Norinaga's belief in the existence of phenomena inexplicable in rational terms, his acceptance of the literal truth of ancient chronicles as faithful accounts of events in the past, and his vituperative denunciation of Confucian wisdom are all aspects of his thought in 1757 that remained characteristic of his later writings. The only feature of his arguments concerning the wondrous that Norinaga later repudiated was his acceptance of the *Nihon shoki* as the authoritative text on the ancient past in Japan. It was when Norinaga turned away from the *Nihon shoki* and turned to the philological analysis of the *Kojiki* that he became a linguistic *kokugakusha* in the vein of Kamo no Mabuchi. The evidence suggests that this shift began during the years immediately following his completion of the "Small Boat" and his return to Matsusaka.

The beliefs of the precocious Norinaga were thus well formed by the close of 1757 when he was still in his late twenties, and, though individual elements were later altered and revised, the initial outlines of his thought were clear and remarkably consistent with the mainstream of nativist thought as articulated at this time by Kamo no Mabuchi. Norinaga regarded Shinto as the "great Way" of Japan, a Way that coursed naturally through the life of his archaic forebears and enabled them to behave morally without moral instruction and as good citizens without civic training; he believed that this "great Way" declined with an attendant loss of the moral blessings that accompanied it; he valued verse not just for its aesthetically pleasing qualities but also for what he presumed to be its indirect value to the individual and the polity; his understanding of the past was based on his acceptance of ancient chronicles from the native tradition as literal truth; he perceived the world of the present to be no less infused with the divine and wondrous than the world of the ancient past; and he castigated Confucians for what he regarded as their naive and mistaken confidence in the resources of the human intellect. In all these respects, Norinaga—fresh from five years of instruction in Confucianism—was already a nativist. What remained was for him to ground his theories on the ancient Way in the philological analysis of the *Kojiki*.

As mentioned previously, as soon as Norinaga returned to Matsusaka, he established his practice as a physician, a profession into which he had been initiated two years earlier and whose traditional hairstyle and garb he had assumed. Norinaga specialized in pediatric and internal medicine, and the evidence suggests that his practice was lucrative but otherwise undistinguished.[19]

Norinaga, however, did not long neglect his literary pursuits. Within a few months he joined a Waka group that met twice monthly at a local Buddhist temple, and, despite his relative youth, he was soon leading the group. In 1758, he began a series of lectures to his fellow members on *The Tale of Genji;* in 1759, he lectured on the *Tales of Ise;* and, in the following years, he lectured on such other classics as the *Tosa nikki, Hyakunin isshu, Pillowbook of Sei Shōnagon* (all in 1760), and the *Man'yōshū* (1761). Norinaga generally lectured to the group eight or nine times per month in the evenings, with the lectures on a single work in most instances being completed within a few months. The major exception to this was the series on the *Man'yōshū*, which met three times per month for a period of thirteen years.

These were also eventful years in Norinaga's personal life, as he had reached an age when it was regarded as appropriate for him to be a married householder. Both his former teacher in medicine, Takegawa Kōjun, and a friend from Hori Keizan's school had written to Norinaga after his return to Matsusaka suggesting that he consent to adoption arrangements in Kyoto which were intended to enable him to reside again in the more stimulating environment of the capital. In 1758, Norinaga returned to Kyoto in order to explore one such opportunity; the arrangements were apparently un-

---

[19] Jōfuku, pp. 53–55.

satisfactory, since he was soon back in Matsusaka. In 1760, a marriage was arranged for Norinaga to Murata Mika, daughter of a Matsusaka merchant, but, for reasons never made explicit, the marriage ended in divorce after three months. Then, in 1762, he married Kusubuka Tami (b. 1741), daughter of a prominent physician. On the day of their marriage, Tami assumed the new given name of Katsu, the name of Norinaga's mother, and, one year later, their first child was born, a son, Motoori Haruniwa (1763–1828).

The year 1763 was fruitful in other ways as well. In the 5th month, Norinaga had his first and apparently only meeting with Kamo no Mabuchi. Known as the "evening in Matsusaka," the meeting occurred while Mabuchi was spending the night at the Shinjōya Inn after having toured the Ise Shrines earlier in the day. As early as 1757, Norinaga had read Mabuchi's *On Poetic Epithets* (*Kanji kō*) in which Mabuchi explained his reasons for giving priority to the *Kojiki* over the more commonly used *Nihon shoki;* it appears that one of Norinaga's purposes in soliciting the meeting was to secure from Mabuchi an endorsement of Norinaga's proposed study of the *Kojiki*. At the time, of course, Mabuchi was the best known nativist scholar in Japan, and Norinaga, some thirty-three years Mabuchi's junior, had only a local reputation.

The only account of what transpired that evening was written by Norinaga some three decades after the event. According to his recollection, he began the discussion by expressing his intention to write a commentary on the *Kojiki*. Norinaga recorded Mabuchi's response as follows:

"I also originally thought that I would explicate the *Book of the Gods* (*kami no mifumi,* [that is, the *Kojiki*]), but first I had to purify myself of the Chinese heart (*Karagokoro*) and learn about the true heart (*magokoro*) of ancient times. However, before I could understand the true heart, I had to learn ancient words, and the best way to learn ancient words is to study the *Man'yōshū*. Thus, from the very start I tried to clarify the *Man'yōshū*, but meanwhile I became an old man and have only a few more years left, and so I shall not live to explicate the *Book of the Gods*. You, however, are still young with your life in front of you, and so, if you diligently pursue your studies from now on, you will accomplish what you wish to do. However, when one looks at scholars today, one sees that they all want to reach the heights immediately before they have completed their preliminary studies, so that they do not even reach the valleys much less the heights. . . . This is the principal reason why I have not yet explicated the *Book of the Gods*."[20]

There are several reasons why Norinaga's recollection of Mabuchi's remarks is improbable as a verbatim account. First, in no work does Mabuchi ever refer to the *Kojiki* as the *Book of the Gods;* second, the concept of the "Chinese heart" *(Karagokoro)* was entirely Norinaga's (Mabuchi never used the term in his writings), though it does not appear in Norinaga's writings until 1771, from which time he used it, by way of contrast to the "true heart" of a Japanese, to refer to what he alleged to be a Chinese propensity toward evil and infatuation with rationalism; third, Mabuchi was never elsewhere recorded as having described one's purification from the polluting effects of Chinese thought and behavior as a prerequisite for *learning* about the true heart and ancient spirit; and, fourth, it is most unlikely that Mabuchi, who taught that the verses of the *Man'yōshū* were the most effective medium for communicating the ancient spirit, would have described the study of the *Kojiki* as an advance over one's study of the *Man'yōshū*.

Norinaga's account suggests, and his subsequent correspondence confirms, that there was an initial and never fully resolved tension between the two concerning Norinaga's ambition of doing for the *Kojiki* what Mabuchi had done for the *Man'yōshū* and Mabuchi's insistence that Norinaga first master the *Man'yōshū*. While Mabuchi may have in principle approved of and perhaps even delighted in Norinaga's proposed work on the *Kojiki*—rumor had it that Mabuchi was so pleased at having encountered so promising a student that he held a banquet to celebrate the occasion soon after returning to Edo[21]—he seems to have felt that Norinaga lacked the training to undertake so ambitious a scholarly venture, at least without having first mastered the *Man'yōshū* as Mabuchi himself had done. For

---

[20] *Tamakatsuma, MNZ,* I, p. 86. For an imaginative reconstruction of the "evening in Matsusaka," see Sasaki, pp. 175–178.

[21] See Muraoka, *Motoori Norinaga,* p. 28. Mabuchi mentions Norinaga's promise in his (1776) *Manabi no agetsurai,* in *KKMZ:SH,* II, 897–898.

his part, Norinaga may have felt that, on the one hand, there was little to be gained by repeating Mabuchi's work on the *Man'yōshū* and, on the other, that, having lectured on the anthology for two years, he was far from unfamiliar with it. Norinaga appears to have assented, at least outwardly, to Mabuchi's wishes, for, some eight months later in 1764, Norinaga formally registered in Mabuchi's school while also, somewhat discreetly, beginning work on what became a thirty-year study of the *Kojiki;* during the remaining five years of Mabuchi's life, the two carried on a lively and at times bitter correspondence.

Mabuchi was, in fact, often less than helpful to Norinaga's researches on either the *Kojiki* or the *Man'yōshū.* For example, when Norinaga began his *Kojiki* researches by seeking to compare the various available manuscript editions of the work, he wrote to Mabuchi in 1765 for permission to borrow one of his annotated versions of the text. Mabuchi ignored the request, which Norinaga repeated numerous times during the following years until Mabuchi finally loaned him the work. Their exchanges concerning the *Man'-yōshū* were likewise strained. Mabuchi criticized what he regarded as Norinaga's "tendency to propose a distorted view," insisting that the *Man'yōshū* "cannot be understood well unless one has studied it for twenty years," and, in 1766, Mabuchi wrote to Norinaga that "I do not see why you raise such objections to my view when you have not yet enough knowledge of the *Man'yōshū* and other old texts. If you still continue this attitude," Mabuchi threatened, "you should ask no more questions of me."[22] Furthermore, Mabuchi repeatedly expressed dissatisfaction with Norinaga's verses composed in imitation of *Man'yō* styles, an exercise Mabuchi required of his students. "I do not like any of them," wrote Mabuchi in one of his harshest letters. "If you like such poems, you should discontinue questions about the *Man'yōshū*, since the *Man'yōshū* would be of no use to you with such taste."[23] Mabuchi's discouraging words on Norinaga's *Man'yō* studies are ironic, since Norinaga in all likeli-

[22] Quoted in Matsumoto Shigeru, *Motoori Norinaga, 1730–1801,* p. 71.
[23] Quoted in ibid., p. 74.

hood would have appreciated an opportunity to dispense with further *Man'yō* researches in order to carry on with his primary interest, the *Kojiki*.[24]

It appears that at the time Norinaga accepted Mabuchi's rebukes with respectful silence, though in later years he was less reticent about criticizing his nominal teacher in nativism. For example, several decades later, in a reminiscence of his correspondence with Mabuchi, Norinaga wrote:

> It goes without saying that it was this great man who pioneered the path of ancient learning . . . but his life's work was primarily addressed to the *Man'yōshū*, and his opinions on the *Kojiki* and *Nihon shoki* were not exceptionally profound and contain numerous inaccuracies. Consequently, his theories on the Way were largely inconclusive, since they were based on these inaccuracies, and those theories were merely arbitrary conjectures. Likewise, his inability to rid himself completely of the Chinese spirit (*Karagokoro*) naturally had the result of occasionally allowing that Chinese spirit to infect his writings.[25]

In view of the extraordinary work on the *Kojiki* which Norinaga had completed by the time he brushed these words, his critique of Mabuchi has a certain justification. Mabuchi's philology was often more intuitive than scientific, at least by comparison with Norinaga's. Norinaga was also accurate in characterizing Mabuchi more as a classicist than a fundamentalist, a possible reflection of Mabuchi's decision to focus on a corpus of poetry which, unlike the *Kojiki* or *Nihon shoki*, did not lend itself to literal interpretation. Furthermore, the insinuation concerning Mabuchi's less than wholly native spirit may be an accurate reference by Norinaga to Mabuchi's relative sympathy for the writing of the Chinese classical Taoist philosophers. Nonetheless, Norinaga's assertion in this context that Mabuchi had allowed the *Karagokoro* to infect himself and his writings remains a startlingly candid (if somewhat isolated) revelation of the

---

[24] Norinaga's only substantive written research on the *Man'yōshū* was his *Man'yōshū tama no ogoto*, a largely unoriginal but respectful restatement of Kamo no Mabuchi's views, completed one decade after Mabuchi's death.

[25] *Tamakatsuma*, in *MNZ*, I, 87.

measure of Norinaga's ideological as well as intellectual disdain for his acknowledged mentor.[26]

One month after Norinaga first met Mabuchi on that evening in Matsusaka, he completed a work titled *Essentials of The Tale of Genji (Shibun yōryō)*, in which he applied the concept of *mono no aware* to literary criticism, and later in that same year of 1763 he applied this concept to a theory of poetics in a study titled *Personal Views on Poetry (Isonokami sasamegoto)*. The two works are milestones in the development of Norinaga's literary criticism, since they articulate views that remained for the most part unchanged during the next three and a half decades of Norinaga's scholarly career.[27] Though his *Essentials* was completed after the "evening in Matsusaka," its polished prose and analysis suggest that Norinaga had been at work on the essay long before his meeting with Mabuchi. His *Personal Views,* however, contains several points that represent challenges to Mabuchi's poetics.

The term *mono no aware* defies satisfactory translation. In its most literal sense, it meant an awareness and appreciation of the "sadness" or "pity" *(aware)* of "things" *(mono)*. Its implication, however, was one of an acute sensitivity to the affective and emotional qualities of life—the person who possesses *mono no aware* has a seemingly instinctive sympathy with human actions, a sympathy that transcends and obviates the passing of moral judgment upon the implications of those actions. In his *Personal Views on Poetry*, Norinaga explained the concept by writing that, "when men speak of what they feel in their hearts, this is an awareness of *mono no aware.*"[28]

In his *Essentials,* Norinaga offered a sophisticated extension of certain attitudes toward literature that were evident as early as his *Small Boat:* He declared that what made the *Genji* a great work of

---

[26] For a more favorable reminiscence, written perhaps a year or two later, see Norinaga's *Uiyamabumi* (MNZ, I, 11) in which he wrote, "My teacher, Kamo no Mabuchi, was one scholar in this world who understood well the evil of the *Karagokoro,* and he earnestly studied it and taught others about it."

[27] Norinaga's *Genji monogatari tama no ogushi,* written during the years 1793–1796, was his most comprehensive statement on the *Genji* and *mono no aware,* but it represents principally an amplification (but not a modification) of the views he presented in *Shibun yōryō.*

[28] *Isonokami sasamegoto,* in MNZ, II, 99.

literature was the author's ability to express *mono no aware* through her realistic depiction of those emotive elements that inspire and transfuse life's major events; and he asserted that this appreciation of *mono no aware* drew the reader into a state of sympathy with the novel's characters, which made didactic or moralistic interpretation of the work meaningless. According to Norinaga, when a character in the *Genji* commits an act or expresses an emotion, one's response should not be to ask whether the feeling or action is somehow "right" or "wrong," but, rather, one should look within oneself to determine the extent to which one has shared this emotion or participated in such an action. According to Norinaga's *Essentials,* it is a literary work's capacity to stimulate the cultivation of this quality of sensitivity, and not its potential utility for promoting moral edification, that is the only legitimate criterion for evaluating a work of literature. This perspective on the *Genji* continues today to shape literary criticism on that classic, and, though Kamo no Mabuchi might have disapproved of extolling the merits of a work he felt communicated the spirit of an effeminate age, he would most likely have approved of Norinaga's affirmation of emotion in both one's life and one's art.

It was Norinaga's *Personal Views on Poetry,* however, that brought him into a direct confrontation with Mabuchi on the question of poetics. There were only two points in Norinaga's essay with which Mabuchi would most likely have agreed. The first was that old Waka were more to be esteemed than later verses—Norinaga described older Waka as "exceptional" and criticized the "vulgarity of the words and spirit of contemporary Waka and popular verse"[29]— though by "old" Norinaga did not mean "ancient," as Mabuchi would have preferred, and, as we shall see, Norinaga's reasons for preferring older verses were utterly different from Mabuchi's. The second likely point of agreement concerned Norinaga's theory of the origins of Waka. Norinaga wrote that Waka arose from an "awareness of *mono no aware*" in a circumstance or situation, and that the composition of verse occurred when "an individual could no longer

---

[29] Ibid., II, 87.

bear the *mono no aware.*[30] For Norinaga, this represented an extension of views he had presented earlier in the "Small Boat" essay in which he described the indirect benefits of verse by virtue of its capacity to inform others of one's inmost feelings. In this sense, Norinaga's position resembled that of Mabuchi who had written of verse's capacity to promote individual peace and social harmony by venting those "undiluted yearnings," that is, those powerful emotions which, if left untended, might erupt in disruptive behavior. It goes without saying, however, that Mabuchi never articulated this position, as Norinaga did, in terms of the concept of *mono no aware.*

Norinaga's differences with Mabuchi's poetics far outweighed these seeming points of agreement. While Mabuchi prized the *Man'yōshū* as the premier repository of Japanese verse, Norinaga extolled the poetics of the *Shin kokinshū;*[31] where Mabuchi had cherished ancient verses for their apparent purity of word and spirit, Norinaga valued them more for their elegance and refinement *(miyabiyaka);*[32] and, where Mabuchi had extolled ancient verse for (among other qualities) its masculinity, Norinaga called attention to the graceful and seemingly feminine sophistication *(aya)* of classical verse.[33] Perhaps their most fundamental disagreement, however, stemmed from the fact that, where Mabuchi regarded verse as the primary medium for the communication of the spirit of the age in which the verse was composed, Norinaga tended to value a poem as a distinct entity with an artistic integrity independent of the time and place of its composition. For Mabuchi, the composition of verse was originally an altogether natural and spontaneous event, and thus every verse

---

[30] Ibid., II, 99, 108.

[31] Hence Norinaga's identification with the socalled *Shin kokin* faction among Mabuchi's students. See above, Ch. 5, pp. 157.

[32] In the *Isonokami sasamegoto (MNZ,* II, 87) Norinaga wrote: "Old Waka are exceptional because of the elegance and refinement of their words and spirit. It is the vulgarity of the words and spirit of contemporary Waka and popular verse that sets them apart. Thus, while the form may be the same, the image is what creates the distinction between the old and the new, the refined and the crude."

[33] "If one has to say what makes poetry unique for the expression of otherwise inexpressible feelings, then it is because of the sophistication applied to the words. It is this sophistication that enables one to express an infinite range of *aware.*" (Ibid., II, 113).

was, at least in some measure, a reflection of its age. Norinaga, however, regarded the composition of verse as a more conscious and deliberate action *(waza)* which arose in response to the *aware* of a situation.[34] Accordingly, while for Mabuchi it was not possible fully to dissociate one's estimation of a verse from one's estimation of that verse's age of composition (unless, of course, it was composed in imitation of ancient modes), Norinaga's poetics enabled him to judge a verse without necessary reference to the age in which it was composed. This shift was subtle but significant, since it made, at least in theory, objective and ahistorical critical assessments of verse possible for Norinaga where they had not been so for Mabuchi.

For our purposes and in terms of the development of Norinaga's ancient Way thought, there are two points concerning his poetics that merit attention. First by desanctifying the Waka, that is, by dissociating it from either metaphysical or theological concerns, Norinaga not only created a highly sophisticated and influential theory of poetics but also shifted the focus of eighteenth-century nativism back to prose works, a shift that endured well into the twentieth century. It will be recalled that Kada no Azumamaro had also emphasized prose works, especially the *Nihon shoki,* in the formulation of his ancient Way thought, and, in this sense, Kamo no Mabuchi's concentration on the *Man'yōshū* may be regarded as an aberration from a broader pattern in eighteenth-century ancient Way thought. Second, what appears to be Norinaga's specific repudiation of several points in Mabuchi's poetics, especially coming as it does on the heels of the "evening in Matsusaka," indicates Norinaga's intellectual and ideological independence from the man in whose school he was shortly to register. Norinaga liberally incorporated numerous assumptions formulated by Mabuchi in his ancient Way thought, but, in the final analysis, Norinaga's formulation of the ancient Way is more striking for its differences from Mabuchi's "natural Way of heaven and earth" than for its similarities.

That Norinaga already anticipated his future researches on the *Kojiki* is attested to in the "Personal Views on Poetry" by his rever-

---

[34] Ibid., II, 108.

sal of his previously expressed preference for the *Nihon shoki.* Norinaga now wrote that the *"Kojiki* should be regarded as the primary
text, while the *Nihon shoki* should be treated as a commentary on
the *Kojiki."*[35] His argument at this stage was principally linguistic:
"Since the *Nihon shoki* was written entirely in classical Chinese, it
disregards ancient usage, and there are many passages in which style
has priority over content. The *Kojiki* gave priority to ancient usage
and was not concerned with style."[36] Norinaga's regard for the *Kojiki* as a Japanese-language text, at least by comparison with the
Chinese-language *Nihon shoki,* was accurate though somewhat ex-
aggerated; yet this reversal of the stance taken in the *Small Boat*
cleared the path for Norinaga's future *Kojiki* researches and the attendant bifurcation of his literary and nostalgic ideals.[37]

   From 1764 to 1771, the primary focus of Norinaga's intellectual
energies was on the *Kojiki.* During these years, he continued his
lectures on other Japanese classics to students who were all from Ise
province—and indication that Norinaga's reputation was still prin-

---

[35] Ibid., II, 92.

[36] Ibid. Norinaga summarized his reasons for preferring the *Kojiki* in a later (though undated) essay, "Inishie fumidomo no subete no sada," attached to the *Kojiki den.*

[37] In his *The Japanese Language,* Roy Andrew Miller has described the language of the *Kojiki*
as follows (p. 32):

   "The text itself is written entirely in Chinese characters but in an extremely perplexing
blending of styles and, indeed, of languages. It contains some passages in pure literary
Chinese, some direct quotations of speeches, 112 poems, and a great many proper and
place names in Japanese transcribed phonetically in *man'yōgana,* as well as almost every
possible variety of mixed Japanese and Chinese writing and language between these two
extremes. . . . The total result is a curious variety of non-language that is intelligible
today thanks only to the herculean labors of generations of scholiasts and hermeneuts."

   As Miller indicates, Norinaga was correct in regarding the *Kojiki's* language as "Japanese" relative to the language of the *Nihon shoki,* but the distinction often drawn between
the "Japanese" *Kojiki* and the "Chinese" *Nihon shoki* is somewhat simplistic.

   "One senses that Norinaga would have been incensed by the conclusions of David
Pollack concerning the significance of the *Kojiki* being written with Chinese script:
The dissonances that resulted from the harnessing together of two forces as powerfully
antagonistic to each other as . . . Japanese matter and Chinese script . . . created a primitive and almost geological strain that permanently fractured the surface of the entire
semiotic field of culture. This important semiotic fracture continued thereafter to spread
itself over a thousand years and more of Japanese cultural history."

   See his *The Fracture of Meaning: Japan's Synthesis of China from the Eighth through the
Eighteenth Centuries,* p. 15.

cipally local—and he also produced several minor essays on other ancient works, including the *Man'yōshū*. In 1768, Norinaga's mother died, as did Kamo no Mabuchi in the following year. Though Norinaga rarely wrote of emotions in his diary, preferring a simple record of events, on the occasion of learning of Mabuchi's death he described himself as "unbearably sad."[38] Pressing on with his research, Norinaga in 1771 completed his study of the divine age chapters of the *Kojiki*—those chapters richest in mythological and cosmological content—and in that year wrote his first comprehensive treatise on the ancient Way. Titled *The Rectifying Spirit (Naobi no mitama)*, the work reveals the influence of Mabuchi but nonetheless remains distinctively Norinaga's own product.

One feature of Norinaga's intellectual career is that his theoretical contributions, whether on literature or the ancient Way, were initially presented in remarkably developed forms, and *The Rectifying Spirit* is no exception. Nozaki Morihide (b. 1934), one of several modern scholars engaged in examining afresh Norinaga's ancient Way thought, has suggested that Norinaga's attaching this work as a Preface to his *Kojiki den* commentary and giving lectures on it from 1774 on attest to his regard for it as "a record of the essential aspects of his thought."[39] In later years (as described in the next chapter), Norinaga did, in fact, refine certain arguments and reexamine certain definitions originally presented in *The Rectifying Spirit*, but it remains nonetheless an unusually polished work which presents in mature form the essential aspects of his nostalgic perspectives on the past.[40]

---

[38] Quoted in Matsumoto Shigeru, *Motoori Norinaga, 1730–1801*, p. 75. Author of the only psycho-biographical study of Norinaga, Matsumoto described this record (ibid.) as "brief—in just four Chinese characters—but significant, because Norinaga, after returning home from Kyoto, normally filled his diary only with simple records of events and seldom wrote anything involving emotion."

[39] Nozaki Morihide, *Motoori Norinaga no sekai*, p. 80.

[40] Muraoka Tsunetsugu's position that Norinaga's ancient Way thought demonstrates no further development after his completion in 1786 of the *Tamaboko hyakushu* is generally accurate, although Norinaga continued to add minor refinements to and amplifications of this thought throughout the 1790s. See Muraoka, *Studies in Shinto Thought*, p. 142.

Since the differences between Norinaga's and Mabuchi's positions
will become evident in the discussion that follows, it is important
first to note their points of agreement; the most significant was their
shared view of an idealized ancient past. In words with which Mabuchi would have wholeheartedly agreed, Norinaga wrote that, "in
ancient imperial Japan, there were none of these annoying didactic
teachings, but there was no disruption at any level of society, the
state was peacefully governed, and the heavenly sun succession [of
divine emperors] was perpetuated on to the immeasurably distant
future."[41] Like Mabuchi, Norinaga regarded the ancient past as a
time when untutored perfection in personal behavior was the rule
rather then the exception, and the polity enjoyed the blessings of
spontaneous harmony. Again echoing Mabuchi, Norinaga declared
that those same virtues Confucians "smugly" attributed to the influence of the Confucian Way were "all aspects necessary to human
beings, and so they are necessarily matters people naturally *(onozukara)* know, even if they are not provided with instruction in them."[42]
In short, life in the ancient past was beatific, in that it was inherently moral without morality or moral instruction.[43]

Norinaga also agreed with Mabuchi that there was an indigenous
native Way in ancient Japan, that this Way made personal and
societal behavior correct, and that it was the introduction of foreign
Ways that disrupted conformity to the native Way. In much the

---

[41] *Naobi no mitama,* in *MNZ,* IX, 52.

[42] Ibid., IX, 59.

[43] An amusing but almost certainly apocryphal anecdote concerning this point is recorded
in Yamada Kanzō's *Motoori Norinaga ō zenden,* p. 386:
It is said that when Tao Weng, a Chinese priest from Chi-pei, came to Matsusaka, he
called on Norinaga and borrowed the divine age chapters of the *Kojiki den.* He studied
them carefully back in his rooms, and, when he called on Norinaga in order to return the
book, he said, "I have nothing but utter admiration for your work. What I wish to ask
you, *sensei* (teacher), is what did the Japanese in ancient times regard as their Way and
what teachings did they follow? Please answer me this one question."
Norinaga replied, "Ancient Japanese had neither a man-made Way nor any men's teachings," whereupon Tao Weng slapped his knee and exclaimed, "Good heavens, *sensei,* my
respect for your wisdom has grown even greater! How glad I am that the notions of a
foolish priest like myself should agree with your own."
At this point Norinaga slowly and deliberatly said, "A man who receives my words will
not be led astray by notions of the Chinese heart and is truly a man who knows the Way."

same manner in which Mabuchi had sought to demonstrate that the absence of native Japanese words for Confucian virtues "proved" that those virtues had existed in and were natural to ancient Japan, Norinaga argued that the proof that there was a Way in ancient Japan was the fact that the ancient word *michi* (way) had meant only an ordinary footpath.[44] According to Norinaga, this ancient Way was so comprehensive and pervasive that it was not until foreign Ways were introduced that "the ancient practices of our own land were set aside" and recognized as a Way.[45] Furthermore, Norinaga agreed with Mabuchi that the introduction of these foreign Ways was responsible for a change toward the worse in the hearts of ancient Japanese. As Norinaga described it: "In due course time passed by and writings were introduced. People began studying these writings, and later imitated the Chinese practices that lay behind those writings, until eventually countless aspects of Chinese life were adopted."[46] The consequence, he claimed, was that people's hearts (*kokoro*) were changed and their once "straightforward and pure" (*naoku kiyoki*) actions were "defiled" (*kitanaki*), so that, as matters continued to worsen, people turned naively and in desperation to the Confucian Way of the sages, not realizing that this was the Way responsible for their morally and socially reduced circumstances.[47] Norinaga also shared with Mabuchi the optimistic conviction that the consequences of this Fall from an ancient state of grace were reversible—that the perfection enjoyed *in illo tempore* was recoverable through the study of ancient writings—for, according to Norinaga, "if you do this, you will automatically (*onozukara*) learn about the Way that should be adopted and practiced."[48] In this manner and through the adoption of this Way, the temporal distance separating man from his archaic forebears will diminish, and the comprehensive benefits of the Way will be demonstrated afresh in the present.

---

[44] *Naobi no mitama*, in MNZ, IX, 51–52.
[45] Ibid., IX, 53.
[46] Ibid.
[47] Ibid.
[48] Ibid., IX, 63.

Norinaga was also in essential agreement with Mabuchi (and Ogyū Sorai) concerning the relationship between the Chinese Confucian Way and the Chinese sage. Like Sorai, Norinaga defined the Chinese Way as a set of practices established by men known as sages in order to govern the realm; he also wrote that it was a "grievous error to think of these men called sages as if they were superior beings like gods, or as if they were endowed with extraordinary virtue."[49] Norinaga agreed with Mabuchi and Sorai that the sages were just men, but for Mabuchi and Norinaga this meant that the products of the sages' intelligence, their Way, however wise and profound, was nonetheless subject to the limits of human fallibility. Norinaga shared with Mabuchi the perception that the major shortcoming of the Way of the sages was this "invented" or man-made quality, and that historically Confucians had, in a sense, duped others into obedience with their Way. In this context, Norinaga wrote that, if one asked Confucians what their Way of the sages is all about,"they will rattle on about all the virtues that have been established, like benevolence, righteousness, propriety, deference, filial piety, faithfulness, sincerity, and so on, and they will identify this Way as the tool for teaching people discipline," but the truth of the matter was that the Way of the sages was "merely a weapon that generations of Confucians have arrogantly used to criticize others . . . a method for seizing the land of others, or for preventing others from seizing one's own land."[50] Norinaga, accordingly, arrived at the same conclusion that Mabuchi had—that, far from being a source of order in the world, the Way of the sages "had the reverse effect of being a source of disorder."[51]

Again like Mabuchi, Norinaga related his vilification of the Chinese Way of the sages to a broader argument for Japanese superiority. Like Mabuchi, Norinaga described Chinese history as a relentless tale of upheaval and disorder, and he ridiculed the Chinese proclivity for citing the Confucian classics as authority for the existence of

---

[49] Ibid., IX, 53.
[50] Ibid., IX, 51.
[51] Ibid., IX, 52.

a well-governed polity in the past. Such claims, Norinaga asserted, had "absolutely no relation to the truth," for the fact was that the Chinese people were innately deficient in virtue, and it was in order to remedy this deficiency that they resorted to the invented Way of the sages.[52] The Chinese, he explained, were like a man with little talent who constantly boasts of precisely those qualities he lacks; the truly superior man (Japan), by contrast, makes few claims for himself, since he has secured confidence in his own superior merit.[53] Along these same lines, Norinaga lampooned the Confucian belief in the "will of heaven" (C., *t'ien-ming;* J., *tenmei*) by asking rhetorically how heaven could have allowed a vulgar person like Emperor Ch'in Shih Huang-ti (r. 221–207 B.C.) to terrorize the Chinese people, or why heaven allowed the Chinese to suffer the humiliation of foreign dynasties under first the Mongols and, in his own age, the Manchus.[54] It will be recalled that this kind of pseudo-historical argument had been popular with both Kada no Azumamaro and Mabuchi, and it remained so in Norinaga's writings.[55]

It is thus evident that, in *The Rectifying Spirit,* a work completed two years after Mabuchi's death, Norinaga replicated many of the assumptions and arguments that had characterized the ancient Way thought of his teacher—the idealization of the ancient past, the attribution to ancient man of untutored and inherent virtues, the belief in both a comprehensive and all-pervasive ancient Way, a Fall from the ancient state of grace attributable to the influence of Confucian writings, the castigation of the Chinese for their historical unruliness and innate wickedness, ridicule of the Chinese Confucian Way as a mere product of human invention, and the conviction that

---

[52] Ibid., IX, 51.
[53] Ibid., IX, 52.
[54] Ibid., IX, 54, 57.
[55] Norinaga frequently criticized the Chinese for not leaving well enough alone and having an unjustified confidence in their own ingenuity. One example he chose in later years concerned the change in the calendrical reckoning of the first lunar month when the Chinese Hsia dynasty was superceded by the Yin, and again when the Yin dynasty was displaced by the Chou. Norinaga claimed that this contrasted vividly with the situation in ancient Japan, where farmers understood perfectly well when to plant and when to harvest without any calendar at all. See his *Shinreki kō* (1782), in *MNZ,* VIII, 203, 206–207, 214.

the effects of the Fall were reversible through immersion in ancient writings.

Despite these points of agreement, however, Norinaga was no slavish follower of Mabuchi, as he demonstrated in the formulation of his novel poetics and literary criticism. Time and again Norinaga constructed positions that were different from, if not direct repudiations of, those of Mabuchi. The analysis that follows examines these differences, using *The Rectifying Spirit* as the primary source for Norinaga's views, while amplifying Norinaga's positions with excerpts from his later writings when they represent clarification of views evident but not fully explicit in *The Rectifying Spirit,* that is to say, by using Norinaga to explicate Norinaga.

Perhaps the most significant difference between Norinaga's and Mabuchi's ancient Way thought concerned their perception of the Way itself. In *The Rectifying Spirit,* Norinaga dispensed with his earlier notion of "natural Shinto" and proclaimed that the Way was "not the natural Way of heaven and earth," as Kamo no Mabuchi had asserted, "nor was it a Way created by man," but rather the Way of the gods *(kami no michi)* "created by the miraculous power of the god Takami Musubi, and all things and affairs in the world without exception are created by his miraculous power."[56] Numerous analysts of Norinaga, reluctant to acknowledge the possibility of a bifurcation between his literary criticism and his ancient Way thought, have sought to reconcile these respective ideals by suggesting that both can be subsumed under the rubric of "nature" or naturalism.[57] The difficulty with this approach is that Norinaga is unambiguous in his rejection of the notion of the ancient Way as a natural creation, though he recognized that it appeared "natural" relative to products of human invention. Norinaga made this explicit in his *Arrowroot (Kuzubana)* of 1780: "There is a Way that was not invented by men and that has existed naturally ever since

---

[56] *Naobi no mitama,* in *MNZ,* IX, 57.

[57] To cite just one example, Sasazuki Kiyomi has written that, "it is nature that, within the context of its contradistinction with Confucian and Buddhist notions of invention, provides the bond that links Norinaga's ancient Way and his literary criticism." See his *Motoori Norinaga no kenkyū,* p. 206.

the divine age. It is a Way created by gods and, strictly speaking, is not a natural Way, but, when compared with what humans create, it does resemble nature."[58] The ancient Way, according to Norinaga, was thus Shinto, "Shinto" being the Sino-Japanese reading of those characters Norinaga, always the linguistic purist, preferred to pronounce in their archaic native Japanese reading of *kami no michi,* the Way of the gods; is was a Way that has existed in Japan "naturally" ever since the primordially distant past, but it was nonetheless a product of supernatural divine invention; and, emphatically, it was not to be confused with the "natural" Way as Kamo no Mabuchi had perceived and characterized it.

Norinaga asserted that all things, affairs, and acts of creation stem from the miraculous power of the deity Takami Musubi. Ever faithful to the *Kojiki* account of the cosmogonic myth, Norinaga attributed the creation of the world to the pairing of the brother-sister deities Izanagi and Izanami, but he attributed the *power* of creation—that force which enabled the process of physical creation to take place—to Takami Musubi on the basis of his linguistic analysis of the deity's name. From the root meaning of the word *musubi,* "union" or "joining," Norinaga extrapolated from Takami Musubi's name a concept of a mysterious and divine power that underlay all creation and production, and he attributed this power to Takami Musubi. He explained that the Way created by virtue of Takami Musubi's power was inherited by the sun goddess Amaterasu and bequeathed by her to her descendants, the generations of divine emperors who exercised the Way on earth. In its simplest sense, explained Norinaga, the Way was merely the way things were during the divine age, but at another level it also represented a direct link between terrestrial man and the most primal and divine force of the cosmos.[59]

Norinaga used certain teleological implications of divine creation to arrive at a highly deterministic view of human activity. He declared not only that every human act was made possible by the miraculous power of Takami Musubi, but also that "everything that

---

[58] *Kuzubana,* in MNZ, VIII, 158.
[59] *Naobi no mitama,* in MNZ, IX, 57–58.

exists between heaven and earth without exception is part of the
will of the gods, and every event and action . . . is an act of the
gods.[60] Norinaga accounted for the existence of evil by pointing out
that "among the gods there are both good ones and bad ones," and
he attributed man's wicked acts to the influence of wicked gods,
especially the deity Magatsubi.[61] "Things that do not work or are
broken," he wrote, "each and every affair or matter that has not
followed correct principles, the many instances of wickedness in the
world, all these partake of the spirit of [Magatsubi],"[62] and, as
historical examples of Magatsubi's influence, he offered such figures
as Hōjō Yoshitoki (1163–1224) and Ashikaga Takauji (1305–1358),
both regarded during Norinaga's age as notorious subverters of imperial will.[63] Norinaga maintained that the power of Magatsubi was
so great that even good gods were no match for it, much less the
capacity of an individual human, and he ridiculed the Confucian
attempt to explain misfortune through the concept of the "will of
heaven" as a "stupid" invention resorted to out of ignorance of the
true chronicles of the past.[64]

Norinaga was sensitive to certain paradoxes within his ancient
Way theology: that the Way was both simple and profound, or that
man might understand good and evil by explaining these forces in
terms of the only partially comprehensible wishes of gods. He wrote
that, in other countries, men worshiped gods but always sought to
make sense of their religion, insisting that there were natural and
discernible principles coursing through the cosmos. Japanese faith,
according to Norinaga, was, on the one hand, simpler, since all
action was attributable to the influence of the gods, but on the other
hand, more complex, since the manner in which the gods operated
was beyond human ken. He argued that it was incumbent upon the

---

[60] Ibid., IX, 54.
[61] Ibid.
[62] Ibid., IX, 55.
[63] Ibid., IX, 56. Hōjō Yoshitoki was a key figure in the repression of Emperor Gotoba's
attempt to buttress imperial authority during the so-called Jōkyū Incident; and Ashikaga
Takauji was regarded as having set up the "puppet" line of "northern" emperors during
the period of a divided imperial court in the fourteenth century.
[64] Ibid., IX, 55.

individual to understand what was understandable and to recognize that the rest belonged to the realm of the mysterious and wondrous.[65] He wrote that, since the principles of heaven and earth and the actions of the gods are "exceedingly marvellous, extraordinary, and supernatural, they are beyond the comprehension of human reasoning; so how can one expect to understand them completely?"[66] The Way of the gods, according to Norinaga's fundamentalist interpretation, was thus understandable only to the extent that one might discern its activity in the divine age as chronicled in ancient texts like the *Kojiki,* but it was not reducible either to fixed principles or to the conventional terms of rational explication.

Under these circumstances, explained Norinaga, the primary responsibility incumbent upon man was to seek to act *kannagara,* that is, in accordance with the Way of the gods. He explained that acting in accordance with the divine Way "means that the proper governing of the world is accomplished in accordance with the way things have been done ever since the divine age and that there is not one bit of personal shrewdness (*sakashira*) involved."[67] For Norinaga, the only authority appropriate for informing human action was the authority of ancient precedent: The Way of the gods was the way things were in the divine age; what one can understand of it can be learned through accounts of the divine age in works like the *Kojiki;* and, since human reasoning is inherently incapable of fully comprehending the divine, ingenuity or "shrewdness' have no place in informing man's attempts to accord with the Way of the gods. If a man sincerely wishes to conform his life to the Way of the gods, then his responsibility is to study the records of that Way and to place himself at the discretion of the wishes of the gods.

---

[65] Ibid., IX, 61.

[66] Ibid., IX, 52. In "Arrowroot," Norinaga described this as follows: "The acts of the gods cannot be measured by ordinary human reasoning. Man's intellect, however wise, has its limits. It is small, and what is beyond its confines, it cannot know. The acts of the gods are straightforward. That they appear shallow and untrue is due to the limitation of what a man can know." See Tsunoda, et al., II, 19–20.

[67] *Naobi no mitama,* in MNZ, IX, 50. Norinaga's definition of *kannagara* was based on the Emperor Nintoku chapter of the *Nihon shoki,* one of the rare instances in which he cited the *Nihon Shoki* for authority instead of the *Kojiki.*

In contrast to Mabuchi's emphasis on returning to and reanimating the "natural' spirit of the past, Norinaga interpreted human
existence in terms of man's interactions with the divine, which itself
transcended human reason, demanding faith as much as intellectual
or emotional assent. Furthermore, Norinaga's explication of the Way
of the gods contained certain critical implications in terms of the
distance between an idealized past and a fallen present, since man
in the present was no less subject to the wishes of the gods than
man had been in the past, and since conforming oneself to the Way
of the gods by using ancient precedent as one's guide entailed resurrecting the qualities of a numinous past (the divine age) in an
only seemingly secular present. The implications of this narrowing
(if not collapsing) of the distance separating man from his primordial divine forebears is evident in Norinaga's idealized description
of the ancient past.

The past, according to Norinaga, was not remote. He wrote that
"there is no separation between the divine age and the present,"
and meant by this, not that the past and present are identical, but
rather that the present is linked to and shares certain qualities with
the past.[68] Of all such links, Norinaga regarded that of the imperial
institution as the single most important, since it stood midway
between the human and the divine in Norinaga's hierophany: The
Way was bequeathed by Amaterasu to her descendants, the emperors, together with her divine mandate to rule in perpetuity coeval with heaven and earth; and the emperors exercised their mandate
to rule using loyal ministers who directly governed the people.

Norinaga based his portrait of Amaterasu in *The Rectifying Spirit*
on his researches into the divine age chapters of the *Kojiki,* where
she appears as a maternal and forgiving figure in contrast to her
unruly brother Susanoo. Perhaps his most controversial statement
about Amaterasu was Norinaga's insistence that she is not just the
sun goddess, but also, in what he insisted to be an ultimately inexplicable manner, equivalent to the sun itself. He declared that,
from her vantage point in the Plain of High Heaven (Takamaga-

---

[68] Ibid., IX, 49.

hara), she pours down her beneficent radiance in the form of sunshine upon all creatures and unselfishly sustains all life with her
light and warmth. As a result, claimed Norinaga, all persons
throughout the world owe gratitude to Amaterasu and, by implication, to Japan as well.

In addition to this gift of warmth and light, however, Amaterasu
was also linked to earth by virtue of the fact that her descendants
were believed to have ruled Japan as emperors under the principles
and according to the mandate of the inviolate "heavenly sun succession" *(amatsu hitsugi).* "The principle that our imperial line, which
has been perpetuated by the heavenly sun succession, should exist
coeval with heaven and earth," wrote Norinaga, "was established
early on in accordance with the promises made by Amaterasu when
her grandson [Ninigi] declared that this land be governed by his
descendants in perpetuity."[69] One prerogative of the heavenly sun
succession, according to Norinaga, was that emperors are endowed
with "heavenly god hearts" *(amatsu kami no mikokoro),* so that the
hearts of emperors are identical to the hearts of those wise and beneficent deities resident in the Plain of High Heaven. This identity
of hearts, he explained, enables Japan's divine emperors to be Amaterasu's perfect delegates on earth by "taking the spirit *(kokoro)* of
the sun goddess as their own spirit and perpetuating her imperial
function."[70] In this sense, Norinaga regarded the emperor as both
the progenitor and terrestrial delegate of the solar will, which emperors were capable of discerning in oracular fashion by virtue of
their heavenly god hearts. "When the emperor has a question,"
claimed Norinaga, "he resolves it by using divination to pose the
question to the heavenly god heart."[71] The emperor, in effect, was
an imperial shaman who was genetically and *ex cathedra* capable of
gleaning the wishes of his divine forebears and then putting those
wishes into effect.

Norinaga maintained that the actual exercise of the emperor's

---

[69] Ibid.
[70] Ibid., IX, 56.
[71] Ibid., IX, 49.

terrestrial authority was performed by able and loyal ministers who were themselves descended from aristocratic families of the divine age. These nobles were likewise descendants of gods, though deities subordinate to Amaterasu, and performed the function of translating the imperial will into policy. The consequence of this unbroken delegation of solar will to ministerial functionaries was that, "wherever clouds vie in the sky in our land, there is neither a god who would disrupt the peace nor a man who would not do service."[72] Accordingly, in terms of Norinaga's assertion that there was no separation between the divine age and the present, one observes in *The Rectifying Spirit* the postulation of a hierophany with four principal links—Amaterasu (1) bequeathes her mandate to emperors (2), who delegate their authority to ministers (3), who in turn govern man (4)—and, of these links, all except one have continued inviolate into the present, just as in the past.

According to Norinaga, the weak link, so to speak, and that which distinguishes the present from the divine age, is man. Norinaga insisted that, in ancient times, even ordinary people took the emperor's heart, the heavenly god heart, as their own, and, since people thereby acted in perfect and unselfish accordance with the Way, "subordinates in every instance followed the wishes of their superiors."[73] In other words, by following the divinely inspired dictates of his heart, ancient man's interests were indistinguishable from those divine interests that directed all aspects of the terrestrial and celestial orders under the aegis of the Way of the gods. The religious and political orders were mutually subsumed under the authority of the "true and correct Way," which was passed on from generation to generation, and so, in ancient times, everyone from the emperor down to the lowliest soul engaged in daily observances to the ancestral deities, prayed to good gods for good things and to wicked gods in order to avert evil, and thereby maintained harmony with the divine order. When people in ancient times were bad, Norinaga continued, they performed ablutions to cleanse them-

---

[72] Ibid.
[73] Ibid., IX, 59.

selves physically and spiritually and, in the process, maintained an equilibrium between their religious and emotional requirements.[74]

In this sense, then, it was not that the past had become either remote or separate—indeed, the Way of the gods and the heavenly god heart were as close at hand in the present as they ever had been in the past—but rather that ordinary man no longer conformed himself to the Way or assumed the heavenly god heart as his own; hence man's most immediate link to the divine hierophany and its numinous qualities was cut. Norinaga's nostalgia was less a hearkening back to an idealized ancient past than an exercise in reestablishing man's *relationship* with the divine in the here and now—an attempt, as it were, to bring heaven down to earth.

Where Kamo no Mabuchi had written of the "true heart" (*magokoro*), Norinaga in 1771 preferred the term "Japanese heart" (*mikunigokoro*), which he used with much the same meaning. That is to say, Norinaga, like Mabuchi, believed that contemporary Japanese possessed this Japanese (true) heart as a virtual genetic prerogative, a feature that distinguished the Japanese from less fortunate souls abroad. The difference between Mabuchi and Norinaga in this regard was that, where, for Mabuchi, the reanimation of the true heart represented the fulfillment of the nostalgic quest, for Norinaga, the Japanese heart was more like a piece of racial armament that equipped Japanese man for the task of claiming those blessings that were his birthright. This distinction between Mabuchi's true heart and Norinaga's Japanese heart becomes clearer when examined in the context of their respective views concerning what we have styled the Fall and the methods for its reversal.

For all major eighteenth-century nativists, the loss of certain qualities associated with an idealized past was brought on by exposure to foreign doctrines. In *The Rectifying Spirit*, Norinaga described this Fall in much the same way that Mabuchi had while still in service to Tayasu Munetake, not as a process repeated generationally but as an event that had occurred once in the distant but historical past. It began, according to Norinaga, when ancient man

[74] Ibid., IX, 60–61.

became conscious of his own traditions through exposure to foreign
practices and modes of thought, and this new understanding of
alternatives disrupted what till then had been man's spontaneous
conformity to the Way of the gods. Once ancient man designated
the way in which things had been done in the divine age with the
term "Way of the gods," the practice of the Way declined and
"people began to imitate the Chinese practices behind the [foreign]
writings until, eventually, countless aspects of Chinese life were
adopted."[75] In other words, according to Norinaga, ancient man
lost his innocence. That same quality of naiveté which earlier nativists from Keichū through Mabuchi had attributed to ancient man
was, in Norinaga's terms, responsible for man's observance of the
Way of the gods, since ancient man knew nothing else. Echoing
Ogyū Sorai, Norinaga described the Way as a "comprehensive term,"
an inclusive referent for all aspects of life in the divine age, and so,
unconscious of alternatives, ancient man simply conformed in a
spontaneous and automatic manner to the traditional practices, not
regarding them as a Way until foreign writings and Ways were
introduced.

Norinaga, however, differed with his philologically oriented nativist predecessors by describing the consequences of the loss of the
Way, as well as the means for its retrieval, in the terminology of
Shinto, with certain embellishments distinctly his own. He wrote
that, since the hearts of ancient men were won over by the Chinese
heart *(Karagokoro),* "people no longer took the magnificent heart of
the emperor as their own, and it was this shift to thinking only of
their individual schemes that marked their transition to the Chinese
heart."[76] In a later work of one hundred poems on the ancient Way,
the *Tamaboko hyakushu* of 1786, Norinaga described this as follows:

> By the taint   Karazama no
> Of the Chinese   sakashiragokoro
> Crafty heart   utsurite zo

---

[75] Ibid., IX, 53.
[76] Ibid.

Has the heart of man	yo no hito no kokoro
Been corrupted.	ashiku narinu.[77]

On the one hand, ancient man's observance of the practices of the Way was disrupted, and, on the other, his identification with the heavenly god heart of the emperor was displaced by his assumption of the Chinese heart, and so man lost his two most fundamental links to the numinous foundations of his idealized circumstances. According to Norinaga, people's hearts, once straightforward and pure *(naoku kiyoki)*, became defiled *(kitanaki)* when ancient man committed the Shinto offense *(tsumi)* of turning to the Confucian Way of the sages. Norinaga dated this sequence of events to the mid-seventh century during the reign of Emperor Kōtoku (r. 645–654), after which the only attention to ancient matters and practices was in the context of religious ceremonies.[78]

Norinaga, of course, shared the optimistic conviction of all major nativists that the effects of this loss were reversible:

> If one earnestly wishes to enquire further into these matters, I suggest that one first cleanse oneself *(harai kiyomete)* of any defiled notions one may have acquired from reading Chinese texts, and then, holding fast to one's pristine Japanese heart, study our ancient texts well. If one does this, one will automatically *(onozukara)* learn about the Way that should be adopted and practiced. To know these things is to adopt and practice the Way of the gods."[79]

Where Mabuchi had regarded the study and recitation of ancient texts as the initial step in this process, Norinaga advised that one first exorcise *(harai)* the polluting stain of Chinese writings from one's person; then, once reequipped with the pristine Japanese heart, one might advance to studying the Way, whereupon one's practice of the Way would proceed automatically. Thus, unlike Mabuchi, whose nostalgic quest was completed through the reanimation of a

---

[77] In *MNZ*, XVIII, 323; translation adapted from Muraoka, *Studies in Shinto Thought*, p. 147.
[78] *Naobi no mitama*, in *MNZ*, IX, 53.
[79] Ibid., IX, 63.

latent element of perfection, Norinaga sought to reestablish those
same primordial links between man and the divine hierophany that
had blessed life in the ancient past.

It is curious, however, that, despite Norinaga's condemnation of
Chinese writings for their responsibility in disrupting the ancient
hierophany, in *The Rectifying Spirit* he did not discourage the reading of Chinese works and encouraged those with spare time to read
them in order to expand their knowledge of Chinese characters: "As
long as you hold fast to your Japanese spirit and do not lower your
defenses, no harm will come of it."[80] In his later writings, however,
Norinaga was less than consistent on this point. For example, in his
collection of short essays titled *Tamakatsuma,* written during the
last years of his life, Norinaga repeated this argument, emphasizing
the potential benefits to one's scholarship of studying Chinese works
by enhancing one's knowledge of literary Chinese: "As long as one
understands that Chinese practices are thoroughly evil and one
maintains unwavering dedication to one's Japanese spirit *(mikuni
damashii),* the heart will not be led astray even if one reads those
texts day and night."[81] Elsewhere, however, he counseled in verse
that there may be danger in such an exercise:

Though he may think himself	Karagokoro
Rid of the Chinese heart	nashi to omoedo
The heart of a man	fumira yomo
Who reads Chinese	hito no kokoro wa
Is still Chinese.	nao zo Kara naru.[82]

If the question of the potential hazards or benefits of reading Chinese
works remains somewhat unclear in Norinaga's writings, however,
he left no ambiguity about his dislike of the Taoists.

Unlike Kamo no Mabuchi, who appreciated the Taoist regard for
the natural and spontaneous, Norinaga was particularly alarmed by
the writings of the Taoists, precisely because he understood that

---

[80] Ibid., IX, 59.
[81] *Tamakatsuma,* in MNZ, I, 59.
[82] *Tamaboko hyakushu,* in MNZ, XVIII, 323. Translation adapted from Muraoka, *Studies
in Shinto Thought,* p. 148.

their reverence for the natural resembled certain key concepts in his own understanding of the ancient Way. Norinaga claimed that Lao Tzu and Chuang Tzu never understood the fundamental principle that all things arise in response to the wishes of the gods, and he insisted that, "since they were born in a defiled land which was not the land of Amaterasu, and since they were accustomed to hearing the theories of generations of sages, what they thought to be natural was actually a view of nature based on the thought of the sages."[83] Here again, one observes Norinaga distancing himself from the naturalism not only of the Taoists but also of Kamo no Mabuchi. The ancient Way, as Norinaga envisioned it from his reading of the *Kojiki,* was decidely not a "natural" Way, neither Mabuchi's natural Way of heaven and earth nor the Taoists' Way of non-purposive action, but rather a Way created by gods in the divine age and bequeathed in perpetuity by Amaterasu through divine emperors and their loyal ministers to man.

Finally, in terms of the development through 1771 of Norinaga's ancient Way thought as represented in *The Rectifying Spirit,* just as the goddess Amaterasu stood at the fount of Norinaga's hierophany, she was also a key figure in his articulation of Japan's superiority to China and the rest of the world. In the opening words of *The Rectifying Spirit,* Norinaga proclaimed: "This grand imperial country is the home of the august and awesome divine ancestress, the great goddess Amaterasu, and this is the primary reason why our country is superior to all others. There is not a country in the world that does not enjoy the blessings of this goddess."[84] Generations of Japanese nativists, at least as far back as Kitabatake Chikafusa in the fourteenth century, had asserted that what distinguished Japan from other lands what that Japan was the "divine country" or "land of the gods" (*shinkoku*), but for Norinaga this meant above all that Japan was the abode of Amaterasu. "Other lands," he wrote, "are not the home of the great goddess Amaterasu, and so they have no established principle of rulership. . . . Men's hearts are evil, and

---

[83] *Naobi no mitama,* in MNZ, IX, 62.
[84] Ibid., IX, 49.

their behavior is unruly."[85] Basing his theories on his reading of the *Kojiki,* Norinaga regarded Amaterasu's blessings as twofold: To Japan and the Japanese, Amaterasu bequeathed the Way of the gods, as well as the imperial heavenly god heart which others were then able to assume for themselves; and to all the world, Amaterasu bestowed the gifts of radiant warmth and sunshine. Accordingly, the world as a whole, but Japan in particular, owed the goddess an unspoken debt of gratitude.

In his later writings, Norinaga added a cosmogonic argument to this cosmological assertion of Japanese superiority. He claimed that, since the Japanese gods Izanagi and Izanami were responsible for the creation of the phenomenal world, empowered as they were by the mysterious and divine *and* Japanese force of creation, it stood to reason that Japan, whose gods formed the world and whose goddess sustains all life, should have a unique position in the world. Articulating this in terms of an ancestral relationship with the rest of the world, Norinaga described Japan, in 1786, as the "original, great, and primal source" *(genpon taiso)* of all other countries and, in 1798, as the "original ancestral country" *(moto tsu sokoku)* for the entire world.[86] Japan, according to Norinaga, thus enjoyed an ancestral relationship with the rest of the world by virtue of having been the first of all lands to be created and by being the abode of the gods responsible for all creation and sustenance of life. It was, of course unnecessary for Norinaga to add that civilized countries, like civilized men, should reverence their ancestors.

By according the Japanese cosmogonic myth, as recorded in the *Kojiki,* the status of a true and universal myth, Norinaga transformed the "traditional" nativist articulation of Japanese superiority to China into a more comprehensive assertion of Japan's qualitative advantage and privileged position in the world as a whole. It was, in short, a myth of national and racial superiority: Japan was better than other countries because of its cosmogonic priority, and because

---

[85] Ibid., IX, 50.
[86] Respectively, from his *Tamakushige (MNZ,* VIII, 311) and *Ise nikū sakitake no ben (MNZ,* VIII, 478).

its native gods created and sustained all life; and the Japanese were better people because others had evil hearts and behaved improperly. Such myths, of course, contain a virulence all their own, and Norinaga's arguments for Japanese superiority at times lapsed into trivialities as, for example, when he asserted in the late 1780s that Japanese rice was so superior to all other strains of rice that "all people should pause to consider this blessing of the imperial gods while they enjoy such exceptional rice during their meals."[87] Myths, of course, merit belief as much as assent, and a myth of Japanese superiority was compelling in a way that no mere argument could ever match. The ramifications of this became increasingly apparent during the nineteenth and first half of the twentieth centuries.[88]

The Rectifying Spirit was, thus, an exceptionally important work both in the context of the development of Norinaga's thought and in terms of eighteenth-century nativism as a whole. It identified Norinaga with the ancient Way thought of Kamo no Mabuchi in an apparent lineage that extended methodologically to Keichū and ideologically to Kada no Azumamaro; and, at the same time, it distanced Norinaga from the thought of these earlier figures and established his intellectual independence. In much the same way that Norinaga's *Essentials of The Tale of Genji* and *Personal Views on Poetry* in 1763 heralded his growing reputation as a literary critic, *The Rectifying Spirit* played a comparable role in his reputation as an authority on the *Kojiki* and theoretician of Japan's ancient Way.

The Rectifying Spirit, however, is an exceedingly difficult work to contextualize. Its points of contact with the writings and assumptions of Mabuchi and the Sorai school have already been noted, and most analysts agree that these are the most significant; and yet there

---

[87] See his *Kokugo kō* (1787, in *MNZ*, VIII, 451), and also his *Tamakushige* (1786, in *MNZ*, VIII, 311).

[88] Among Norinaga's students, Shirako Shōhei was particularly interested in mythological arguments for Japanese superiority and, in 1791, wrote the Preface to the published edition of Norinaga's *Gyojū gaigen* (*MNZ*, VIII, 21). Norinaga's posthumous disciple, Hirata Atsutane (1776–1843), was the most successful popularizer of the superiority myth, using numerous arguments developed by Norinaga but restating and elaborating them in ways that attracted a large following.

appear to be other referrants for situating the text within the contemporary discourse. For example, Norinaga's critique of the Confucian Way of the sages as a "weapon" for Confucians to criticize others or as a "method" for either appropriating the land of others or preventing the seizure of one's own land seems unconsciously to echo the views of Andō Shōeki (1703–1762?), a physician and social philosopher from Dewa. In a defense of peasant cultivators, Shōeki urged a return to the Way of nature, which he accused the sages of having violated, and wrote that the sages' "desire to rob the world and the state . . . plunged the world into war."[89] In his denunciation of Confucian sages, Shōeki even included such Japanese Confucians as Hayashi Razan and Ogyū Sorai, castigating them as non-tillers of the soil who "violated the way of heaven by robbing the common people who engage in direct cultivation."[90] Shōeki was prone to utopian flights of fantasy comparable to those of Mabuchi and Norinaga, though, as one scholar has observed, Shōeki's utopia was "less a possible alternative to the Tokugawa system than a conceptual tool which he could use in his attacks on the society of his day," and what "scholars of National Learning found in the ideal realm of an imaginary past, Shōeki found in an infinitely distant land."[91]

Where Kamo no Mabuchi appears to have sought a psychological refuge from a seemingly fallen reality, Norinaga's formulations suggest a more deliberate though veiled critique of his society and the Ways that informed it. By the eighteenth century, it was apparent that the Neo-Confucian vision of the social order was inadequate as a description of a reality far more pluralistic than Neo-Confucianism suggested and in which merchants had ascended to a social position far higher than its dictates prescribed—hence the historicism of Ogyū Sorai, who argued that the Way was an "invention" of mortal minds, and that, just as it was devised to address specific problems in the past, it had to be modified appropriately if it was to meet the

---

[89] See Maruyama, *Studies in the Intellectual History of Tokugawa Japan*, pp. 254–255.
[90] Quoted ibid., p. 255.
[91] Shuichi Kato, *A History of Japanese Literature: The Years of Isoloation*, p. 142.

needs of a changed social order in the present. Accordingly, the Confucian Way, which had been domesticated during the seventeenth century to provide a satisfactory description and justification of Japanese political realities, was further modified during the first half of the eighteenth century to address changing social realities.

By the 1760s and early 1770s, however, no interpretation of the Confucian Way adequately addressed the deteriorating circumstances of the bakufu. There had not been a strong shogun since 1745 when Yoshimune had retired, and authority was increasingly concentrated in the hands of chamberlains like Ōoka Tadamitsu and Tanuma Okitsugu. Other than by issuing largely disregarded decrees (four from 1767 to 1771), the government was displaying an inability to deal with the problem of agrarian uprisings, which in earlier decades had been dealt with promptly and often cruelly; even nature itself seemed to be conspiring against the agricultural heart of the economy with a severe drought in 1770–1771. Under these circumstances the notion that there might be natural beneficent principles governing the polity seemed to many no more convincing than the conviction that human ingenuity was sufficient to address disorder of such magnitude.

In this context, Norinaga's exhortation that one embrace the Way of the gods, exorcise the Chinese heart, cling fast to one's Japanese heart, and reestablish an identification between one's own heart and the heavenly imparted heart of a divine emperor represented a radical approach. This was neither an invocation of a natural principled order nor an embracing of a set of devised policies based on historicist arguments; it was, instead, an appeal for a supernatural solution to perceived problems. By castigating one or another of the Confucian Ways as means of theft and deceit, Norinaga was in fact challenging the ideological justification for the legitimacy of the status quo, though one senses that he would have been the first to deny such intentions. We shall return to these issues in the next chapter when we examine Norinaga's political thought more closely, but it is evident that *The Rectifying Spirit* contains the nucleus of certain assumptions with considerable political significance, irrespective of Norinaga's intent.

SEVEN

The House of Bells: Post-1771 Developments in Norinaga's Ancient Way Thought

Since *The Rectifying Spirit* was, at the time of its composition, and remained for several decades an important statement of Norinaga's ancient Way thought, it is understandable that it provoked a host of challenges and responses. Not fewer than five major attacks on the work were brushed by figures as ideologically diverse as Ichikawa Tatsumaro (1739–1795), identified with the Sorai school, and Aizawa Seishisai (1782–1863), of Mito school fame, who was not even born until eleven years after Norinaga wrote *The Rectifying Spirit*.[1] Norinaga chose to rebut Ichikawa Tatsumaro in his *Arrowroot (Kuzubana)* of 1780, in which he referred condescendingly to Tatsumaro as a "man who seems to know a few things about native learning" but is handicapped by an inability to regard the ancient matters of Japan other than through the constricted eyes of a Confucian.[2] Others as well wrote defenses of *The Rectifying Spirit,* though the "battle" surrounding the text was for the most part a posthumous one.[3]

---

[1] See Matsumoto Sannosuke, *Kokugaku seiji shisō no kenkyū,* p. 83n. The attacks included Ichikawa Tatsumaro's *Maganohire* (1780), Numada Jungi's *Kyūchō kofū* (1830), Yamada Korenori's *Shintō hōshō ben* (1833), Minamoto Yasushi's *Naobi no mitama seii kaikojun* (1838), and Aizawa Seishisai's *Doku naobi no mitama* (1858).

[2] *Kuzubana,* in MNZ, VIII, 123.

[3] Other defenses of *The Rectifying Spirit* included Hirata Atsutane's *Kamōsho* (1803), Take-

From the point of view of contemporary Shinto theology, two of the most controversial issues raised in the work were that the ancient Way contained no moral teachings and that the sun goddess was also the sun. Tanikawa Kotosuga (1709–1776)—from Ise and a follower of Yamazaki Ansai's Suika Shinto teachings, whose writings on the *Nihon shoki* Norinaga had read during his Kyoto years—challenged the former opinion in 1772 in a letter to Norinaga: "I cannot accept what you have stated to the effect that there are no teachings for the heart in our Shinto."[4] The controversy surrounding the precise nature of Amaterasu, in turn, had begun with an undated and unsigned work titled *Chronicle of a Separate Source for Gods (Shin beppongi)*, which declared that Amaterasu's capital was located in the town of Nakatsu in Buzen province. In 1767, an unidentified scholar wrote a work in rebuttal to this called *Arguments Concerning the Capital of the Heavenly Ancestor (Tenso tojō ben)*, in which it was claimed that Amaterasu's capital was actually located in Yamato province. Norinaga restated his position that Amaterasu simultaneously is the sun and the sun goddess in his own rebuttal titled *Refutation of the Arguments Concerning the Capital of the Heavenly Ancestor (Tenso tojō benben)*, written in 1788 and revised in 1796. In this work, Norinaga declared that, as a deity, Amaterasu resided with the other heavenly deities in the Plain of High Heaven and that any allegation to the contrary is a heresy inspired by the study of Yamazaki Ansai's Suika Shinto.[5] In a later work, the *Straight Talk on the Two Ise Shrines (Ise nikū sakitake no ben)* of 1798, Norinaga wrote that two of the most prominent heresies concerning Amaterasu were that she is the sun goddess but not the sun and that she lived in Yamato province—an argument which he in this work claimed to have come about from reading too many works in Chinese.[6]

---

mura Shigeo's *Naobi no mitama furoku ichimei dōshu no hyō* (1829), and Sugehara Sadao's *Hana no shiragami* (1838). See Matsumoto Sannosuke, *Kokugaku seiji shisō no kenkyū*, p. 83n.

[4] Quoted in Matsumoto Sannosuke, *Kokugaku seiji shisō no kenkyū*, p. 63. In the same letter, Kotosuga went on: "The records of the divine age contain passages on the pure and spontaneous heart. I feel that the Izumo poems also describe purity of the heart."

[5] See *MNZ*, VIII, 3–17.

[6] See *MNZ*, VIII, 475.

In 1782, Norinaga had a second story added to his home in Matsusaka and used this addition as both a study and a venue for Waka gatherings. The architecture suggests a further compartmentalization of Norinaga's life, since he used the ground-floor veranda and "living room" for seeing patients and the upstairs exclusively for his research and related scholarly activities; it is apparent that his scholarship and not his medical profession had become his primary vocation.[7] It was said that, when Norinaga grew weary of his long hours of study, he amused himself by ringing a small set of bells hung from a wooden tablet—a practice that resulted in the sobriquet "Suzunoya" (House of Bells) for him and his school.

Norinaga's popularity as a teacher and fame as a scholar grew exponentially during the three decades following his completion of *The Rectifying Spirit*. From some 45 students (all from Ise) in 1773, the figure roughly doubled during the next decade, with students from outside Ise approaching 10 percent of the total. By 1793, his school claimed over 300 registrants, of whom one-half were drawn from outside Ise; and, at the time of Norinaga's death in 1801, the rolls of the Suzunoya recorded over 500 entries with nearly 60 percent of students from beyond the borders of Norinaga's native province of Ise.[8] Not only did Norinaga's reputation become one of considerable national celebrity, but he achieved this while living virtually his entire adult life outside of one or another of Japan's major metropolises—an indication of both widespread interest in nativist topics throughout Japan and the impressive penetration of the nativist academy as a popular cultural activity into non-urban environments.[9] Furthermore, these students represented remarkable diversity in terms of class background and vocation but not

---

[7] The entire edifice has been transported from its original site to a hilltop plot adjacent to Matsusaka castle, where it forms part of the Motoori Norinaga Memorial Hall (Motoori Norinaga Kinenkan).

[8] These figures follow those given in the chart in Matsumoto Shigeru, *Motoori Norinaga. 1730–1801*, p. 125. Matsumoto's source is the *Motoori Norinaga monjin roku* and disregards a decrease in number due to death of students.

[9] For a chart showing the geographical distribution of students in the Suzunoya, see Haga, *Bakumatsu kokugaku no tenkai*, pp. 290–291. The chart is reproduced in Rubinger, p. 164.

gender: The majority were either merchants (34 percent) or agriculturalists (23 percent), the latter most likely of village-headman
(*shōya*) status; these groups, in turn, were followed in equal propor-
ation by samurai and Shinto priests (14 percent each), with smaller
representation by physicians (5 percent) and Buddhist clergy (5 percent); it is clear, however, that unlike Mabuchi's academy, which
had a remarkable percentage of women students, the Suzunoya was
overwhelmingly (95 percent) a male institution.[10] One point of significance revealed by these figures is that those groups who might
have derived a measure of vocational advantage through enrollment
in Norinaga's school, the samurai and Shinto priests, represent only
slightly more than one-fourth of the total, suggesting other moti-
vations, such as personal intellectual enrichment and even curiosity
on the part of sightseers to the Ise Shrines for the overwhelming
majority of Norinaga's students.[11]

The instruction by Norinaga took a variety of forms. Many of his
students from more distant provinces communicated their questions
to him by mail (just as Norinaga himself had done with Kamo no
Mabuchi), and these students often enrolled as a result of hearing
Norinaga speak during one or another of his frequent lecture tours
in Nagoya, Kyoto, and Kii province—indications of both the relative sophistication of the communications infrastructure in the late-
eighteenth century and the contribution of this infrastructure to the
development of the rural private academy. Norinaga gave his lectures in Matsusaka in the evenings, thereby encouraging part-time
students rather than professional scholars, and it is believed that the
average number of students present at any one evening's lecture was
roughly a dozen. The schedule of lectures was announced in advance

[10] Following the figures in Haga Noboru, *Bakumatsu kokugaku no kenkyū*, p. 47, with
percentages added.
[11] One such sightseer recorded his experience as follows: "I went to the Ise Shrine and then
went sightseeing in the area. I arrived in Matsuzaka at noon and went to Norinaga's
school. There was a poetry session meeting somewhere else and so he was not in. I waited,
and that night I heard his lecture on the *Man'yōshū* at his home. The school appeared to
be very prosperous. There were scholars from Kumamoto and from various other parts of
the country in attendance." Quoted in Rubinger, pp. 168–169.

with lectures on a single classic extending at times over several years, and Norinaga repeated some series, like those on the *Genji*, as many as four times during his career. Within the Suzunoya, administrative matters like grading or evaluation appear to have been irregular and at best rudimentary, with an informal atmosphere prevailing on such matters as attendance or advancement in one's studies.[12] It is impossible to determine with certainty whether Norinaga's students were drawn to his school more by his views on literary and poetic classics or by his thoughts on the ancient Way, but, since he appears to have lectured more frequently on the former, it may be that the study of the ancient Way formed something of a specialized discipline in the Suzunoya.

Norinaga's *The Rectifying Spirit* was a key work in establishing his reputation and represents his first comprehensive statement on the ancient Way based on his study of the *Kojiki*, but it was not Norinaga's final statement on ancient Way thought. During the three decades of his life following the completion of *The Rectifying Spirit*, Norinaga revised certain concepts, by belatedly adopting Mabuchi's concept of the true heart and by writing of not one but two Musubi deities; he further developed certain concepts such as the wondrous and numinous qualities of life; and he added altogether new concepts, like his postulation of an ancient Way eschatology. These revisions, developments, and innovations all contributed to enhancing the religious dimensions of Norinaga's ancient Way thought and brought it to the verge of becoming a contemporary religion.[13]

---

[12] Based on ibid., pp. 166–171.

[13] The most useful texts for analyzing Norinaga's post-1771 ancient Way thought are the following (the translation of titles generally follows that of Matsumoto Shigeru in *Motoori Norinaga*, pp. 237–239): *Gyojū gaigen* (Complaint on the failure to bridle the Chinese), 1778; *Kuzuhana* (Arrowroot), 1780; *Shinreki kō* (On the true calendar), 1782; *Tamaboko hyakushu* (One hundred verses on the Way), 1786; *Tamakushige* (Jeweled comb box), 1786; *Hihon tamakushige* (Secret book of the jeweled comb box), 1787; *Kami no yo no masagoto* (True words on the divine age), 1789; *Tamakatsuma* (Jeweled bamboo basket), 1793–1801; *Tenso tojō benben* (Refutation of the arguments concerning the capital of the heavenly ancestor), 1796; *Ise nikū sakitake no ben* (Straight talk on the two Ise Shrines), 1798; *Uiyamabumi* (First steps on the mountain of learning), 1798; *Kojiki den* (Commentary on the *Kojiki*), 1798; *Shindō* (Way of the vassal), 1800; "Yuigon sho" (Last will and testa-

In his later writings, Norinaga came into agreement with Kamo
no Mabuchi on the position that, for the individual, the loss of the
primordial perfection meant the abeyance of the true heart *(magokoro)* into a dormant state, but, while Mabuchi had regarded the
true heart as an attribute of the natural Way of heaven and earth,
Norinaga described it as a gift of the Musubi deities, Takami Musubi and Kami Musubi, whom he now jointly recognized as the
gods whose mysterious creative power lay behind all acts of creativity and production.[14] According to Norinaga, humans and gods
alike were endowed with true hearts, but those true hearts represented a considerable range of propensity toward either good or
wicked behavior:

> The true heart is that heart with which one is born by virtue of the Musubi
> gods. Within this concept of the "true heart" are included wise hearts and
> clumsy ones, good ones and bad ones, and every possible variation thereon,
> since people in this world are not all the same. Thus, even the gods of the
> divine age were some good and some bad, for they all behaved in accord-
> ance with their individual true hearts.[15]

Thus, while the true heart represented for Norinaga a latent element of numinosity within each individual, it did not assure that

---

ment), 1800; *Maiasa haishin shiki* (Order for morning worship), undated; and *Suzunoya
tōmon roku* (Questions and answers in the House of Bells), published posthumously. For
additional works relevant to this study, see Muraoka, *Motoori Norinaga*. pp. 245–254.

In the *Uiyamabumi* (MNZ. I, 5), a curriculum for study of the ancient Way, Norinaga
advised his students to pay special attention to his *True Words on the Divine Age* and to read
the work ten times in order to get the flavor of ancient Japanese words; then *The Rectifying
Spirit* and *One Hundred Verses on the Way*. followed by *Jeweled Comb Box* and *Arrowroot. True
Words on the Divine Age* was written at the promoting of Yokoi Chiaki (1738–1801), a
Nagoya samurai, who enrolled in Norinaga's school in 1785 and encouraged his teacher
to write a synopsis in simple language of the divine age myths; Chiaki underwrote the
publication costs for Norinaga's *Kojiki den* and held considerable influence in the Suzunoya.
Norinaga dedicated *Jeweled Comb Box* to Tokugawa Harusada (1728–1789), lord of Kii
and father of Tokugawa Harutomi, a patron of Norinaga's researches after 1789.

[14] In the *Tamaboko hyakushu* (MNZ. XVIII, 324), Norinaga described the Musubi gods in
verse as follows:

All that exists	Moromoro no
Owes its existence	narizuru mono was
To the divine linkage	Kami Musubi
Of Kami Musubi	Takami Musubi no
And Takami Musubi.	kami no musubi zo.

[15] *Kuzubana*. in MNZ. VIII, 147.

human behavior would accord with conventional notions of goodness but rather that human behavior would accord with the Way of gods who are themselves some good and some bad.

Norinaga, however, did believe that the true heart endowed man with the capacity to distinguish good behavior from bad, and that it thereby obviated the need for external moral codes to guide man's actions. Since humans were created by the power of the Musubi gods, they were "aware of and able to do what they should."[16] That man might not actually do good at times was, of course, due to man's subjection to the deterministic forces of both good and wicked gods. The nostalgic quest for Norinaga was thus no longer simply an attempt to take the emperor's heart as one's own but rather, as it had been for Kamo no Mabuchi, the aspiration to reanimate one's true heart in order to recapture the beatific blessings that derive from its activation.

In *The Rectifying Spirit,* Norinaga had dated the loss of these blessings to the mid-seventh century when, he alleged, ancient man read Chinese writings, became convinced of their truth, assumed the Chinese heart, and lost his identification with the imperial heavenly god heart; but, in his later writings, Norinaga modified this view as well. The key features of this revised interpretation were that Norinaga now regarded the Fall as both a more ancient and more gradual process, repeated generationally and not directly related to one's reading of works in Chinese. He wrote that the changes began during the reign of Emperor Ōjin (r. 270–310) and were more or less complete by the reign of Emperor Tenmu (r. 673–686), whereupon people increasingly turned to the Way of the sages until their only knowledge of ancient Japanese practices came from the *Nihon shoki,* a work written in imitation of Chinese historiographic practices and itself a contributing factor in the Sinification of ancient man's perspectives.[17]

According to Norinaga, heaven—not, of course, the "heaven" of an afterlife but rather the Plain of High Heaven—became remote

---

[16] *Tamakushige,* in Tsunoda, II, 16.
[17] *Kuzubana,* in MNZ, VIII, 126.

during this four-century-long process. He asserted that, during the divine age and prior to the descent to earth of Amaterasu's grandson, Ninigi, it had been possible to travel between this heaven and earth and that, even afterwards, heaven remained in proximity as a result of the various links—the true heart, the Way of the gods, and so on—which bonded men to their gods.[18] In a sense, prior to the commencement of terrestrial rule by divine emperors, heaven *was* earth since, according to Norinaga, "the gods of the divine age were men," and all components of life and existence—all creatures and all things—were believed by him to have been divine.[19] Norinaga speculated that, even after the separation of heaven from earth, when travel between the two was no longer possible, heaven, though physically remote, remained accessible, and it was the disruption to the metaphysical links enabling man to participate in the divine hierophany that represented the apparent termination of the relationship between the human and the divine.

Norinaga further explained that, while the introduction of Chinese writings and their attendant insinuation of the Chinese heart into ancient Japanese man were initially responsible for the severance of this relationship, the Fall was not directly contingent upon having read such works. He expanded his description of the symptoms of the Chinese heart to include, not just preferring Chinese practices or exalting China at the expense of Japan, but also "such things as the widespread habit of arguing over right and wrong, and good and bad, and searching for the principle of things;"[20] and he insisted that, even though the assumptions of the Chinese heart were embedded in Chinese writings, "even illiterate farmers who could not read a single character lost their true hearts in middle antiquity" through their indirect exposure to the contagion of Chinese writings.[21]

Norinaga's earlier description in *The Rectifying Spirit* of how one might reclaim one's true Japanese heart had contained certain ele-

---

[18] Ibid., VIII, 128.
[19] Ibid., VIII, 158.
[20] *Tamakatsuma*, in *MNZ*, I, 48.
[21] *Kuzubana*, in *MNZ*, VIII, 154.

mentary contradictions. He wrote there, on the one hand, of the need first to exorcise the Chinese heart and then to immerse oneself in the texts of high antiquity; but he also wrote of the instinctiveness of ancient man's conformity to the Way and the futility of human endeavor in a world in which all action was the result of the wishes of the gods. Norinaga sought to resolve these contradictions in his later writings by making the recovery of the true heart contingent upon the healing powers of the god Naobi and by acknowledging that, since "man originally did not know the Way by studying it," it was not something ultimately to be apprehended through the medium of texts.[22] He counseled that, if man expunged the Chinese heart by placing his trust in the healing powers of Naobi, then this was sufficient for his reattaining the true heart he had at birth and being again at "one with the Way."[23] In 1786, Norinaga summed up this revised counsel in verse:

Rid yourself of	Karagokoro
The Chinese heart and	naoshi tamae to
Worship only the	ōnaobi
Healing powers of the	kami no naobi o
Great god Naobi.	koi nomi matsure.[24]

In other words, faith and trust had displaced scholarship as components of Norinaga's nostalgic quest, and, whether these revisions represent simply a desire for theological consistency or whether they reveal the influence of those Pure Land Buddhist teachings that emphasized man's ineffectuality in securing his own salvation and dependence on the Amida Buddha—doctrines with which Norinaga had been raised and continued, somewhat surreptitiously, to practice in later life—remains an issue disputed by Norinaga's biographers.

It is evident that, for Norinaga, some questions were answerable while others were not. Since he had a fundamentalist's attitude toward the literal truth of the *Kojiki,* and since the divine age chapters of

---

[22] *Tamakatsuma,* in MNZ, I, 47.
[23] Ibid.
[24] *Tamaboko hyakushu,* in MNZ, XVII, 323.

the *Kojiki* were more mythological than theological in content, Norinaga was obliged to acknowledge that some questions are unanswerable. Further, since the activities of the gods, according to Norinaga, were no less a factor in the present than they had been *in illo tempore,* and since the gods were not fully fathomable by human minds other than to the extent that ancient texts shed light upon them, Norinaga perceived the world—each action, gesture, thought, and feeling—to be infused with the divine and thus, however familiar, nonetheless irreducible and elusive. Nowhere in the writings of eighteenth-century nativism does the lyrical beauty of this wondrous attitude toward life find better expression than in Norinaga's *Arrowroot* of 1780:

> Consider also the human body: It has eyes to see, ears to hear, a mouth to speak, feet to walk, and hands to do a thousand things. Are they not truly wonderful? Birds and insects fly in the sky, plants and trees bloom and bear fruit—they are all wonderful. When insentient beings change into sentient beings like birds or insects, or when foxes and badgers take on human form—are these not the strangest of all things? Thus the universe and all things therein are without a single exception strange and wondrous when examined carefully. Even the sage would be incapable of explaining these phenomena. Thus, one must acknowledge that human intelligence is puny while the acts of the gods are illimitable and wondrous.[25]

Elsewhere in the same work, Norinaga described how there are things one cannot see but can smell, or things like the wind that one can neither see, hear, nor smell but can nonetheless feel; there are the promptings of the heart that exist but cannot be verified or measured scientifically (Norinaga, of course, was a physician); and in the same manner, the gods which are invisible today were plainly visible in the divine age, just as Amaterasu remains visible to anyone who will but turn his head toward the daytime sky.[26] All these, for Norinaga, were evidence of the enduring potency of the divine in his own environs, "but, because we are accustomed to their pre-

---

[25] *Kuzubana,* in Tsunoda, II, 20–21.
[26] *Kuzubana,* in MNZ, VIII, 160.

sent form and have always lived in their midst, we cease to be aware of their wondrous quality."[27]

Norinaga applied his fundamentalist's approach, though with less pleasing conclusions, to the question of eschatology. Over the centuries, Shinto theologians had maintained a conspicuous silence concerning an afterlife, and in this respect Shinto has been a relatively comfortless creed. One reason for this silence was the fact that the divine age chapters of both the *Kojiki* and *Nihon shoki* described in graphic detail Izanami's terrifying descent to the forbidding Hades-like afterworld of Yomi, and this remained the only scripturally based eschatology for a Shintoist. Most Japanese, in fact, had turned to Buddhism for insight on what occurs after the death of the body, and Pure Land Buddhists like Norinaga believed that one's entry into paradise could not begin until one's physical death. From his study of the *Kojiki,* Norinaga concluded that "everyone in the world, whether noble or base, good or bad, must one and all go to the land of Yomi when they die." Norinaga recognized that it "may sound callous or even unfounded" to state this, but he insisted that his conclusions were "all based on the true legends of the divine age, and, since they are founded on a mysterious principle, they are not something upon which man, with his limited reason, can speculate."[28] He acknowledged that this destiny was a "terribly sad matter," since Yomi lay deep beneath the earth and was "an exceedingly filthy and bad land."[29] He described the moment of death as the final and irrevocable separation of a man from his wife, children, property, friends, relatives, and anything he might hold dear, but in the same breath he denigrated other creeds as "fallacious foreign Ways" for their promises of a glorious afterlife and insisted that acceptance of this grim portrait of Yomi was essential to one's understanding of the "truth of the divine imperial Way."[30] The this-worldly orientation of both Shinto and

---

[27] *Kuzubana,* in Tsunoda, II, 20–21.
[28] *Tamakushige,* in MNZ, VIII, 315.
[29] Ibid.
[30] Ibid., VIII, 316.

Norinaga's ancient Way theology is evident in the following poem
by Norinaga:

> Polluted Yomi   Kitanakuni
> Bourne of darkness—   yomi no kunibe
> How dirty and disgusting!   inashikome
> I want to stay in this world   chi yo toko to wa ni
> A thousand ages evermore!   kono yonomogamo.[31]

Norinaga was nothing if not consistent in the formulation and depiction of this eschatology. That he did not shy away from analysis
of this subject and description of Yomi attests to the uncompromis-
ing integrity of his fundamentalist commitment to the *Kojiki*. Furthermore, his conclusion that all humans without exception proceed
to Yomi was consistent with the implications of both universal Japanese possession of the true heart and divine determinism of all
human activity: If all Japanese were divinely endowed with a true
heart, which might be good or bad or anywhere in between, and if
human actions were determined by the wishes of the gods, then
anything other than a uniformly destined afterlife would have been
indefensible. Norinaga's teachings on these matters, however, may
have contributed to the failure of his ancient Way theology to rad-
icate as a contemporary religion, since the sheer unpleasantness of
this eschatology was inescapable.

The issues of divine determinism and fundamentalism posed other
problems for Norinaga in, for example, his explanation of such matters as illness and sages. When asked by one of his students whether
illness, like wickedness, was attributable to the god Magatsubi,
Norinaga declared that illness was due to a "god of illness," but
that the "inspiration" for illness came from Magatsubi. However,
since there were no instances of illness recorded in the *Kojiki*, Norinaga further explained that the "god of illness must have come to
Japan from elsewhere," and that, since "he does not appear to have
existed in China in ancient times, he must have come to that country as well from elsewhere."[32] At other times, however, Norinaga

---

[31] *Tamaboko hyakushu*, in Muraoka, *Studies in Shinto Thought*, p. 151.
[32] *Suzunoya tōmon roku*, in MNZ, I, 537–539.

accepted the identification of native deities with the gods of other countries. Generally, however, Norinaga insisted upon the paramountcy of Japanese deities as, for example, when he described Shen Nung and Fu Hsi, respectively the Chinese mythological culture-heroes of agriculture and animal husbandry, as offshoots or derivatives of Toyouke, the Japanese god of the five grains.[33]

Norinaga encountered a comparable dilemna when he was asked to account for the presence of foreign sages and their teachings in a world governed by Japanese divine forces. Rather than simply attributing the Way of the sages to the manipulations of Magatsubi and refuting his earlier critique of the Chinese Way as a product of human ingenuity, Norinaga chose instead to make quasi gods out of the sages. He postulated a distinction between the "revealed" state of the sages as men and their "concealed" state as deities. Norinaga claimed that the Way of the sages was thus a Way created by malevolent deities when the sages were in their concealed state, but, since the sages were in their revealed state when they fashioned their Way, it was still correct to think of their Way as man-made and inferior.[34] Whether Norinaga's students found this bit of sophistry convincing is impossible to determine, since the record of questions and answers from which is drawn was not compiled until more than three decades after Norinaga's death.

Norinaga, ever the precisian, also showed an increased concern for definitions and terminology in his post-1771 writings on the ancient Way. One example is his definition of *kami* (deities) which he did not write until the final decade of his life in the 1790s. After modestly disclaiming perfect understanding of the matter (a theological impossibility, according to Norinaga), he wrote:

> Speaking in general, however, it may be said that the word *kami* signifies first the deities of heaven and earth who appear in the ancient records and the spirits of the shrines where they are worshiped. It is unnecessary to add that it includes birds and beasts, trees and plants, seas and mountains, and so forth. In ancient usage, anything whatsoever which was outside the

---

[33] *Ise nikū sakitake no ben*, in *MNZ*, VIII, 478.
[34] *Suzunoya tōmon roku*, in *MNZ*, VIII, 544.

ordinary, which possessed superior power or was awe-inspiring was called *kami*. Eminence here does not refer merely to the superiority of nobility, goodness, or meritorious deeds. Evil and mysterious things, if they are extraordinary and dreadful, are also called *kami*. Among human beings who are called *kami*, the successive generations of divine emperors are all included. The fact that emperors are also called "distant gods" (*tōtsu kami*) is because they are far-separated, majestic, and worthy of reverence. In lesser degree we find in the present as well as in ancient times human beings who are *kami*. Although they may not be accepted as such throughout the country, yet in each province, village, and family there are human beings who are *kami*, each one according to his own proper position. The *kami* of the divine age were for the most part human beings of that time, and, because the people of that time were all divine, it is called the divine age.[35]

This explication and definition by Norinaga of as elusive a subject as *kami* is so lucid and comprehensive that it has continued into modern times to be widely cited in both Japanese and non-Japanese scholarship on Shinto.

Norinaga was no less concerned about the terminology to be used in discussions of the ancient Way. He objected to references to China as either Chūgoku (Central Kingdom) or Chūka (Central Florescence) and preferred what he regarded as the more neutral term, Kara. He likewise objected to references to China as "Great China" since, in his view, the country had no claim to such grandeur, and also to references to Japan as "Great Japan," on the grounds that such practices aped the Chinese proclivity toward self-aggrandizement.[36] In the same manner, Norinaga in his post-1771 writings objected to references to the study of things Japanese as either National Learning (*kokugaku*) or Japanese Studies (*Wagaku*), preferring instead the simpler term "scholarship" (*mono manabi*).[37] It had long been the practice in Japan to refer to Chinese studies as "scholarship" and to designate nativist or other studies as a separate subject. In response to this, Norinaga wrote that, "for over one thousand years, Japanese scholars have drunk the poisonous wine of Chinese writings . . . until they have all forgotten how wildly drunk it has

---

[35] From the *Kojiki den*, translation adapted from Tsunoda, I, 21–22.
[36] *Gyojū gaigen*, in MNZ, VIII, 67–69; and *Kokugo kō*, in MNZ, VIII, 470–471.
[37] *Uiyamabumi*, in MNZ, I, 7.

made them," and he felt that a first step in redressing this wrong was for one to regard the study of Japan and not the study of China as the primary foundation and focus of one's scholarship.[38] Yet another example of Norinaga's concern with disallowing traditional terminology to imply either priority or equality of the foreign with the native was his inclination in later years not to use the term "Way of the gods" for the ancient Way—a term whose origins lay in the desire to distinguish the previously unnamed native Way from the new imported Ways—and to refer to it instead as the "true Way" (*makoto no michi*), the "original true Way" (*moto no makoto no michi*), or the "orignal true and correct Way" (*moto no makoto no masamichi*).[39] He further defined the study of the Way as being comprised of three sub-disciplines, with each representative of one branch of the field: Shinto studies (*shingaku*), which he regarded as largely the domain of Shinto theologians; antiquarian studies (*yūsoku no gaku*) of imperial-court offices and ceremonial, legal codes, ancient customs and practices, and so on; and ancient studies (*kogaku*), by which he meant the study of ancient Japanese histories and poetry anthologies.[40]

Norinaga's concerns in these revisions were neither petty nor pedantic. His intent was to revise the entire vocabulary and apparatus of one's approach to the study of the national past and its Way. Furthermore, as the philologist par excellence of his age, Norinaga believed that words themselves possessed more than simply literal or suggestive value. In particular, he was intrigued by special words called *kotodama*, spells or incantations which Norinaga and others believed capable of granting wishes and regarded as "bridges" between the ordinary world of human affairs and the supernatural realm of numinous phenomena. The word *kotodama* had its locus classicus in one of the verses of the *Man'yōshū*, where it was suggested that *kotodama* were linked to the maintenance of the national weal, and Norinaga believed that *kotodama* had the power to trans-

---

[38] *Kuzubana*, in *MNZ*, VIII, 123.
[39] See, for example, *Tamakushige*, in *MNZ*, VIII, 309.
[40] *Uiyamabumi*, in *MNZ*, I, 5.

port one, at least on a spiritual level, from the sullied present to the divine age.[41]

During the last decade and a half of his life, when his celebrity became widespread and the number of his students more than quadrupled, Norinaga's advice and political counsel were actively sought by high-ranking domainal officials, and Norinaga himself pursued contacts with members of the Kyoto nobility who were affiliated with an inner circle of imperial loyalists. The explicit content of Norinaga's political thought, however, was extraordinary not for any measure of radicalism as these associations during the last Tokugawa century might suggest, but rather for its conservatism and near-constant affirmation of the status quo. Politics, for Norinaga, was synonymous with respect for the ruler, but this "ruler" was not the emperor in Kyoto as nineteenth-century restorationists argued but rather the Tokugawa shogun in Edo. As one biographer of Norinaga described this feature of his thought, "The Way of respect for the ruler [for Norinaga] meant *the exercise of loyalty toward the bakufu.*"[42]

Norinaga's political thought was consistent with the implications of his deterministic theology. He taught that, since one's actions are determined by the gods, one's limited initiative should be channeled into respect for the gods' presence and obedience to the dictates of Amaterasu's terrestrial instruments, the emperor and shogun. In terms of the role of the scholar, he taught that the responsibility of scholars was to enquire into the Way, while the role of rulers was to practice the Way, and that, "for better or worse, the obligation of those who are ruled is to follow their ruler," for to do otherwise represented "a selfish act inconsistent with the spirit of the Way."[43] According to this view, reverence for the gods was inseparable from reverence for the divinely ordained political

---

[41] See *Kuzubana,* in *MNZ,* VIII, 125. The *Man'yōshū* verse is number 3254 which reads: "The Land of Yamato is a land/Where the word-soul *(kotodama)* gives us aid;/Be happy, fare you well!" In Japan Society for the Promotion of Scientific Research, tr., *Man'yōshū,* p. 59.

[42] Muraoka, *Motoori Norinaga,* p. 331. Original emphasis retained.

[43] *Tamakatsuma,* in *MNZ,* I, 74.

order from which all blessings flow, as in the following verse in which Norinaga played upon the similarity between the words for gods *(kami)* and rulers *(kimi):*

The food that sustains life,	Inochi tsugu
Our clothes, our dwellings—	kuimono kimono
These are the blessings	sumi ie ra
Of our ruler,	kimi no megumi zo
Of our gods.[44]	kami no megumi zo

Norinaga was likewise emphatic in his praise for the first Tokugawa shogun, Ieyasu, and the existing political order:

> The reason why our age is so excellently governed is chiefly because the eastern-illuminating divine ancestor [Tokugawa Ieyasu] took the magnificent heart of Amaterasu as his own heart and restored the condition of her imperial descendants whose fortunes had waned in the medieval period. . . . His feat of bringing peace to the land was due to his conformity to the true Way and his reverence for the gods of heaven and earth.[45]

He described the present age as one in which the shogun conducted the affairs of state and the administration of the territories in a fiduciary capacity on behalf of Amaterasu, and his conclusion was that Ieyasu's laws and decrees as well as those of his successors "are the laws and decrees of Amaterasu."[46]

Though any analysis of Norinaga's political thought must draw a distinction between his private and public pronouncements—a distinction examined below—one cannot dismiss the possibility that factors other than an intellectual concern for consistency between his political ideology and his ancient Way theology influenced Norinaga's formulation of such passive politics. One such factor may have been the arraignment and imprisonment of Takenouchi Shikibu, who initially expounded his views in Kyoto concerning reverence for the emperor while Norinaga was near the end of his student years there. The execution of Yamagata Daini a decade later, as well as Shikibu's death in exile in the same year, were likewise events

---

[44] *Tamaboko hyakushu,* translation adapted from Muraoka, *Studies in Shinto Thought,* p. 160.
[45] *Shindō,* in MNZ, VIII, 505–506.
[46] *Tamakushige,* in MNZ, VIII, 366–367.

that probably captured Norinaga's attention at formative stages of the development of his thought and that exhibited in unambiguous terms the bakufu's attitude toward potentially subversive teachings.[47]

In 1790, there arose within the bakufu a controversy over intellectual orthodoxy whose ripples extended to Norinaga himself. The controversy concerned a document called the "Prohibition of Heterodox Studies" ("Kansei igaku no kin"). The "Prohibition" was promulgated by Matsudaira Sadanobu (1758–1829), son of Tayasu Munetake, who replaced Tanuma Okitsugu as head of the Council of Elders (Rōjū) following Tanuma's ouster in 1786 from that position upon the death of the shogun Ieharu. Sadanobu addressed the "Prohibition" to the head of the Shōheikō, the Confucian College founded by the Hayashi as an intended bastion of fidelity to orthodox Neo-Confucian teachings and patronized for over a century by successive generations of Tokugawa shogun. The "Prohibition" was, in fact, nothing less than a demand for such fidelity which had apparently waned since the College's founding.[48]

Matsudaira Sadanobu's policies were characterized by retrenchment on numerous fronts and were a response to what was perceived within the bakufu to be serious social disintegration during the preceding decade. There had, in fact, been several dramatic indications of widespread unrest during the tenure of Tanuma Okitsugu as head of the Council of Elders, and, while some blamed this unrest on allegations of bribery and corruption during the Tanuma years, there had also been a succession of bad harvests which strained both the bakufu treasury and the economies of numerous domains. In 1783, famine struck, and in the wake of the famine came epidemics.[49] The rate of peasant uprisings accelerated with at least 147

---

[47] See Muraoka, *Motoori Norinaga,* p. 23; and Shigeru Matsumoto, *Motoori Norinaga, 1730–1801* p. 118. The deaths of Takenouchi Shikibu and Yamagata Daini came midway between the "evening in Matsusaka" and completion of *The Rectifying Spirit.*

[48] See Herman Ooms, *Charismatic Bureaucrat: A Political Biography of Matsudaira Sadanobu, 1758–1829,* pp. 122–150; and Tsunoda, I, 493–496.

[49] In *Epidemics and Mortality in Early Modern Japan,* Ann Bowman Jannetta disputes the assumption of a cause-and-effect relationship between famines and epidemics in Tokugawa Japan. The epidemics of the 1780s were, nonetheless, immediately preceded by famines.

such incidents between 1781 and 1788, and with 35 uprisings in 1787 alone. And, in the summer of that year, a four-day riot broke out in Edo, and, according to an entry in Norinaga's diary, "Every corner of Edo was involved in this unprecedented disturbance."[50]

Matsudaira Sadanobu's response was to base his economic policies on the principles of frugality, fiscal retrenchment, and an emphasis on agriculture—policies reminiscent of those of the founders of the Tokugawa bakufu—and his policy toward intellectuals was likewise based on what Sadanobu believed to be seventeenth-century precedents. The "Prohibition" represented an attempt to restore the orthodox Neo-Confucian teachings of Chu Hsi to a position of primacy in the Shōheikō, and Nishiyama Sessai (1735–1795), an instrumental figure in persuading Sadanobu to promulgate the "Prohibition," made it clear that it was intended to purge the proponents of Confucian Ancient Learning from the hallowed college. According to Sessai, figures like Itō Jinsai and Ogyū Sorai were guilty of sophistry, while their "second-rate" successors were guilty of having insisted upon their "own mistaken interpretations of the classics and slandered the Chu Hsi school."[51]

Even Norinaga felt the wrath of Sessai's brush and the ripples of the controversy, though not without a measure of irony. "Norinaga," claimed Sessai, "constantly writes works critical of the Confucianism of the Duke of Chou and Confucius. In his discussions, he includes information about the sage emperors of our imperial court and covertly attempts to arouse public feeling."[52] As early as 1788, Yokoi Chiaki (1738–1801), one of Norinaga's leading students, had tried unsuccessfully to introduce Norinaga's teachings to Matsudaira Sadanobu in the hope that Sadanobu would base his future policies on the ancient native Way rather than on Chinese Neo-Confucianism. No official action was taken against Norinaga as a result of either Chiaki's efforts or the "Prohibition," and in this respect Norinaga was more fortunate than his celebrated contem-

---

[50] See Shigeru Matsumoto, *Motoori Norinaga, 1730–1801*, pp. 118–123.
[51] From a letter to Akamatsu Sōshū (1721–1801), adapted from Tsunoda, I, 495.
[52] Quoted in Maruyama Masao, *Studies in the Intellectual History of Tokugawa Japan*, p. 282.

porary, Hayashi Shihei (1738–1793), whose arrest for harboring "fantastic and unorthodox" views was ordered by Sadanobu himself.[53] The irony, of course, is that, when removed from their nativist context, Norinaga's public pronouncements of his political theory were utterly conservative and largely consistent with Sadanobu's own notions of political, economic, and social retrenchment.[54] Norinaga's, however, was but one voice among many during the late-eighteenth century who were seeking in various ways to "rectify the world" *(yonaoshi)*.

Despite his apparent reticence concerning explicitly political statements, Norinaga readily cultivated associations with prominent political figures, and his counsel in turn was likewise sought by a number of daimyo. In 1787, Tokugawa Harusada (1728–1789), lord of Kii, took the unprecedented step of soliciting Norinaga's views on politics and economics. It will be recalled that Keichū had served Tokugawa Mitsukuni on the *Man'yōshū* project, Kada no Azumamaro had actively sought the sponsorship of the shogun for a nativist academy, and Kamo no Mabuchi had spent fourteen years as a specialist in Japanese studies in the service of Tayasu Munetake; but no major nativist had ever been retained as a political counselor, since such matters in Tokugawa Japan had traditionally been entrusted to Confucian advisors of one persuasion or another. Norinaga's response was first to dedicate to Harusada a work he had completed the previous year, *Jeweled Comb Box (Tamakushige)*, which contained

---

[53] In his *Military Proposals for a Maritime Nation (Kaikoku heidan)*, Hayashi Shihei wrote in 1791 that, in order to prevent incursions by foreign enemies, Japan urgently required improved maritime defenses. His punishment for asserting this self-evident fact was a 6-month sentence in an Edo prison. See Donald Keene, *The Japanese Discovery of Europe, 1720–1850*, pp. 39–45. Keene (ibid., p. 43) states that Shihei was arrested for having published a book "dealing with affairs of state and advocating the violation of existing laws." Ooms, however (*Charismatic Bureaucrat*, p. 141), believes that Shihei's work "was judged too alarming because it might spread unnecessary fears about national security" and implies that Shihei's arrest was the result of his violation of a decree by Sadanobu that "all new publications must be registered with the city magistrate."

[54] For example, Sadanobu's assertion in 1788 that "the Way was established by the sages. . . . It is not the natural Way of heaven and earth and nature" (from his *Seigo*, quoted in Maruyama Masao, *Studies in the Intellectual History of Tokugawa Japan*, p. 284) was consistent with both Norinaga's and the Sorai school's critique of orthodox Neo-Confucianism and might have failed Sadanobu's own test of orthodoxy.

a concise statement of Norinaga's publicly espoused views on such matters as Amaterasu and the divine hierophany, the human responsibility of obedience to the divinely ordained political order, the importance of conforming one's behavior to the Way, and so on. Then, in the 12th month of 1787, Norinaga presented Harusada with a comprehensive confidential statement of his views on economics and administration, the *Secret Book of the Jeweled Comb Box (Hihon tamakushige)*. The work was not published until 1851, exactly fifty years after Norinaga's death, and it represents the single most important statement of Norinaga's private political views.

In all of Norinaga's works known within or publicly without the Suzunoya, one searches almost in vain for utterances that might be construed as political. The closest Norinaga comes in these public writings to challenging the status quo are the following two statements: In the "Jeweled Comb Box" he reminds daimyo that, since the residents of their domains were entrusted to them by Amaterasu, they "should make much of these people and treat them with care and lenience,"[55] then, in the *Jeweled Comb Basket (Tamakatsuma)* collection of essays, completed during his last years, Norinaga laments the dilapidated condition of Shinto shrines in many domains, as well as the disregard for traditional Shinto festivals, and remarks that "people today have no idea how much things have changed since ancient times when all they see is what exists now."[56] Neither of these remarks, however, was likely to provoke suspicions of subversive intent, even in the ideologically charged atmosphere that prevailed during Matsudaira Sadanobu's years as head of the Council of Elders.

If not actually subversive, Norinaga was somewhat bolder and more explicit in his pronouncements in the *Secret Book of the Jeweled Comb Box*. The essence of the work restates Norinaga's conviction that, since one's ability to fathom the mysterious forces that activate the world is limited, one's only true guide in the formulation of policy is an understanding of ancient practices and precedent: "So

---

[55] Quoted in Shigeru Matsumoto, *Motoori Norinaga, 1730–1801*, p. 139.
[56] *Tamakatsuma*, in MNZ, I, 210–211.

long as government does not run counter to the pattern of the times
and seeks to maintain the practices of the past, then there may be
an occasional abuse but, by and large, there will be no major loss."[57]
Norinaga told Harusada that a ruler must concern himself with the
"basics" *(moto)* of an issue and must make his policies "farsighted"
(matsu o fusegu), by which he meant that policies must not only
conform to ancient precedents but also take into account the long-
term benefits that derive from the restoration of ancient practices;
and he cautioned that the repeated use of "palliative measures" *(kufū)*
was as fruitless a pursuit as "shooing flies from rice."[58] Norinaga
placed the responsibility for the enactment of such policies squarely
on the shoulders of the ruler and promised that, if these adminstra-
tive principles were followed, then the laws and practices of the
domain "will automatically conform to the ancient spirit of our
land."[59]

The two "basics" Norinaga emphasized in the *Secret Book* were,
first, a concern with social class and the economic ramifications of
behavior inappropriate to one's station in life, and, second, the importance of planning for the future so that, by prudent allocation of
resources in the present, the future consequences of adversity or
misfortune might be reduced. He wrote that all people have a specific status within the social hierarchy and that there is a corre-
sponding mode of behavior appropriate to everyone's status, that is,
a specific degree of luxury and ostentation that each individual should
maintain but under no circumstances exceed. He warned that the
responsibility for living within one's means grew more serious as
one ascended the social ranks: For an ordinary person, extravagance
was largely a matter of personal foolishness, but, for those in positions of authority, the burden of their excesses was borne by those
who lived within their territories and whose taxes or rents wre used
to support such extravagance. In the same manner, Norinaga also
advised Harusada that the responsibility for planning for the future

---

[57] *Hihon tamakushige*, in MNZ, VIII, 331–332.
[58] Ibid., VIII, 329–330, 342.
[59] Ibid., VIII, 362.

likewise grew greater in proportion to one's social standing. He argued that farmers should plan their household economies with an ever-watchful eye toward the possibility of bad harvests, and that rulers should keep a close eye on their agricultural cultivators, the fruits of whose labor sustained and supported the entire social edifice. If daimyo engaged in such planning at the domainal level, and if the shogun did so at the national level, then, explained Norinaga, the people would be able to turn for help to their rulers just as they had in ancient times when suffering was averted.[60]

It must be noted that, thus far, Norinaga's advice to Tokugawa Harusada in the *Secret Book* was scarcely distinguishable from that of most traditional Confucian counselors whom he nonetheless disparaged. Norinaga claimed that Confucians were unfit for the task of political counsel, since they allegedly examine ancient laws and practices, study how they have been modified over the centuries, and assume that "then no harm will come of it if they are still further altered."[61] Nowhere in this argument, however, does Norinaga indicate that his criticisms of Confucian counselors applied more to the Sorai school than to traditional Neo-Confucians who tended to share the conviction that the practices and policies of the past were true informants of the present and that the past was the most appropriate model for the formulation of contemporary policy. In fact, Norinaga's counsel thus far was in most respects consistent with the sumptuary laws, policies of fiscal retrenchment, and emphasis on primary modes of production adopted by Matsudaira Sadanobu several years later.

Norinaga's concern with preserving the secrecy of his confidential advice to Tokugawa Harusada appears excessive until one considers two areas in which Norinaga proposed actual changes to existing government policy, since, as a non-offical, it was illegal for him to make such suggestions. Norinaga's first proposal concerned relaxing the requirements of the *sankin kōtai* whereby daimyo were required to spend alternate periods of residence in Edo under the watchful

---

[60] Ibid., VIII, 333–338.
[61] Ibid., VIII, 362.

eye of the bakufu. Norinaga criticized this policy on the grounds that it was responsible for unnecessary expenditure—he wrote of the "self-aggrandizement and ostentation" of daimyo who insisted on being accompanied to and from Edo by large retinues of servants and retainers[62]—and that these expenditures brought unwarranted hardship to the peasant cultivators. In itself, this was not an altogether radical proposal, since Tokugawa Yoshimune (Matsudaira Sadanobu's grandfather and model for some of Sadanobu's conservative reforms) had likewise sought, in 1722, to reduce the requirements of the *sankin kōtai,* only to have his reforms reversed some nine years later. Norinaga's second proposal was more radical. He recommended that Shinto shrines be reinvigorated and used as centers for local community activities. Norinaga explained this proposal by stating that worship of the gods of Japan would enhance that kind of respect for authority he believed local governments needed, and some domains (Mito in particular) were already known for such pro-shrine policies. Norinaga's attempt to unify the political and spiritual altars was, in fact, an early version of what a century later was known as Shrine Shinto, a government program for the dissemination of policy and propaganda through the local shrine structure.[63]

His suggested changes notwithstanding, Norinaga's proposals in the *Secret Book* cannot be construed as a challenge to the authority of the bakufu, even though they do imply certain oblique criticisms, and the fact that Norinaga was not a member of the bakufu or domainal government appears to be the principal reason for his obsessive secrecy concerning the work. The predominant characteristic of Norinaga's political thought was its unwavering support for the existing structure of authority, and it is thus a point of some irony that, decades after his death, those who regarded themselves as the heirs of his ancient Way thought were instrumental in pro-

---

[62] Ibid., VIII, 336.
[63] On Shrine Shinto, see Helen Hardacre, "Creating State Shinto: The Great Promulgation Campaign."

viding the ideological rationale for the overthrow of the old order and the resumption of imperial rule.

Norinaga continued to associate with other domainal lords through the 1790s. In early 1792, Maeda Harunaga, lord of Kaga, invited Norinaga to head the Japanese-studies program in his domainal school, but Norinaga declined the offer on the grounds that it would have required his leaving Matsusaka. Later that same year, Tokugawa Harutomi, lord of Kii and Harusada's successor there, invited Norinaga to be his official physician, while allowing Norinaga to continue to reside in Matsusaka. Norinaga accepted this invitation and, in 1794, lectured to Harutomi for three days on such diverse subjects as poetics and Shinto liturgy. In 1795, Norinaga also met with Matsudaira Yasusada, lord of Hamada, when Yasusada was visiting the Ise Shrines, and Norinaga lectured to him on *The Tale of Genji*. Two of Yasusada's retainers had studied under Norinaga, and Yasusada later requested and subsidized the publication of Norinaga's major study of *The Tale of Genji, Genji monogatari tama no ogushi*.[64]

Norinaga, however, appears to have been even more eager to establish relationships with members of the Kyoto aristocracy than the domainal elites, especially after his visit to Kyoto in 1793 when he met the imperial Prince Myōhōin, to whom he presented copies of his writings. Probably the most politically provocative of all his associations was, on his last visit to Kyoto in 1801, with Nakayama Naruchika (1741–1817). Naruchika had attained a measure of notoriety for his involvement in what was known as the Title Incident (*songō jiken*). Emperor Kōkaku (r. 1780–1817) had ascended the throne upon the death of Emperor Gomomozono (r. 1771–1779), but the succession was unconventional, since Gomomozono had died without male issue and Kōkaku was selected as successor from one of the collateral branches of the imperial family. In 1789, Emperor Kōkaku attempted to confer upon his father, Prince Sukehito (d. 1794), the title of *dajō tennō,* ordinarily reserved for abdicated emperors. Since Prince Sukehito was the father of the regnant emperor

[64] Shigeru Matsumoto, *Motoori Norinaga, 1730–1801,* p. 131.

but had not himself reigned, the bakufu rejected the petition Kō-kaku's supporters had drafted on the grounds that their cited precedents had all occurred during periods of upheaval and were thus invalid in a time of peace. Undaunted, the imperial court pressed its claims again in 1791 and 1792, and, as the issue grew increasingly aggravated, the bakufu resolved upon a course of punishment for Nakayama Naruchika, whom it regarded as the principal instigator of the growing number of court nobles rallying to the emperor's cause. Meted out in 1793, the sentence consisted of one hundred days of house arrest for Naruchika, after which the incident died down without conferral of the title, much as Matsudaira Sadanobu had predicted.[65]

During the seventy or so days Norinaga spent in Kyoto in 1801, he met with Naruchika at Naruchika's home, where he also presented several lectures on Shinto liturgies and the ancient Way to Naruchika and other nobles in attendance. After the first lecture, Norinaga described his joy over the day's events as follows in a letter to his sons in Matsusaka:

> I am pleased that the study of the ancient Way has been gradually growing in Kyoto, too. . . . The venerable Nakayama is a hero and intellectual of our time whom the emperor especially trusts and who is foremost among all the nobles, and so I was particularly glad of today's lecture. I hope the ancient Way will gradually spread among the court. The nobles present took notes of my lecture, looking impressed by it, and I am told to come again to lecture.[66]

Though Norinaga was evidently pleased with his reception among the Kyoto aristocracy and hoped to spend more time there, his visit was cut short by the death of his sister, Shun, in Matsusaka; Norinaga returned there after canceling his remaining scheduled lectures.

One final question in this examination of Norinaga's post-1771 ancient Way thought is the issue of his personal faith. It is evident that faith and scholarship stand like twin pillars in Norinaga's in-

[65] See Ooms's excellent account of the Title Incident in his *Charismatic Bureaucrat*, pp. 106–119.
[66] Adapted from Shigeru Matsumoto, *Motoori Norinaga, 1730–1801*, pp. 134–135.

tellectual career, but the nature of Norinaga's own faith is problematic. The difficulty stems from an evident disparity between what Norinaga preached and what he actually practiced. The ancient Way thought of Norinaga and other major nativists has often (though somewhat misleadingly) been referred to in English-language studies as a "Shinto revival."[67] Shinto, in fact, was not in need of a "revival," since, in its various permutations and transformations, it had continued to remain a vital and even popular religion during the Tokugawa period.[68] Norinaga's ancient Way thought advocated a return to a "reconstructed" Shinto, that is, Shinto as Norinaga imagined it to have been in primordially distant times and as he understood it from his reading of the *Kojiki* and other ancient liturgical works. Furthermore, it is evident that, more than any other major eighteenth-century nativist, Norinaga demanded faith from his students of the Way: faith in the rectifying and healing power of the god Naobi, faith in the sacred authority of divine emperors and their terrestrial delegates, faith in the context of one's trust in the beneficent determinism of the native gods, and so on. In order to give expression to and reinforcement of this faith, Norinaga prescribed a sequence of daily religious observances in an undated work titled *An Order for Morning Worship (Maiasa haishin shiki)*. In it, he described a precise order for morning devotions to twenty deities, beginning with Amaterasu while facing east by southeast and proceeding counter-clockwise until one concludes worship with obeissance for the local tutelary mountain deity, Yama.

It is not known when Norinaga began the daily devotions outlined in *An Order for Morning Worship,* but it is clear that, throughout his life, he also maintained the religious practices of the Buddhist Pure Land denomination with which he had been raised. Furthermore, despite his insistence that all persons proceed to Yomi upon the death of the physical body and despite his condemnation of exces-

---

[67] This historiographic error may derive from a misunderstanding of the title of Satow's otherwise excellent pioneering study, "The Revival of Pure Shin-tau," in *Transactions of the Asiatic Society of Japan*. See above, p. 79n.

[68] See my "Masuho Zankō (1655–1742): A Shinto Popularizer between Nativism and National Learning," in *Confucianism and Tokugawa Culture.*

sive attention to one's funeral arrangements,[69] Norinaga appears to have been almost obsessively concerned with the arrangements for his own somewhat bizarre funeral. In his will, Norinaga specified that his funeral be conducted according to Buddhist custom, with a standard service at his family temple, the Jukyōji; he also insisted, however, that his actual remains be secretly interred at a different Pure Land temple, the Myōrakuji, several miles south of Matsusaka. These requests perplexed both the local magistrate in Matsusaka and Norinaga's adopted son and successor, Motoori Ōhira (1756–1833), and their implications for the analysis of Norinaga's personal faith elude convincing resolution. Since there is no way to reconcile Norinaga's practice of Buddhism with the counsel on the ancient Way he provided his followers, one can only conclude that, if he was not actually something of a hypocrite, then at least, on a personal level, Norinaga saw no contradiction in maintaining two different modes of religious piety.[70]

Norinaga died on the 29th day of the 9th month of 1801. In a letter written one month before his death, he observed that "the study of the ancient Way has spread virtually throughout Japan today. In the west, there are a number of followers in Nagasaki and Higo. In the east, there are some in Nanbu. . . . It has also spread to the other provinces."[71] This positive assessment was consistent with the stepped-up pace of lectures and political associations that Norinaga maintained during the last decade and a half of his life. On the evening of the 13th day of the 9th month, just five days before he contracted the disease that claimed his life, Norinaga attended a final gathering to read Waka at the home of Motoori Ōhira. After the gathering, he was escorted home by Hattori Nakatsune (1756–1824), one of his students who concentrated on the study of the ancient Way. During the walk, Nakatsune is reported to have told his teacher of his desire to enter more deeply into the study of

---

[69] *Tamakatsuma*, in MNZ, I, 126–127.
[70] Shigeru Matsumoto has written a thorough discussion of Norinaga's funeral and its possible implications for an understanding of Norinaga's thought in his *Motoori Norinaga*, pp. 166–176.
[71] Quoted in Shigeru Matsumoto, *Motoori Norinaga, 1730–1801*, p. 136.

verse, but Norinaga is said to have objected on the grounds that the Suzunoya was full of students who wished to study literature and poetics, yet not one inclined toward the study of the Way.[72] If that conversation actually occurred, it is ironic, since Nakatsune's writings are known to have influenced the ancient Way cosmology of Hirata Atsutane (1776–1843), who, more than any other Tokugawa nativist, succeeded in reaching a wide audience through his preaching of the ancient Way.

After Norinaga's death, his school did, in fact, become more narrowly focused on the study of literature and poetics. The school's leaders—Motoori Ōhira, whom Norinaga adopted in 1799, and Motoori Haruniwa (1763–1828), Norinaga's gifted first-born son who went blind in 1794—were more interested in literary and philogical pursuits than in their father's researches on the ancient Way. One posthumous student, Ban Nobutomo (1775–1846), wrote extensively on shrine history, ancient court ceremonial, and other antiquarian topics peripherally related to the study of the Way. Nobutomo met Hirata Atsutane, another posthumous student, and the two became close friends from 1805 until 1819, when Nobutomo was angered by Atsutane's quotation in his *Koshi chō* (The meaning of ancient history) of material Nobutomo himself had not yet made public.[73]

---

[72] According to Hirata Atsutane's *Tamadasuki*, in Muromatsu Iwao, et al., eds., *Hirata Atsutane zenshū*, IV, 382. The story is said to have been recorded but kept confidential by Nakatsune until he related it in 1823 to Hirata Atsutane upon the occasion of their first meeting. The story may be apocryphal, since Atsutane had a vested interest in proclaiming himself to be the heir to Norinaga's teachings on the Way—because Atsutane and Norinaga never actually met, Atustane's claims in this regard were strengthened by the suggestion of a measure of despair on the part of Norinaga concerning the alleged absence of an heir to these teachings.

[73] See Tahara Tsuguo, *Hirata Atsutane*, pp. 278–286. Atsutane's publication of the same work in 1829 so incensed Ban Nobutomo that thereafter relations between them were bitter.

EIGHT

Conclusions

The ideological nativism of the eighteenth century known as National Learning took root in highly fertile cultural soil. A number of factors— increased literacy and urbanization, surplus wealth distributed more broadly among a variety of social classes, the development of communications technology and infrastructure, and an attitude of cultural liberality in an otherwise illiberal political environment—contributed to a remarkable outburst of popular cultural activity in the late-seventeenth century. One part of this activity was the rise of the popular private academy. The Confucians, in particular those of the heterodox schools, pioneered this development, which provided vocational advantage to those of the samurai class and the trappings of culture for the ascendant merchants. Since this kind of academy required neither the independent wealth of the educator nor his financial subsidy by a wealthy patron, it marked the rise of a new relationship between academician and student, a relationship analagous to that between the producers and consumers of other varieties of the richly textured popular culture of the Genroku years. The major eighteenth-century *kokugakusha* welcomed and recruited private students, but they also sought, with varying levels of success, to elicit at least the interest if not the financial support of national and domainal elites for their endeavors.

National Learning also represents both a reaction against Confucianism and a focused redefinition of the broader concerns of seventeenth-century nativist activities. In their reaction against Con-

fucianism, the major *kokugakusha* adhered to a number of assumptions
characteristic of their Confucian brethren. They agreed with orthodox Neo-Confucians that the Japanese possessed, at the moment of
their birth, an inherent propensity for goodness which, though obscured or made dormant, was ultimately recoverable. With the Ancient Learning school, they shared the methodological conviction
that ancient truths of contemporary relevance might be gleaned in
their purest form from ancient texts through the application of philological, linguistic, and textual analysis. They agreed with Ogyū
Sorai that the sages were just men and that their Way was a product
of human ingenuity constructed to remedy specific ills. Like most
contemporary schools of Confucianism in Japan, the nativists af-
firmed the validity and value of the emotional and affective realms
of human experience. And, like all Confucians, the major National
Learning figures taught that there had once been an ideal age in the
remote past, and that this age served the needs of the present as a
repository of value, example, and moral lesson.

   Numerous aspects of nativist scholarship in the seventeenth century reappear in altered guise in the ideological nativism of the
eighteenth century. Seventeenth-century Shinto studies began with
attempts to reconcile and update Shinto theology with the assumptions and vocabulary of Neo-Confucianism, and they ended with
efforts to extricate Shinto teachings from those same syncretic formulations, an effort that heralded National Learning's quest for an
unadulterated native ancient Way. Seventeenth-century literary
criticism and poetics in Japan featured a marked revival of interest
in the traditional genre of the Waka, attempts to freshen contemporary verse by incorporating more ancient stylistic elements, a renewed fascination with the *Man'yōshū,* an initial rejection followed
by an eventual embracement of the possible normative value in the
study of literature and verse, and a general popularization of literary
and poetic activity. In addition, the outburst of historical writing
in the seventeenth century, an activity representative of the convergence at that time of Confucian and nativist scholarly ideals, reflected in domesticated form the ethnocentrism characteristic of
Chinese historiography and reinforced eighteenth-century National

Learning's conviction that the past was linked to the present through natural principles or a Way that made the past accessible.

Keichū and Kada no Azumamaro were key figures in the eventual disassociation of nativism from Confucianism and its establishment as an independent field of scholarly inquiry and endeavor, and the major *kokugakusha* of the second-half of the eighteenth century regarded them as the founders of their studies. Keichū's career as a Shingon Buddhist priest in the service of Tokugawa Mitsukuni, daimyo of Mito and the most important patron of scholarship in his age, and his production in that service of a full commentary on the *Man'yōshū* are representative of the subsumption during the seventeenth century of nativist studies within a singular scholarly discourse whose boundaries and contours were defined by Confucians, if not by Confucianism. Conversely, Keichū's conclusions concerning Japan's high antiquity betray the traces of an initial rupture between Confucian and nativist ideals, a fissure that had emerged at a time when China no longer commanded in Japan the allure or respect that had long been its apparent prerogative. Keichū did not depict the divine age in the idealized terms characteristic of eighteenth-century National Learning, but he did portray its features in a manner consistent with the views and perspectives of the later major *kokugakusha*: He regarded the divine age as a simple, naive, and unlettered age infused with a Way people later knew as Shinto; he alluded to the disruption of this guileless simplicity by the introduction from abroad of Buddhist and Confucian doctrines; he attributed to ancient Shinto qualities that made it sufficient for all social needs, including that of governing man; and he asserted that the legacy of this Way was a tradition in Japan of giving priority to the sacred over the temporal. Keichū's nativist successors, in fact, found nothing in this or in him with which to quarrel, with the singular exception of his calling as a Buddhist priest.

The service of the Kada as hereditary wardens of the Shinto Inari Shrine made Azumamaro in some ways a more appropriate candidate as the first of National Learning's so-called "great men." Throughout his adult life, he solicited the support of what he promoted as the new field of National Learning, and he defined this field in terms of an adversarial relationship with the Confucianism with which nativism had coexisted so comfortably during the preceding century. Azumamaro also articulated a number of postures and themes which reverberate in the writings of the later major *kokugakusha*. He asserted the intrinsic moral and political superiority of the Japanese polity over that of "other lands" like China. He justified this stance by asserting that it was inconceivable in Japan that human force could prevail against the divine government of the imperial institution and its delegates, and he criticized countries whose history reveals the violent seizure of power to be a commonplace occurrence. He attributed the stability of the Japanese polity to the influence of its native Way of Shinto. And he criticized Confucianism and Buddhism as rampant and dangerous false doctrines, implying that, unless their teachings were resisted in a resolute and determined manner, Japan's privileged position in relation to China might itself be threatened. In addition to Azumamaro's vigorous promotion of National Learning, the presence of these themes in his writings justifies a regard for him as the first major eighteenth-century *kokugakusha*. The primary "shortcoming" of Azumamaro from the perspectives of his eighteenth-century nativist successors was that, despite his professed intention to elicit an ancient Way from the analysis of the earliest Japanese texts, it is evident that he used this analysis principally to justify his preconceived theological assumptions, rooted for the most part in seventeenth-century Shinto thought.

Kamo no Mabuchi was thus the first major eighteenth-century nativist to utilize the philological examination of ancient texts in order to extract what he believed to be the spirit of an ancient Way, encoded within archaic and linguistically cryptic works. His preferred text was the *Man'yōshū,* and, in the verses of this most ancient of all extant Japanese poetry anthologies, he found his spirit of high antiquity. This quest for an ancient Way emerged from his love of verse: His fondness for poetry was evident during his early years in Hamamatsu; that fondness acquired an antiquarian orientation during his period of study under the tutelage of Azumamaro; then, during his years of service to Tayasu Munetake, his passion for verse came to be linked to a quest for the spirit of antiquity. It reached its most mature form during Mabuchi's final years as the self-styled "old man of the fields," when verse became his medium for transporting one back to the natural and premoral perfection of the ancient past.

Mabuchi's nostalgic perspectives on the past construed that era in near-paradisal terms. He depicted the past as a time when perfection in human behavior, government, and versification reigned in a mutually reinforcing, timeless, and seemingly uninterruptible manner. He described the age as distinguished by an overriding masculinity in which both men and women partook. He alleged that, in their dealings with each other, ancient people were straightforward and truthful, for their words and affairs were few and devoid of contention. He concluded that what he called the natural Way of heaven and earth coursed through and underlay all aspects of existence, manifesting itself within the individual in the form of a true heart. And he asserted that this individual element of perfection, enjoyed then as now as one's birthright, brought ancient man into harmony with birds and beasts, so that they together spontaneously conformed their behavior to the dictates of the natural order.

This idealized ancient condition was disrupted, according to Mabuchi, by the introduction from abroad of the "pernicious" doctrines of Confucianism which made men crafty and undermined their true hearts, with the eventual consequence of the loss of those virtues that supported the terrestrial harmony. Mabuchi contended that, by learning morality from humanly fabricated teachings, ancient man learned immorality and lost his grasp on the natural and spontaneous; he also maintained that this Fall from an ancient state of grace was not an event that had occurred once in the remote yet historical past, but rather a sequence repeated in each generation as successive Japanese acquired the alien crafty spirit of Confucianism, to the detriment of their true hearts. Mabuchi taught, however, that the true heart could be reanimated—that man might be "born again" as it were and the effects of his Fall reversed—through the apprehension of and immersion in the ancient spirit through the medium of the *Man'yōshū,* which served for him as that spirit's repository. He counseled the prospective fellow traveler in this quest to master and recite the verses of the ancient anthology in order to integrate their spirit into his own, and then to reactivate his true heart with all its attendant blessings.

Mabuchi also argued with vigor the case for Japan's superiority to China, using familiar arguments from the past as well as certain more recent lines of argument used by Azumamaro in support of this ideal. China had never been well governed, these arguments ran, because of the fundamental wickedness of its people. In order to check this wickedness, men of crafty wisdom invented doctrines to assist in the maintenance of public order. Called Confucianism, the very presence of these doctrines attested to their need. Japan, in contrast, had no such doctrines or teachings within its native tradition, since it had no need for them, its people being perfectly orderly and obedient as a result of their natural conformity to the Way of heaven and earth. Contrasting the "youthful" innocence and truthfulness of Japan with the "middle-aged" craftiness of China, Mabuchi concluded that Japan was, in every respect, superior to its enormous continental neighbor.

Despite the xenophobic chauvinism of such assertions, Mabuchi's ancient Way thought retained certain benignly enchanting qualities; perhaps the most outstanding feature of this thought was its originality. Our analysis of his thought has sought to situate it within its contemporary social context and to contextualize it in terms of quondam intellectual discourse, and so the various forms of his "ideological indebtedness" have been duly noted. Nonetheless, his cosmology of the ancient past and immediate present were remarkably different from any preceding and comparable formulations: This concept and depiction of the true heart, the idealized near-paradisiac past, Chinese responsibility for what we have termed the Fall, and the potential resurrection of ancient beatific qualities in the present all originated with Kamo no Mabuchi and, together with his assertions of Japanese superiority, figured prominently in the mainstream of later National Learning ancient Way thought. That Mabuchi achieved and sought to justify such formulations by his analysis of a poetry anthology, as opposed to such mytho-historical works as the *Kojiki* or *Nihon shoki*, further attests to the intuitive originality of his formulations, and the National Learning thought of decades to follow represents, in significant measure, the transformation and retransformation of concepts and themes first articulated by Mabuchi.

The twenty-five years between 1746, when Mabuchi entered the service of Tayasu Munetake, and 1771, when Motoori Norinaga completed *The Rectifying Spirit*, constitute the most significant period for the development of National Learning thought. During these years, philological method became central to National Learning, and the themes of the nostalgia for an idealized past and the assertion of Japanese priority over China came to represent the core of its ancient Way thought. We have seen how Norinaga refashioned much of this thought in the direction of the religious. Where Mabuchi's nostalgic quest devolved from his study of the *Man'yōshū*, Norinaga's centered on the more ancient and mythologically rich divine age chapters of the *Kojiki*, a shift that enabled Norinaga to approach his key text with the confident zeal and faith of a fundamentalist. For Mabuchi, the *Man'yōshū* was at best a source book of ancient values, and his cosmological formulations owed more to his imaginative reconstruction of an ancient spirit than to any single text. Norinaga, however, regarded the *Kojiki* as a True Book, a document with scriptural authority, and he sought, whenever possible, to ground his ancient Way thought in the work. This link between text and thought was, in fact, stronger in Norinaga than in any other major eighteenth-century nativist.

Norinaga's fundamentalism was just one of a number of aspects in which his ancient Way thought inclined toward the religious. Tetsuo Najita has described the ideological field of eighteenth-century Japanese thought in terms of a dialectic between "those who claimed that 'nature' was the ultimate source of knowledge and those who claimed 'history' was the source"[1] but, for Norinaga, the source of all such knowledge was the gods. He regarded the true

---

[1] Najita, *Visions of Virtue in Tokugawa Japan*, p. 10.

Way as neither man-made nor, strictly speaking, a "natural" Way, but rather as the divine Way of the gods fashioned by those deities responsible for the creation of the world at the primordial time of beginnings. He believed the *kami* were likewise responsible for all thought, word, and activity in the world, and that actions of the gods were not reducible to terms fully comprehensible to man's limited intellect. He regarded man's most fundamental responsibility to be his resignation to and acceptance of the dictates of the divine presence both within and about him, counseling that one abandon all attempts to influence one's own destiny through personal initiative or shrewd manipulation. And, in order to discipline those who inclined toward this faith, he even constructed a liturgy for daily personal or corporate worship. Furthermore, Norinaga sought through his study of the *Kojiki* to provide answers to certain ultimate questions Mabuchi had never raised. For example, ever faithful to the *Kojiki,* he formulated a comfortless eschatology according to which all proceeded to Yomi upon the death of the physical body. And, he attempted to account for the presence of evil in a world wholly determined by the wishes of the gods by attributing all manifestations of evil and wickedness to the god Magatsubi.

Where Mabuchi had regarded the true heart as a natural attribute of humankind, Norinaga regarded it as a genetic prerogative of being Japanese and thereby having been created by the Musubi deities. Where Mabuchi viewed the loss of one's true heart as a consequence of one's exposure to Chinese writings, Norinaga regarded it a process of defilement which involved, on the one hand, the acquisition of the Chinese heart as a result of one's exposure to Chinese ways of thinking and, on the other, the negation of those mysterious and wondrous qualities of life that Norinaga found so compelling. By losing one's true heart, according to Norinaga, one lost one's identification with and participation in a divine hierophany which extended vertically as far as Amaterasu and the Musubi gods. Like Mabuchi, Norinaga regarded these effects as reversible, but, where Mabuchi had counseled one to exert effort in the reading and recitation of ancient works like the *Man'yōshū,* Norinaga taught that human effort was of no avail and that one had to rely on the healing and rectifying power of the deity Naobi in order to exorcise the Chinese heart and to fortify and reanimate one's true heart. For Norinaga, the study of ancient texts and immersion in an ancient spirit—practices of paramount importance to Mabuchi—were no more than optional adjuncts in the nostalgic quest.

This same inclination toward the religious is evident in Norinaga's assertions of Japanese superiority. For Mabuchi, such assertions had been the expression of an ideality, but, for Norinaga, they acquired the vigor and force of a myth: Japan was superior because it was the primordial home of Amaterasu, the sun-goddess/sun, and the world thus owed gratitude to Japan for Amaterasu's radiant and life-sustaining warmth and sunshine; and, since all gods were believed to be Japanese gods, Japan ranked as the original ancestral country, a global progenitrix as it were, with the implication that the rest of the world's relationship to Japan should resemble that of children toward their parents.

Norinaga's expansion of the National Learning theme of Japanese superiority to include the entire world and not just the countries of Asia came at a remarkable time in Japanese history just prior to Japan's ineluctable entry into a larger orbit of nations with which Norinaga was at best only dimly familiar. Despite the mythic vigor of his ancient Way thought, however, it failed during his lifetime to command the belief of either a coherent legion of followers or even the complete conviction of Norinaga himself. However great Norinaga may have been as an explicator or teacher, the propagation of the ancient Way *as a contemporary religion* remained for those who were to assume the mantle of his religious thought, and, of these, the most important was Hirata Atsutane. Though the two never met, Atsutane, during the early decades of the nineteenth century, became the outstanding preacher of the major assumptions and themes of National Learning's ancient Way thought, but with a number of variations which captured the interest of an ever greater audience and demonstrated National Learning's somewhat belated entry into the arena of political thought.

One such symbolic variation concerns Norinaga's and Atsutane's respective liturgies for worship. It will be recalled that, in his *Order*

for Morning Worship (Maiasa haishin shiki), Norinaga recommended
that one begin by facing toward the Ise Shrines as the abode of
Amaterasu; by way of contrast, Atsutane specified, in his *Morning
Order for Worship (Maiasa shinhai shiki)* that one start by facing toward
the abode of the living god who dwelled in the imperial palace in
Kyoto.[2] In much the same way that the religious thought of National Learning was gradually acquiring the status of a contemporary religious movement, National Learning was about to shed its
fundamentally apolitical character and enter into the arena of political thought, with consequences which, in the nineteenth century,
spelled the end of much of the old order.

National Learning, however, was not alone in its contribution to
the political ideology of those activists who led the Meiji Restoration, and the transformations and permutations of National Learning's ancient Way thought in the complex matrix of restorationist
ideology reflected a number of ironies. For one thing, many of the
nativist assumptions concerning an ancient Way were fused with
those assumptions of duty and loyalty to one's sovereign which formed
the mainstream of Confucian thought in the early decades of the
nineteenth century. It will be recalled that it was the positing of an
adversarial relationship between nativism and Confucianism that
contributed to the emergence in the early eighteenth century of
National Learning as an independent mode of thought; conversely,
in the nineteenth century, it was the eventual reconvergence of
Confucian and nativist goals that provided the underpinnings for an
ideology of sufficient appeal to Japan's disgruntled elites to justify
the replacement of the Tokugawa bakufu with a new government
that claimed the imperial institution as its true head. Again, it will
be recalled that it was in Keichū's work on the *Man'yōshū*—scholarship sponsored in Mito by Tokugawa Mitsukuni, the greatest of
all Tokugawa-period patrons of scholarship—that we detected the
initial rupture of Confucianism and nativism, which had coexisted
harmoniously and with mutual benefit during most of the seven-

---

[2] *Maiasa shinhai shiki,* in Muromatsu Iwao, et al., eds., *Hirata Atsutane zenshū* IV, Ch1,
3.

tions of the major eighteenth-century nativists, like the "study of reality" attributed to Hirata Atsutane, were capable of enchanting the disenchanted and inspiring marvelous and heroic actions, but, when they ceased to be dreams—when the "study" of the myth was confused with the apprehension of "reality"—those myths became a most serious folly.

teenth century; however, it was the nineteenth-century reading of *The History of Great Japan,* which Mitsukuni had initiated, in which the imperial loyalists of Mito found justification for their devotion to the imperial institution, as well as their xenophobic regard for all things foreign, perspectives they reinforced through their understanding of National Learning teachings on the ancient Way. Furthermore, even the study in Japan of the secular learning of the West—a field initiated during the eighteenth century, which accelerated during the nineteenth—fostered not an admiration for the West, as one might expect, but rather an involuted contempt for foreign ways which thus melded neatly with the similar conclusions of the proponents of National Learning. It is in this sense only apparently ironic that as xenophobic a figure as Hirata Atsutane advised his students: "Even if you study foreign things, the primary focus of all paths of learning should be to select that which is good and to apply it to our country. It is perfectly correct to study foreign learning so long as you study with our country as your paramount concern."[3] His words have a peculiarly and almost deceptively familiar ring to them, since the relatively young group of men who became the technocratic and oligarchic rulers of Japan half a century later shared this view that foreign learning was vital so long as it benefited the construction of a "new" Japan destined to assume its "rightful" place in the first rank of the family of nations.

During the early decades of the twentieth century, a number of assumptions characteristic of the National Learning formulations of Mabuchi and Norinaga—in particular, those concerning the divinity and mission of the imperial institution, the existence of a pristine and unsullied age in the primordially distant past, and arguments concerning Japan's privileged position vis-à-vis the rest of the world—contributed to the formation of an ultranationalist state ideology which supported, with disastrous consequences, Japan's international excesses in the 1930s and early 1940s. Then, in the immediate aftermath of Japan's defeat in World War II, the discussion and even historical study of these themes became virtually ta-

[3] *Ibuki oroshi,* in *Hirata Atsutane zenshū,* I, Ch. 10, 4.

boo in both university circles and the popular culture. The mysti-
fication of Japan and the Japanese was recast domestically and
reproduced internationally during the 1950s and 1960s in the san-
itized terms of the "mysterious" ethnographic and racial origins of
the Japanese people, their "natural" inclination toward harmony
and consensus, the "elusive" and "eliptic" properties of their language and related "thought patterns," the "uniqueness" of their
culture, and similar themes.

In more recent times, this discussion has again been transformed,
though in more familiar, that is, traditional terms. During the 1970s,
when Japan's economic strength and international importance came
to be more fully recognized and appreciated both at home and abroad,
there emerged what in the 1980s was referred to variously in the
popular press as a "new" nationalism.[4] The once taboo subjects became no longer so, and it became possible, even fashionable, in the
popular press, to discuss such subjects as Japan's destiny and, in the
scholarly press, to recount the history of nativist-related topics.[5]
During these years, "memorial museums"—the contemporary
equivalent of what in the eighteenth century were called shrines—
were erected in Hamamatsu and Matsusaka to house the collected
memorabilia of Kamo no Mabuchi and Motoori Norinaga and have
even become prominent local tourist attractions as well as important
archival resources.

---

[4]See, for example, Ian Buruma's "A New Japanese Nationalism" in "The New York Times
Magazine," 12 April 1987; and the series of articles by Antonio Kamiya, Charles Whip-
ple, and Jonathan Lloyd-Owen under the cover story of "Nationalism: Is Japan Turning
to the Right?" *PHP Intersect: Where Japan Meets the World* 3.2 (February 1987).

[5]Tokugawa-period nativism during these decades became again a subject of serious scholarly enquiry; after almost vanishing during the period from 1946 through the early 1970s,
the number of published scholarly book-length studies of Tokugawa nativism and the
major nativists and the publication of collections of their writings returned during the
late-1970s and the 1980s to annual levels roughly identical to those of the 1930s. In the
popular press, articles like Ishii Takemochi's "The Japan Corridor, Cradle of Tomorrow's
Civilization," and Fukuda Tsuneari's and Saeki Shoichi's "The Betrayal of Japanese Culture" (both in *Japan Echo* 14:2 [summer 1987]) are not uncommon. Spanning the two is
a work like the celebrated critic Kobayashi Hideo's *Motoori Norinaga,* an extended medi-
tation on and study of Motoori Norinaga, which first appeared in serial form in 62 issues
of the monthly periodical *Shinchō* (October 1971 through December 1976) and was later
reprinted in book form (Shinchōsha, 1977).

Nostalgic themes remain conspicuous in the popular
manifestations of nativism in the 1980s. Two indications of
ular interest are called the *furusato buumu* (the renewed inte
periodic visits to what one identifies as one's traditional hom
the *Edo buumu* (a new interest in the culture and history
Tokugawa period). The *furusato buumu* represents that most o
manifestation of nostalgia in the form of homesickness, nos
for a condition from which one is removed spatially but not
porally; conversely, the Edo *buumu* represents a nostalgic orienta
toward that from which one is separated by the distance of time
not space. Taken individually, the *furusato buumu* suggests a n
talgic response to the anomie characteristic of life in the less p
sonal environment of urban Japan, while the *Edo buumu* may in
cate a renewed fascination with the native roots of Japan's moderni
in its "early modern" period; taken together, they confirm that no
talgia continues in the second half of the twentieth century as
major theme in the long and distinguished history of Japanese culture.

Like the nostalgic "booms" of Japan in the 1980s, those of the
eighteenth century existed alongside patriotic and ultimately nar-
cissistic articulations of a privileged position for Japan and its people. In 1823, Ikuta Yorozu (1801–1837), a student of Hirata Atsutane and, for a brief period, his adopted son, wrote: "Time and
again, our teacher, the great [Atsutane], lectured to us on the importance of 'the study of reality' (*jijitsugaku*). . . . Great learning
is, first of all, pondering feverishly over the ancient legends and
receiving the great Way; then all that one has learned must be
accepted as reality."[6] The inspiration generations of nativists drew
form the simple centuries-old equation of Japan with the land of
the gods remains in its variously reconstituted forms a potent force
in contemporary Japan, since the power of any myth lies in its
ability to motivate dreams and to harness aspirations in a manner
no mere history can replicate. As dreams, the nostalgic construc-

---

[6]From his *Manabi naobi,* quoted in Matsumoto Sannosuke, *Kokugaku seiji shisō no kenkyū,*
pp. 104–105.

Bibliography
Index

Bibliography

N.B. The place of publication for all Japanese-language works is Tokyo, unless otherwise indicated.

Abe Akio. "Keichū, Azumamaro, Mabuchi." In *Kinsei Shintōron zenki kokugaku.* Eds. Taira Shigemichi and Abe Akio. NST no. 39. Iwanami Shoten 1972.

Abe Yoshio. *Nihon Shushigaku to Chōsen.* Tōkyō Daigaku Shuppankai, 1965.

———. "Development of Neo-Confucianism in Japan, Korea and China: A Comparative Study," *Acta Asiatica* 19:16–39 (1970).

Akai Tatsurō. "Genrokuki no toshi seikatsu to minshu bunka." In *Iwanami kōza Nihon rekishi 10: kinsei 2.* Iwanami Shoten, 1975.

Arai Hakuseki. *Told Round a Brushwood Fire.* Tr. Joyce Ackroyd. Tokyo: University of Tokyo Press, 1979.

———. *Lessons from History: Arai Hakuseki's Tokushi Yoron.* Tr. Joyce Ackroyd. St. Lucia, London, and New York: University of Queensland Press, 1982.

Araki Yoshio. *Kamo no Mabuchi no hito to shisō.* Kōsei Kaku, 1943.

Arano Yasunori. "18 seiki no Higashi Ajia to Nihon." In Rekishigaku Kenkyūkai and Nihonshi Kenkyūkai, comps., *Kōza Nihon rekishi 6: kinsei 2.* Tōkyō Daigaku Shuppankai, 1985.

Asukai Masamichi. "Norinagateki kansei no seiritsu," *Bungaku* 41:1–15 (November 1973).

Bellah, Robert N. *Tokugawa Religion: The Values of Pre-industrial Japan.* Glencoe: Free Press, 1957.

Bitō Masahide. *Nihon hōken shisōshi keukyū.* Aoki Shoten, 1961.

———. "Andō Shōeki to Motoori Norinaga," *Bungaku* 36:8–20 (August 1968).

———. "Kōkoku shikan no seiritsu." In Sagara Tōru, Bitō Masahide, and Akiyama Ken, comps. *Kōza Nihon shisō 4: jikan.* Tōkyō Daigaku Shuppankai, 1984.

Bix, Herbert B. *Peasant Protest in Japan, 1590–1884.* New Haven: Yale University Press, 1986.

Bolitho, Harold. *Treasures among Men*. New Haven: Yale University Press, 1974.

Borgen, Robert. *Sugawara no Michizane and the Early Heian Court*. Cambridge: Council on East Asian Studies, Harvard University, 1986.

Brownlee, John S. "The Jeweled Comb-box: Motoori Norinaga's *Tamakushige*," *Monumenta Nipponica* 43.1:35−61 (1988).

Chamberlain, B. H. "Notes by Motoori on the Japanese and Chinese Art," *Transactions of the Asiatic Society of Japan* 12, Pt. 3: 221−229 (1883).

Chan, Wing-tsit, tr. and comp. *A Source Book in Chinese Philosophy*. Princeton: Princeton University Press, 1963.

Cooper, Michael, ed. *They Came to Japan: An Anthology of European Reports on Japan, 1543−1640*. Berkeley: University of California Press, 1965.

Craig, Albert M., and Donald H. Shively, eds. *Personality in Japanese History*. Berkeley and Los Angeles: University of California Press, 1970.

Creel, Herrlee G. *Chinese Thought from Confucius to Mao Tse-tung*. Chicago: University of Chicago Press, 1953.

deBary, Wm. Theodore. "Some Common Tendencies in Neo-Confucianism." In *Confucianism in Action*. Eds. David S. Nivison and Arthur Wright. Stanford: Stanford University Press, 1959.

──────, Wing-tsit Chan, and Burton Watson, comps. *Sources of Chinese Tradition*. New York: Columbia University Press, 1960.

Dore, Ronald P. *Education in Tokugawa Japan*. London: Routledge & Kegan Paul, 1965.

Dumoulin, Heinrich. "Motoori Norinaga," *Nippon*, 5.4:193−197 (1939).

──────. *Kamo Mabuchi (1697−1769): Ein Betrag zur japanischen Religions- und Geistesgeschichte*. Tokyo, 1943.

Earl, David Magarey. *Emperor and Nation in Japan: Political Thinkers of the Tokugawa Period*. Seattle: University of Washington Press, 1964.

Eliade, Mircea. *The Myth of the Eternal Return*. Tr. W. R. Trask. London: Routledge & Kegan Paul, 1955.

──────. *Myths, Dreams, and Mysteries*. Tr. P. Mairet. London: Fontana, 1968.

Elison, George. *Deus Destroyed*. Cambridge: Harvard University Press, 1973.

──────, and B. L. Smith, eds. *Warlords, Artists and Commoners: Japan in the Sixteenth Century*. Honolulu: University of Hawaii Press, 1981.

Endo Motoo. *Kinsei seikatsushi nenpyō*. Yuzankaku, 1982.

Frankel, Charles. "The Foundations of Liberalism," *Seminar Reports* 5:1 (1976). Columbia University Program of General Education in the Humanities.

French, Cal. *Shiba Kokan: Artist, Innovator, and Pioneer in the Westernization of Japan*. New York: Weatherhill, 1974.

Fujii Sadafumi. *Edo kokugaku tenseishi no kenkyū*. Yoshikawa Kōbunkan, 1987.

Fujita Tokutarō. *Motoori Norinaga to Hirata Atsutane*. Maruoka Shuppansha, 1943.

Gluck, Carol. *Japan's Modern Myths: Ideology in the Late Meiji Period*. Princeton: Princeton University Press, 1985.

Goodman, Grant. *Japan: The Dutch Experience*. London: The Athlone Press, 1986.

Haga Noboru. *Bakumatsu kokugaku no tenkai*. Hanawa Shobō, 1963.

――――. *Motoori Norinaga*. Sekai Shisōka Zensho, no. 12. Maki Shobō, 1965.

――――. *Motoori Norinaga*. Hito to Rekishi Shiriizu (Nihon), no. 22. Shimizu Shoin, 1972.

――――. *Kokugaku no hitobito――sono kōdō to shisō*. Nihonjin no Kōdō to Shisō, no. 42. Hyōronsha, 1975.

――――. *Bakumatsu kokugaku no kenkyū*. Kyōiku Shuppan Sentā, 1980.

Hall, John Whitney. *Tanuma Okitsugu (1719–1788): Forerunner of Modern Japan*. Cambridge: Harvard University Press, 1955.

――――. "The Confucian Teacher in Tokugawa Japan." In *Confucianism in Action*. Eds. David S. Nivison and Arthur Wright. Stanford: Stanford University Press, 1959.

――――. "The Castle Town and Japan's Modern Urbanization." In *Studies in the Institutional History of Early Modern Japan*. Eds. John W. Hall and Marius B. Jansen. Princeton: Princeton University Press, 1968.

――――, John Whitney Hall, Nagahara Keiji, and Kozo Yamamura, eds. *Japan Before Tokugawa: Political Control and Economic Growth, 1500–1650*. Princeton: Princeton University Press, 1981.

Hani Gorō. *Nihon ni okeru kindai shisō no zentei*. Iwanami Shoten, 1949.

Hanley, Susan B., and Kozo Yamamura, eds. *Economic and Demographic Change in Preindustrial Japan, 1600–1868*. Princeton: Princeton University Press, 1977.

Hardacre, Helen. "Creating State Shinto: The Great Promulgation Campaign," *Journal of Japanese Studies* 12.1:29–64 (Winter 1986).

Harootunian, H. D. *Toward Restoration: The Growth of Political Consciousness in Tokugawa Japan*. Berkeley and Los Angeles: University of California Press, 1970.

――――. "The Functions of China in Tokugawa Thought." In *The Chinese and the Japanese: Essays in Political and Cultural Interactions*. Ed. Akira Iriye. Princeton: Princeton University Press, 1980.

――――. *Things Seen and Unseen: Discourse and Ideology in Tokugawa Nativism*. Chicago: University of Chicago Press, 1988.

Hino Tatsuo. *Norinaga to Akinari*. Chikuma Shobō, 1984.

Hirano Kimihiro. "Kokugaku: kokugakusha ni okeru bungaku ishiki." In *Nihon bungakushi*. Ed. Iwanami Kōza. Iwanami Shoten, 1968. Vol. VIII

Hirata Atsutane zenshū. Ed. Muromatsu Iwao, et al. 15 vols. Itchidō Shoten, 1911–1918.

Hirata Atsutane zenshū. Ed. Ueda Mannen, et al. 10 vols. Naigai Shoseki, 1931–1934.

Hisamatsu Sen'ichi. *Keichū den. Keichū zenshū*. Osaka: Asahi Shinbunsha, 1927. Vol. IX.

――――. *Kokugaku: sono seiritsu to kokubungaku to no kankei*. Shibundō, 1941.

Hisamatsu Sen'ichi. *Keichū.* Jinbutsu Sōsho, no. 110. Yoshikawa Kōbunkan, 1963.

————, ed. *Motoori Norinaga shū.* Koten Nihon Bungaku Zenshū, no. 34. Chikuma Shobō, 1967.

————. *Biographical Dictionary of Japanese Literature.* Tokyo, New York, & San Francisco: Kodansha International, 1976.

Idemaru Tsuneo. *Norinaga no seishun: Kyōto ryūgaku jidai.* Matsusaka: Hikari Shobō, 1977.

————. *Norinaga no botsugo: sono chinkonka.* Matsusaka: Hikari Shobō, 1980.

Ihara Saikaku. *Some Final Words of Advice.* Tr. Peter Nosco. Rutland and Tokyo: Charles E. Tuttle, 1980.

Inoue Minoru. *Kamo no Mabuchi no gakumon.* Yagi Shoten, 1944.

Inoue Tetsujirō. *Nihon kogakuha no tetsugaku.* Fuzanbō, 1931.

Ishida Ichirō, and Kanaya Osamu, eds. *Fujiwara Seika, Hayashi Razan.* NST, no. 28. Iwanami Shoten, 1975.

Ishikawa Jun, comp. *Motoori Norinaga.* Nihon no Meicho, no. 21. Chūō Kōronsha, 1984.

Itō Tasaburō. *Kokugaku no shiteki kōsatsu.* Ōokayama Shoten, 1932.

————. *Sōmō no kokugaku.* Masako Shobō, 1966.

Izumo Fudoki. Tr. Michiko Yamaguchi Aoki. Tokyo: Sophia University, 1971.

Janetta, Ann Bowman. *Epidemics and Mortality in Early Modern Japan.* Princeton: Princeton University Press, 1987.

Jien. *The Future and the Past.* Tr. Delmer Brown and Ishida Ichiro. Berkeley: University of California Press, 1979.

Jōfuku Isamu. *Motoori Norinaga.* Jinbutsu Sōsho, no. 179. Yoshikawa Kōbunkan, 1980.

Johnson, David, Andrew Nathan, and Evelyn S. Rawski, eds. *Popular Culture in Late Imperial China.* Berkeley: University of California Press, 1985.

Jung, C. G. *Psychology and Religion.* New Haven: Yale University Press, 1971.

Kada zenshū. 7 vols. Yoshikawa Kōbunkan, 1928–1938.

Katanuma Seiji. *Jugaku to kokugaku: "shōtō" to "itan" to no seiseiteki kōsatsu.* Ōfūsha, 1984.

Kato, Shuichi. *A History of Japanese Literature: The First Thousand Years.* Tokyo, New York, and San Francisco: Kodansha International, 1983.

————. *A History of Japanese Literature: The Years of Isolation.* Tokyo, New York and San Francisco: Kodansha International, 1983.

————. *Tominaga Nakamoto, A Tokugawa Iconoclast.* Vancouver: University of British Columbia Reprint Series, n.d.

Keene, Donald. *The Japanese Discovery of Europe, 1720–1830.* Rev. ed. Stanford: Stanford University Press, 1969.

————. *World Within Walls: Japanese Literature of the Pre-Modern Era, 1600–1867.* New York: Holt, Rinehart and Winston, 1976.

————. "Characteristic Responses to Confucianism in Tokugawa Literature." In

Confucianism and Tokugawa Culture. Ed. Peter Nosco. Princeton: Princeton University Press, 1984.

Keichū zenshū. Ed. Hisamatsu Sen'ichi, et al. 9 vols. Osaka: Asahi Shinbunsha, 1926–1927.

Kitaoka Shirō. *Kinsei kokugakusha no kenkyū.* Ise: Ko Kitaoka Shirō Kyōju Ikoshu Kankōkai, 1977.

Kiyohara Sadao. *Kokugaku hattatsushi.* Kokusho Kankōkai, 1981.

KKMZ:SH. See *Kōhon Kamo no Mabuchi zenshū: shisō hen.*

Kobayashi Hideo. *Motoori Norinaga.* Shinchōsha, 1977.

Kōhon Kamo no Mabuchi zenshū: shisō hen. 2 vols. Comp. Yamamoto Yutaka. Kōbundō, 1942.

Kokugakusha denki shūsei. Eds. Ogawa Shigeo and Minami Shigeki. 3 vols. Kunimoto Shuppansha, 1934–1936.

Kōno Shōzō. "Kannagara no Michi." *Monumenta Nipponica,* 3 (1940).

———, ed. *Kokugaku no kenkyū.* Ōokayama Shoten, 1932.

Kojiki. Tr. Donald L. Philippi. Princeton: Princeton University Press, 1969.

Koschmann, J. Victor. *The Mito Ideology: Discourse, Reform and Insurrection in Late Tokugawa Japan, 1790–1864.* Berkeley: University of California Press, 1987.

Koyasu Nobukuni. *Norinaga to Atsutane no sekai.* Chūō Kōronsha, 1977.

KSRZK. See Taira, ed., *Kinsei Shintōron, zenki kokugaku.*

Kuno Kyuemon. *Motoori Norinaga.* Hikari Shobō, 1980.

Kuwabara Takeo, ed. *Arai Hakuseki shū.* Nihon no Shisō, no. 13. Chikuma Shobō, 1970.

Kuwano Keiji. "Kokugaku, Waka, shizen." In Sagara Tōru, Bitō Masahide, and Akiyama Ken, comps. *Kōza Nihon shisō 1: shizen.* Tōkyō Daigaku Shuppankai, 1983.

KZ. See *Kada zenshū.*

Levin, Harry. *The Myth of the Golden Age in the Renaissance.* New York: Oxford University Press, 1969.

Levy, Ian Hideo. *Hitomaro and the Birth of Japanese Lyricism.* Princeton: Princeton University Press, 1984.

Lidin, Olaf G. *The Life of Ogyū Sorai, a Tokugawa Confucian Philosopher.* Lund: Scandinavian Institute of Asian Studies, 1973.

Lowenthal, David. *The Past Is a Foreign Country.* Cambridge: Cambridge University Press, 1985.

Manuel, Frank E. and Fritzie P. *Utopian Thought in the Western World.* Cambridge: The Belknap Press of Harvard University Press, 1979.

Manyōshū. Tr. Japan Society for the Promotion of Scientific Research. New York: Columbia University Press, 1969.

Maruyama Masao, ed. *Rekishi shisō shū.* Nihon no Shisō, no. 6. Chikuma Shobō, 1972.

Maruyama Masao. *Studies in the Intellectual History of Tokugawa Japan.* Tr. Mikiso Hane. Tokyo: University of Tokyo Press, 1974.

Maruyama Sueo. *Kokugakushijō no hitobito.* Yoshikawa Kōbunkan, 1979.

———. *Kokugakusha zatsukō.* 2 vols. Yoshikawa Kōbunkan, 1982.

Matsumoto Sannosuke. *Kokugaku seiji shisō no kenkyū.* Miraisha, 1972.

——— and Ogura Yoshihiko. *Kinsei shiron shū. NST,* no. 48. Iwanami Shoten, 1974.

Matsumoto, Shigeru. *Motoori Norinaga, 1730–1801.* Cambridge: Harvard University Press, 1970.

———. *Motoori Norinaga no shisō to shinri: aidentitei tankyū no kiseki.* Tōkyō Daigaku Shuppankai, 1981.

McClain, James. *Kanazawa: A Seventeenth-Century Japanese Castle Town.* New Haven: Yale University Press, 1982.

McEwen, J. R. *The Political Writings of Ogyū Sorai.* Cambridge: Cambridge University Press, 1962.

McLuhan, Marshal. *Understanding Media.* New York: New American Library, 1973.

Miki Shōtarō. *Hirata Atsutane no kenkyū.* Kyoto: Shintōshi Gakkai, 1969.

Miller, Roy Andrew. *The Japanese Language.* Chicago: University of Chicago Press, 1967.

Mills, Douglas E. *A Collection of Tales from Uji: A Study and Translation of Uji shūi monogatari.* Cambridge: Cambridge University Press, 1970.

Miyajima Katsuichi. *Norinaga no tetsugaku.* Kōzan Shoin, 1943.

Miyake Kiyoshi. *Kada no Azumamaro.* Unebi Shobō, 1942.

Miyake Yasutaka. *Kokugaku no undō.* Fūkan Shobō, 1966.

MNZ. See *Motoori Norinaga zenshū.*

Morris, Ivan. *The Nobility of Failure: Tragic Heroes in The History of Japan.* New York: Holt, Rinehart & Winston, 1975.

Motoori Norinaga. *Tamakatsuma.* Ed. Muraoka Tsunetsugu. 2 vols. Iwanami Shoten, 1934.

Motoori Norinaga zenshū. Comps. Ōno Susumu and Ōkubo Tadashi. 20 vols. Chikuma Shobō, 1968–1975.

Motoyama Yukihiko. *Motoori Norinaga.* Hito to Shisō, no. 47. Shimizu Shoin, 1978.

Muraoka Tsunetsugu. *Motoori Norinaga.* Iwanami Shoten, 1928.

———. *Nihon shisōshi kenkyū.* 4 vols. Iwanami Shoten, 1930–1939.

———. *Norinaga to Atsutane.* Sōbunsha, 1957.

———. *Studies in Shinto Thought.* Tr. Delmer M. Brown and James T. Araki. Tokyo: Japanese National Conference for UNESCO, 1964.

Najita, Tetsuo. *Visions of Virtue in Tokugawa Japan: The Kaitokudō Merchant Academy of Osaka.* Chicago: University of Chicago Press, 1987.

———— and Irwin Scheiner, eds. *Japanese Thought in the Tokugawa Period, 1600–1868: Methods and Metaphors.* Chicago: University of Chicago Press, 1978.

Nakagawa Tadamoto. *Motoori Norinaga to Genji monogatari.* Ise no Fūdō to Bungaku, no. 2. Ise, 1978.

Nakai, Kate Wildman. "The Naturalization of Confucianism in Tokugawa Japan: The Problem of Sinocentrism," *Harvard Journal of Asiatic Studies* 40.1:157–199 (1980).

————. "Tokugawa Confucian Historiography: The Hayashi, Early Mito School, and Arai Hakuseki." In *Confucianism and Tokugawa Culture.* Ed. Peter Nosco. Princeton: Princeton University Press, 1984.

————. *Shogunal Politics: Arai Hakuseki and the Premises of Tokugawa Rule.* Cambridge: Council on East Asian Studies, Harvard University, 1988.

Nakamura Yukihiko, ed. *Kinsei bungakuron shū.* Nihon Koten Bungaku Taikei, no. 94. Iwanami Shoten, 1966.

Nihon rinri ihen. Comps. Inoue Tetsujirō and Kanie Yoshimaru. 10 vols. Ikuseikai, 1901–1903.

Nihongi: Chronicles of Japan from the Earliest Times to A.D. 697. Tr. W. G. Aston. Rutland and Tokyo: Charles E. Tuttle, 1972.

Nishimura, Sey. "First Steps into the Mountains: Motoori Norinaga's *Uiyamabumi*," *Monumenta Nipponica* 42.4:449–493 (1987).

Noguchi Takehiko. "Motoori Norinaga ni okeru shigo to kogo," *Bungaku* 38:59–74 (April 1970).

Nomura Hachiro. *Kokugaku zenshi.* 2 vols. Seki Shoin, 1928–1929.

Nosco, Peter. "Keichū (1640–1701): Forerunner of National Learning," *Asian Thought & Society: An International Review* 5:237–252 (1980).

————. "Nature, Invention, and National Learning: The *Kokka hachiron* Controversy, 1742–46," *Harvard Journal of Asiatic Studies* 41.1:75–91 (1981).

————. "*Man'yōshū* Studies in Tokugawa Japan," *Transactions of the Asiatic Society of Japan,* 4th series, 1:109–146 (1986).

————. "The Requisites for Popular Culture in Genroku Japan," *The Occasional Papers of the Virginia Consortium of Asian Studies* 4:68–127 (1987).

————, ed. *Confucianism and Tokugawa Culture.* Princeton: Princeton University Press, 1984.

Nozaki Morihide. *Motoori Norinaga no sekai.* Hanawa Shobō, 1972.

————. *Norinaga to Kobayashi Hideo.* Meicho Kankōkai, 1982.

————. "Motoori Norinaga no uchi ni sumu rekishi no katachi." In Sagara Toru, Bitō Masahide, and Akiyama Ken, comps. *Kōza Nihon shisō 4: jikan.* Tōkyō Daigaku Shuppankai, 1984.

Nunn, G. Raymond. "On the Number of Books Published in Japan from 1600 to 1868." *Asian Studies at Hawaii.* East Asian Occasional Papers, no. 1 (1969).

Ogura Kishi. *Motoori Norinaga no hito oyobi shisō.* Daidō Shoten, 1934.

Ogyū Sorai. *Bendō*. Tr. Olaf G. Lidin. Tokyo: Monumenta Nipponica Monographs, 1971.

Ōishi Arata. *Kamo no Mabuchi*. Yanagihara Shoten, 1942.

Ōkubo Tadashi. *Edo jidai no kokugaku*. Shibundō, 1963.

Ooms, Herman. *Charismatic Bureaucrat: A Political Biography of Matsudaira Sadanobu, 1758–1829*. Chicago: University of Chicago Press, 1975.

————. "Neo-Confucianism and the Formation of Early Tokugawa Ideology: Contours of a Problem." In *Confucianism and Tokugawa Culture*. Ed. Peter Nosco. Princeton: Princeton University Press, 1984.

————. *Tokugawa Ideology: Early Constructs, 1570–1680*. Princeton: Princeton University Press, 1985.

Otto, Rudolph. *The Idea of the Holy*. Tr. J. W. Harvey. Oxford: Oxford University Press, 1923.

Ōyama Tadashi. *Kamo no Mabuchi den*. Shunjūsha, 1938.

Philippi, Donald L., tr. *Norito: A New Translation of Ancient Japanese Ritual Prayers*. Tokyo, 1959.

Plath, David William, ed. *Aware of Utopia*. Urbana: University of Illinois Press, 1971.

Pollack, David. *The Fracture of Meaning: Japan's Synthesis of China from the Eighth through the Eighteenth Centuries*. Princeton: Princeton University Press, 1986.

Prasad, Sajja A. *The Japanologists: A History*. Andhra Pradesh: Samudraiah Prakashan, 1984.

Roberts, John G. *Mitsui: Three Centuries of Japanese Business*. New York: Weatherhill, 1973.

Rozman, Gilbert. *Urban Networks in Ch'ing China and Tokugawa Japan*. Princeton: Princeton University Press, 1973.

Rubinger, Richard. *Private Academies of Tokugawa Japan*. Princeton: Princeton University Press, 1982.

Sagara Tōru. *Motoori Norinaga*. Tōkyō Daigaku Shuppankai, 1978.

————. *Hirata Atsutane*. Nihon no Meicho, no. 24. Chūō Kōronsha, 1984.

Saigō Nobutsuna. *Kokugaku no hihan*. Miraisha, 1965.

Saigusa Yasutaka. *Kamo no Mabuchi*. Jinbutsu Sōsho, no. 93. Yoshikawa Kōbunkan, 1962.

————. *Kokugaku no undō*. Fūkan Shobō, 1966.

Sampson, George. *The Concise Cambridge History of English Literature*. 3rd ed. Cambridge: Cambridge University Press, 1970.

Sano Masami. *Kinsei kokugaku shinshiryō shūkai*. Kyoto: Sanwa Shobō, 1972.

————. *Kokugaku to rangaku*. Yūzankaku, 1973.

Sansom, George B. *A History of Japan, 3* vols. Stanford: Stanford University Press, 1958–1963.

Sasaki Nobutsuna. *Zōtei Kamo no Mabuchi to Motoori Norinaga*. Yugawa Kōbunsha, 1935.

Sasazuki Kiyomi. *Motoori Norinaga no kenkyū.* Iwanami Shoten, 1944.

Satow Ernest. "The Revival of Pure Shin-tau," *Transactions of the Asiatic Society of Japan,* Reprints, no. 2 (1927).

Sheldon, Charles D. *The Rise of the Merchant Class in Tokugawa Japan, 1600–1868.* Locust Valley: J. J. Augustin, 1958.

Shigematsu Nobuhiro. *Kinsei kokugaku no bungaku kenkyū.* Fūkan Shobō, 1974.

Shively, Donald H. *"Bakufu* versus *Kabuki."* In *Studies in the Institutional History of Early Modern Japan.* Eds. John W. Hall and Marius B. Jansen. Princeton: Princeton University Press, 1968.

Smith, Thomas C. *The Agrarian Origins of Modern Japan.* Stanford: Stanford University Press, 1959.

Spae, Joseph John. *Itō Jinsai: A Philosopher, Educator and Sinologist of the Tokugawa Period.* New York: Paragon Reprints, 1967.

Suzuki Jun. "Motoori Norinaga den no seiritsu," *Bungaku* 55:21–39 (January 1987).

Tahara Tsuguo. *Hirata Atsutane.* Jinbutsu Sōsho, no. 111. Yoshikawa Kōbunkan, 1963.

———. *Motoori Norinaga.* Kōdansha Gendai Shinsho, 1968.

———, et al., eds. *Hirata Atsutane, Ban Nobutomo, Ōkuni Takamasa.* NST, no. 50. Iwanami Shoten, 1973.

Taira Shigemichi and Abe Akio, eds. *Kinsei Shintōron, zenki kokugaku.* NST, no. 39. Iwanami Shoten, 1972.

Takada Mamoru. "Norinaga to Akinari," *Bungaku* 36:21–30 (August 1968).

Takeda Yukichi, ed. *Norito.* Nihon Koten Bungaku Taikei, no. 1. Iwanami Shoten, 1958.

Takeoka Katsuya. *Kinseishi no hatten to kokugakusha no undō.* Shibundō, 1927.

———. "Kokugakusha to shite no Masuho Zankō no chii," *Shien* 3 (December 1931).

Terada Yasumasa. *Kamo no Mabuchi—shōgai to gyōseki.* Hamamatsu: Hamamatsu Shiseki Chōsa Kenshokai, 1979.

Toby, Ronald P. *State and Diplomacy in Early Modern Japan: Asia in the Development of the Tokugawa Bakufu.* Princeton: Princeton University Press, 1984.

Totman, Conrad D. *Politics in the Tokugawa Bakufu.* Cambridge: Harvard University Press, 1967.

Tsunoda, Ryusaku, Wm. Theodore de Bary, and Donald Keene, comps. *Sources of Japanese Tradition.* 2 vols. New York: Columbia University Press, 1964.

Tyler, Royall. "The Tokugawa Peace and Popular Religion: Suzuki Shōsan, Kakugyō Tōbutsu, and Jikigyō Miroku." In *Confucianism and Tokugawa Culture.* Ed. Peter Nosco. Princeton: Princeton University Press, 1984.

Uchida, Asahi. "Sugiura Kuniakira no shōgai." In *Kokugakusha kenkyū.* Hokkai Shuppansha, 1942.

Uchino Gorō. *Edoha kokugaku ronkō.* Sōrinsha, 1979.

Ueda, Kenji. "The Idea of 'Restoration' in the Thought of the Kokugaku School," *Philosophical Studies of Japan,* no. 11 (1975). Japan Society for the Promotion of Science.

————. "Kada no Azumamaro no shingaku," *Kokugakuin zasshi* 80.12:1–12 (December 1979); 81.1:131–147 (January 1980); 81.2:54–67 (February 1980).

Uete Michinari. "Edo jidai no rekishi ishiki." In *Rekishi shisō shu.* Ed. Maruyama Masao. Nihon no Shisō, no. 6. Chikuma Shobō, 1972.

Umeya Fumio. "Kokugaku ni okeru gakumonteki jikaku." In *Kōza Nihon shisō 2: chisei.* Eds. Sagara Tōru., Bitō Masahide, and Akiyama Ken. Tōkyō Daigaku Shuppankai, 1983.

Vaporis, Constantine N. "Post Stations and Assisting Villages: Corvee Labor and Peasant Contention," *Monumenta Nipponica* 41.4:377–415 (1986).

Vlastos, Stephen. *Peasant Protests and Uprisings in Tokugawa Japan.* Berkeley: University of California Press, 1986.

Wakabayashi, Bob Tadashi. *Anti-Foreignism and Western Learning in Early-Modern Japan: The* New Theses *of 1825.* Cambridge: Council of East Asian Studies, Harvard University, 1986.

Walthall, Anne. *Social Protest and Popular Culture in Eighteenth-Century Japan.* Association for Asian Studies Monograph, no. 43. Tucson: University of Arizona Press, 1986.

Watanabe Hiroshi. *"Michi* to *miyabi*—Norinagagaku to *kagakuha* kokugaku no seiji shisōshiteki kenkyū," *Kokka Gakkai Zasshi* 87:477–561, 647–721 (1974); 88:238–68, 295–366 (1975).

————. *Kinsei Nihon shakai to Sōgaku.* Tōkyō Daigaku Shuppankai, 1985.

Watt, Ian. *The Rise of the Novel.* Berkeley: University of California Press, 1957.

Webb, Herschel. *The Japanese Imperial Institution in the Tokugawa Period.* New York: Columbia University Press, 1968.

Wills, John E., Jr. "The Waters Red with Blood: Maritime China in Japanese Perspective, 1550–1700." Unpublished conference paper.

Yamada Kanzō. *Motoori Norinaga ō zenden.* Shikai Shobō, 1938.

————. *Motoori Haruniwa.* Matsusaka: Motoori Norinaga Kinenkan, 1983.

Yamada Yoshio. *Kokugaku no hongi.* Unebi Shobō, 1942.

Yamamoto Kasho. *Kamo no Mabuchi ron.* Kyoto: Shoin Shobō, 1963.

Yamamoto Yutaka. See *Kōhon Kamo no Mabuchi zenshū.*

Yamashita, Samuel Hideo. "The Early Life and Thought of Itō Jinsai," *Harvard Journal of Asiatic Studies* 43.2:453–480 (1983).

Yanase Kazuo. *Motoori Norinaga to sono monryū.* Osaka: Izumi Hensho, 1982.

Yokota, Fuyuhiko. "Shokunin to shokunin shūdan." In *Kōza Nihon rekishi 5: kinsei 1.* Eds. Rekishigaku kenkyūkai and Nihonshi kenkyūkai. Tōkyō Daigaku Shuppankai, 1985.

Yoshida Nobuyuki. "Chōnin to machi." In *Kōza Nihon rekishi V: kinsei 1.* Comps.

Rekishigaku kenkyūkai and Nihonshi kenkyūkai. Tōkyō Daigaku Shuppankai, 1985.

Yoshikawa Kōjirō. *Jinsai, Sorai, Norinaga.* Iwanami Shoten, 1975.

————, et al. eds. *Motoori Norinaga.* NST, no. 40. Iwanami Shoten, 1978.

————, ed. *Motoori Norinaga shū.* Nihon no Shisō, no. 15. Chikuma Shobō, 1969.

Young, Blake Morgan. "A Tale of the Western Hills: Takebe Ayatari's *Nishiyama Monogatari,*" *Monumenta Nipponica* 37:77–121 (1982).

Index